Peter Brötzmann

Free Jazz, Revolution
& the Politics of Improvisation

Image © Dawid Laskowski

Peter Brötzmann

Free Jazz, Revolution
& the Politics of Improvisation

By Daniel Spicer

Published by Repeater Books

An imprint of Watkins Media Ltd

Unit 11 Shepperton House

89-93 Shepperton Road

London

N1 3DF

United Kingdom

www.repeaterbooks.com

A Repeater Books paperback original 2025

1

Distributed in the United States by Random House, Inc., New York.

ISBN: 9781915672407

Ebook ISBN: 9781915672414

Printed and bound by CPI Group (UK) Ltd, Croydon, CR0 4YY

Table of Contents

Preface

Waking to the news that Peter Brötzmann had died on June 22, 2023, I was more surprised than I thought I'd be. While his physical health had been in decline for the last few years, there was something about his great, bristling energy that had always made him seem immortal. There was, of course, sadness too. That I would never get to talk to him again. And, especially, that I would never again witness one of his phenomenal live performances.

Over the preceding twenty years, I had probably seen him play more times than any other artist. Certainly, I've written about Brötzmann more than I have anyone else, reviewing dozens of live shows and album releases, both new and reissued, for *Jazzwise* and *The Wire* magazines (adapted excerpts of some of those reviews appear in these pages, with thanks to both publications). It's a task I welcomed. To my mind, Brötzmann remains one of the most fascinating and inspiring personalities in improvised music — not to mention one of the key artistic figures to have emerged from the socio-cultural tumult of the 1960s: a fiercely individual and uncompromising musician and visual artist with a reputation for gruff intensity, who spent half a century on the road forging an ever-widening global network of collaborators and kindred spirits.

In late summer 2012, *The Wire* asked me to write a primer on Brötzmann — an introduction to and overview of his long career based around a dozen or so key recordings — to accompany a lengthy interview feature by David Keenan. Not long after the article's appearance, publisher Tariq Goddard approached me, asking me to expand the piece to a book-length project, the result of which you now hold in your hands. Like that original primer, this book is based on a selection of foundational recordings and is not by any means an attempt to provide an exhaustive account of the hundreds of albums Brötzmann appeared on or the countless working collaborations he appeared in with musicians from all over the world. By the same token, I have resisted the temptation to become bogged down in a complete history of German jazz, not least because, while Brötzmann did indeed arise from that milieu, his sphere of influence and pool of collaborators went on to encompass a far broader purview.

In terms of biography, my emphasis throughout is on his art rather than his personal life. However, I have made it a priority to consider his art in the context of the revolutionary politics that informed both his own music and the free-jazz tradition from which it sprang. While Brötzmann later largely renounced his youthful dabbling in organised leftist thought, he remained convinced of the urgency and importance of the democratic and ultimately liberating models of human interaction suggested by musical cooperation. It's an ideal he devoted his life to, and one which deserves greater scrutiny. Where possible, I have told the story using my own interviews with Brötzmann and several of his key associates — conducted over a period of more than fifteen years — while using a handful of existing source texts for further insight.

In the decade or so after I first accepted the assignment to write about Brötzmann in more depth, our paths crossed many times. I'd like to describe three personal encounters, all of which took place here in Brighton, which reveal an artist with far greater emotional range and complexity than the hackneyed image of the belligerent sonic terrorist that he was all too often saddled with.

The first is from January 2013, when Brötzmann performed with drummer Steve Noble and double-bassist John Edwards at a venue called the Green Door Store, a cavernous, brick-lined Victorian archway underneath the train station, more used to hosting throbbing late-night club vibes. Here's an excerpt from the review I wrote for *Jazzwise*.

"Other than a small amp for the double-bass, the trio perform entirely unplugged, which immediately sets a challenge for Brötzmann: Noble is playing a snappy little kit, favouring sticks over brushes or mallets, and diving immediately into a furious pulse-time barrage. Always an extremely busy drummer, Noble is relentlessly loud tonight, seeming to feed off the energy in the room, whipped up into a non-stop frenzy of activity. It only takes a matter of minutes before Edwards is drenched in sweat, shirt sticking to his back, eyes clamped shut. So, it's especially astonishing just how much savage energy the nearly 72-year-old Brötzmann is capable of generating, largely favouring alto, pumping out wave after wave of high, cascading peals that sing out clearly over the rhythmic turmoil. It's a brittle, jabbing sound this trio makes, like a karate chop to the windpipe. After an hour of it, it's a wonder anyone in the room can breathe."[1]

Afterwards, my band, Bolide, played a late support slot, but no one was under any illusions: it was like trying to start a fire in a vacuum. The night belonged to Brötzmann. During the same brief trip to Brighton, Brötzmann allowed me to take him out for dinner so I could conduct the first of the in-person interviews that have informed this book. During the evening, he was generous, forthcoming and candid in his recollections — as he was for all our later phone calls and meetings.

The second encounter took place in April 2016 when a colleague and I invited the duo of Brötzmann and pedal steel guitarist Heather Leigh to perform in the West Hill Hall, a DIY space with a high stage and the feel of a 1950s village hall, located incongruously in central Brighton. Again, I played a support slot, this time with a trio called In Threads. I'd been curious to note that Brötzmann's rider had requested a bottle of whisky and a bottle of brandy: it was common knowledge that his drinking days had ended long before. All was explained when, after the gig, promoters, performers and various friends were invited backstage and drinks began to flow. Brötzmann sat happily chatting and laughing as the chaos unfolded, serenely bathing in the vicarious fun of seeing those around him finishing off the two bottles he'd requested. I enjoyed myself and don't remember leaving — but even at the time I was aware that this was, again, a generous act from a wise and well-travelled soul.

The third event happened in October 2018, during the third edition of the Brighton Alternative Jazz Festival, of which I was founder and director. It was an all-day gig in a nineteenth-century, high-Anglican church full of stained glass, glittering gold and stern icons. Out of the six acts performing, Brötzmann was scheduled to appear second-to-last with the trio Full Blast, featuring the Swiss rhythm section of Marino Pliakas on electric bass and Michael Wertmueller on drums. The three arrived by taxi from their hotel, not long off the plane, with minutes to spare till showtime. Brötzmann was clearly tired and tense. He prowled around the backstage vestry growling and fuming. He wouldn't look me in the eye. I wondered if he would even perform. Then a miracle occurred. Exactly on time, Full Blast took the stage and delivered a punishing forty-five-minute set of intense, boiling energy music, with Brötzmann roaring like a bull elephant unleashed. After they finished, it was immediately clear that Brötzmann's mood had lifted. He was happy. I have never seen a clearer example of an artist who absolutely *needed* to perform, to marshal the inner demons and drive them out into the light to ensure his own wholeness and sanity.

And this is how I'd like to remember him. Furiously alive. Utterly committed. An eternal star of fierce beauty in the firmament of creative expression.

DS
Brighton
April 2024

Long Story Short

"The total Brötzmann"

In September 2019, six months before the first Covid lockdown called a sudden halt to live shows, London's premier venue for improvised and experimental music, Café OTO, hosted a four-night residency billed as Peter Brötzmann Festival 2019. Since OTO first opened its doors in 2008, Brötzmann had been a regular guest, performing dozens of one-off gigs and several extended residencies. In a very real sense, OTO had become Brötzmann's UK basecamp, serving a pivotal role in his engagement with British audiences. As such, this latest visit felt like a celebration — of that relationship between artist and venue, and simply of Brötzmann's fifty-plus years of trailblazing music-making. Curated by Brötzmann himself, the residency pulled together a rotating cast of collaborators, presented in configurations of varying sizes, which paid tribute to some of his most formative and enduring artistic relationships while, at the same time, highlighting his tireless drive to forge fresh links.

One of Brötzmann's oldest sparring partners, impish Dutch drummer Han Bennink was on hand to play out their cantankerous, half-century relationship in real time — both as a duo and with fellow veteran associate, German pianist Alexander von Schlippenbach. Their performances were distinguished and magisterial, displaying a thorough mastery of a shared improvisatory language yet, despite their long-shared histories, never succumbing to easy familiarity. Where other musicians often showed Brötzmann a certain deference, Bennink was having none of it, constantly attempting to wrong-foot him with gratuitous show-boating and buffoonery. It was hilarious, touching and thrilling all at the same time.

By contrast, twenty-six-year-old French percussionist Camille Emaille played with Brötzmann for the very first time, joining his long-running duo with pedal steel guitarist Heather Leigh. "I just heard her once, one and a half years ago at a little festival," Brötzmann told me the day after her debut. "She played a solo and I was impressed, so I thought this was a good chance to invite her." A former student at the Musik-Akademie of Basel in Switzerland, Emaille studied contemporary music under percussionist Christian Dierstein and improvisation with guitarist Fred Frith. "But she quit," Brötzmann confided. "She realised, 'It's not my thing, not what I want to do.' She has her own hat, which is the most important thing."[1] In the event, Emaille was a revelation. While Brötzmann and Leigh created a diaphanous, cloud-like sound, she added a brutal barrage of clanging gongs and bass drum punctuation that felt like the accompaniment to a Japanese butoh dance or some more obscure ritual. Brötzmann evidently enjoyed it so much that the following evening's scheduled duo performance with Leigh was changed to a second trio performance of equal intensity.

But it was another pair of longstanding comrades who helped provide some of the residency's most exciting encounters. Flown over especially from Japan, pianist Masahiko Satoh and drummer Takeo Moriyama played a rare trio with Brötzmann, in which seventy-four-year-old Moriyama demonstrated his ferociously fast and fleet pulse-time drumming style. It all came together on the fourth and final night, with two sets from a specially convened sextet featuring Moriyama and Satoh, plus bassist John Edwards and (making her first appearance with Brötzmann) American alto saxophonist Matana Roberts — with UK pianist Pat Thomas replacing Satoh for the second set. Both ensembles dived straight to the heart of blissful wholly communion, pouring forth a glorious, tumultuous blast with roots planted firmly in the same fertile soil that produced John Coltrane's epochal free jazz template *Ascension*.

In its bringing together of collaborators from around the world to present not a nostalgic retrospective but a living representation of Brötzmann's current and ongoing preoccupations, the Peter Brötzmann Festival 2019 at Café OTO closely resembled an even more ambitious summit that took place eight years earlier. The 25th iteration of the Unlimited-festival, held in Wels, Austria, in November 2011, was conceived by its organisers as presenting "the total Brötzmann, the whole Brötzmann, something that had never been there before."[2] An exhibition of Brötzmann's visual art ran alongside four days of concerts, curated by Brötzmann, with forty musicians taking part in eighteen performances, nine of which featured Brötzmann himself. Reflecting Brötzmann's globetrotting career, artists were drawn from North America, Europe, East Asia and North Africa.

The entire event is documented in a five-CD box set, released in 2013 under the name *Long Story Short*. It's an apt title: crammed into a few hours of music, it offers what the festival organisers describe as "a representation of the contemporary musical spheres that Brötzmann and his comrades are investigating today."[3] Moreover, the set is just as notable for some of the artists not included, as saxophonist Ken Vandermark remarks: "It was very interesting that in this huge festival, centred around all the different kinds of work Peter was doing in a contemporary way, he didn't, say, do a reunion with Han Bennink or Fred Van Hove. It was really about people that he had a history with but that he was still working with now."[4]

Sure enough, Brötzmann appears with several of his regular, ongoing groups from the time. His Chicago Tentet, featuring Vandermark and several other luminaries from both the US and Europe, makes a huge, sprawling sound, with special guest and free jazz originator John Tchicai momentarily confounding the ensemble by introducing a delicate, wavering flute into the full rambunctious flow. Brötzmann also makes a steamrolling, armour-plated attack with his trio Full Blast (featuring Swiss musicians Michael Wertmüller on drums and bass guitarist Marino Pliakas) and with multinational quartet Hairy Bones (with Japanese trumpeter Toshinori Kondo, Italian bassist Massimo Pupillo and Norwegian drummer Paal Nilssen-Love). Brötzmann also appears in a couple of trios that bring him closer to traditional free jazz than he usually allows: a set with Satoh and Moriyama is an intimately charged summit, with Satoh's leaping chords and prancing hooks summoning the spirit of the New Thing; while New Yorkers Eric Revis (playing double bass) and Nasheet Waits (on drums) stir up an acoustic barrage with hints of Milford Graves's radical rewiring of the rhythmic imperative.

However, some of the box set's most interesting moments come when the music moves further away from jazz: for instance, Mats Gustaffson's sax and electronics sparring with turntablist Dieb13 and guitarist Martin Siewert, or the string trio that brings Japanese koto player Michiyo Yagi into a brittle and austere conversation with South Korean cellist Okkyung Lee and Chinese musician Xu Fengxia playing the zither-like guzheng. Most exciting, though, are the collaborations featuring Moroccan gnawa master Maalem Mokhtar Gania's burbling guimbri. His tumbling, earthbound rhythms on the ancient bass lute catalyse a multicultural synthesis, transforming Joe McPhee's sax into a whinnying shenai while encouraging Fred Lonberg-Holm's cello to fall into a sarangi-like drone. Playing with Brötzmann, drummer Hamid Drake and bassist Bill Laswell, Gania opens up buoyant rhythmic possibilities that lead bass and drums into funky breaks and even a cheeky disco vamp that bends the saxophone's phrases into joyous, upward curls.

At the heart of the box set — and the festival itself — sits the Concert for Fukushima, a fundraising gig by the Chicago Tentet in aid of organisations supporting the Japanese people in recovering from the earthquake, tsunami and ensuing nuclear catastrophe of March 2011. Here, guest Michiyo Yagi's koto provides a focal point as her harp-like glissandi and sparkling dissonances sketch turbulent seas while massed horns rise up in wailing lamentation, building a statement of wrenching sorrow and horror. In the box set's liner notes, festival organiser, Wolfgang Wasserbauer observes: "Social commitment and solidarity are important to Brötzmann — no empty words and no contradiction to his radical aesthetic dispositions."[5]

The fact that events like these were staged in Brötzmann's honour reveals the enormous status — even celebrity — he enjoyed in the world of improvised music. After emerging as a musician in the mid-1960s, he played with virtually every major figure in avant-garde jazz, while also leaving his mark on extreme rock and noise scenes, in the process amassing a dizzyingly diverse discography and appearing on over a hundred albums. He was the undisputed heavyweight elder statesman of European free music, infamously cited by former US president and baby-boomer amateur saxophonist Bill Clinton as "one of the greatest alive."[6] Self-taught on saxophones, clarinets and the Hungarian tarogato, Brötzmann was a rugged individualist who continued to inspire younger generations of saxophonists, from the UK's Colin Webster to Swedish firebrand Mats Gustafsson. "He was the real reason why I started to make research in creative music," says Gustafsson.

> "What he makes on stage with his music, his story-telling, his focus, his dedication and his tone, is something you don't easily find anywhere else. How is it possible to put that much knowledge and depth into your music? I'm still trying to figure it out. No other musician has taught me so much, on and off stage."[7]

Yet, to the end, he remained a somewhat divisive figure. On 7 September 2021, US late-night talk-show host Jimmy Fallon included Brötzmann's 1969 album *Nipples* in a juvenile and mean-spirited section of his *Tonight Show* which he calls the "Do Not Play List" — essentially mocking albums and artists he advises his audience to avoid. Fallon smirked at the idea of German jazz, then played a few seconds of the album's cacophonous high-energy attack before cutting it short and commenting that it sounded "like a Guitar Centre on a busy Saturday," while his musical director, Questlove of hiphop/R&B band the Roots, mugged and guffawed. In the days that followed, Brötzmann fans took to social media to show their displeasure. A meme surfaced showing a black and white photo of Brötzmann glaring into the camera with barely restrained, smouldering aggression, together with the text: "A certain late-night host apparently made fun of Peter Brötzmann tonight, and all I can think about is how easily an 80-year old Peter Brötzmann could snap Jimmy Fallon's fucking neck like a twig."[8] On YouTube, the clip garnered some choice comments. One user remarked: "I have never had any respect for Jimmy Fallon and this only proves me correct all along. Brötzmann is a legend and Fallon is lukewarm milk."[9] Others directed their displeasure at Questlove, who directed the 2021 documentary *Summer of Soul*, about the 1969 Harlem Cultural Festival, which featured footage of Brötzmann collaborator guitarist Sonny Sharrock. As one user put it: "Huh? Questlove acting like he didn't just put out a concert movie with Sonny Sharrock in it, who played in bands with Peter Brötzmann for YEARS."[10] Brötzmann, for his part, remained sanguine about the debacle, telling *Rolling Stone*: "We both know that the world is full of ignorants and stupidos, one more or less, who cares."[11]

"We have to do it together"

A life spent on the road as pioneer and dogged envoy of high-energy free music spawned many tales. Off stage, Brötzmann was, for many years, the old-school, heavy-drinking hellraiser. On stage, he was legendary for his fierce stamina and the raw, incendiary ferocity of his huge sound; an aural assault characterised by shrieking overtones and brutish multiphonic distortions; a physical force of astonishing, elemental power and directness. Said to have once cracked a rib on stage through the sheer strength of his blowing,[12] for years Brötzmann was lauded with the cartoonish title of "Loudest Saxophonist in The World." Indeed, his volume and power were such defining features that they were notorious even among his fellow musicians. "I knew he was a very loud player," guitarist Fred Frith recalls, "and before we went on stage in New York, I told him, you know the great thing with playing the guitar is that I'll always be louder than you. And during the concert, he came and put his tenor sax in front of my ear and blew. It was very painful."[13]

Perhaps it's unsurprising that Brötzmann's ferocity is particularly legendary among fellow saxophonists: "Brötzmann is about pure sound and energy through the saxophone, he's just a force of nature directly through the saxophone,"[14] says erstwhile collaborator Evan Parker. "The first time I heard Peter I was frightened to death. I'd never heard a saxophone make that much sound. Such a huge sound. That was something I had to try and deal with very quickly, how to match that and bring my sound up to that."[15] Improv pioneer Trevor Watts has a similar story to tell: "One gig I was in, I was standing and playing next to Brötzmann at a gig in Berlin in the 1960s. Nearly perforated my eardrums!"[16] And later: "At some point I remember seeing that he had taken his octave key off his saxophone. I never asked him why, but I suspect it helps with the volume thing. He blows on the natural overtones that you can get on the sax."[17]

This modification is something that drummer Steve Noble also noticed:

"The first time I played with Peter, I think in 1990, I saw he had no octave key on his saxophone. Ordinarily, you press a lever with your thumb and it opens up so you can go up an octave. It wasn't there. It was broken off. He didn't need it, he blows so hard. You just think, 'Fuck.' He's one of the unique originals. He's got a style that has not been replicated by anybody."[18]

It's an opinion echoed by another drummer, Brötzmann's longstanding friend and collaborator of more than half a century Han Bennink: "What I like about Peter is that you recognise him from one note. [Thelonious] Monk you recognise by one note, Miles [Davis], Charlie Parker — all those people — but also Brötzmann. You recognise him right away."[19]

Despite Brötzmann's reputation for loudness, his harsh, fanfaric bray was rarely, if ever, used for volume's sake alone. In its almost unbearable rage and pain, it is a defiantly human cry. It is the blues, channelling all the anguish and absurd horrors of a post-Auschwitz Europe into a concentrated, alchemical shriek, transmuting suffering into a bright, illuminating blade of redemption. Moreover, if his unfettered roar is the voice for which he is still best known, it has become almost as much of a cliché to observe how he was equally capable of communicating great tenderness and lyricism.

Perhaps we shouldn't be surprised. Brötzmann's half century on the fringes of jazz can be seen as a quest to fully realise a particular form of deeply compassionate humanism. The festivals he curated in London and Wels are emblematic of a drive towards internationalism. In many ways, his reputation as an *éminence grise* of the global avant-garde sprang as much from his role as catalyst and bridge builder between various international communities as it did from his playing. Over the decades, Brötzmann touched, enlivened and connected so many key scenes, while enacting a kind of practical utopianism through a life lived on the road in the company of friends and co-conspirators. On a more immediate level, his commitment to artistic collaboration and group improvisation provides clues as to how humans can better organise themselves, to borrow William Parker's phrase, in order to survive. We can, if we like, view Brötzmann's life as embodied example of how to make the world a better place. "I was, as a kid, fascinated by the music," Brötzmann told me,

"and, because I started with a lot of blues and wasn't so interested in the musical form and theory, I was interested in musicians' lives, where they came from, why they did what they did and so on. So, for me, jazz music was always not only a musical form, it was always a kind of social reaction to the society these guys had to live in. I started getting interested in Sun Ra's way of doing things, and my main guy Duke Ellington. Both of them — Ellington and Ra — found different ways to present music, but not only music: the way they lived together, the way they worked together. And, I think, in a very unconscious way, when we started in the '60s, we had the same feeling: we have to do it together. In our kind of life and cultural society, we were always the outcasts. So we had to develop our things — everything — ourselves. And this doing together, not only playing together but developing things together and reaching something together, I think jazz music is the only music where you really have that kind of feeling."[20]

For Adolphe Sax

"We tried to organise"

The world Brötzmann arrived into was sorely in need of change. Hitler's armies were rampaging through Europe and beginning their attempted invasion of Russia. British cities bore the nightly onslaught of the Blitz. Allied and Axis troops clashed in North Africa. The planet seemed consumed by war, with humanity descending into violent madness.

Brötzmann was born on 6 March 1941, in the town of Remscheid in the western German state of North Rhine-Westphalia. The year before, his father had been conscripted into the army and sent first to France and then to the Eastern Front, where he was captured and transported to a prisoner of war camp in Siberia. In 1943, baby Peter, his mother and his sister were evacuated to the eastern part of the Greater German Reich, and settled in what is now Poland in the small town of Schlawe (Sławno, in Polish). Brötzmann claimed that his earliest memory was seeing captured Russian soldiers on display in the marketplace in Schlawe.

"And some months later, the same marketplace was full of other people wearing uniforms, German uniforms. That was the time the Russians came to the West. So it was time for my mother to leave. We left Schlawe on my fourth birthday on the sixth of March 1945, with my sister, my mother's mother and other members of the family — most of them died on the way to the west. When I looked round, I remember the whole town was burning. It took us several months to get to Remscheid."[1]

Back in ruined Remscheid, while his mother struggled to make ends meet, young Peter, with the resilience of youth, enjoyed roaming the streets with a gang of older boys, stealing fruit from the local grocery, spending afternoons at the cinema watching Westerns and getting into fights with other street gangs.

"Everybody was so busy surviving that we were able to do just what we wanted; we had all the freedom we wanted…I found my own way of being independent and making my own decisions about my daily life, I still like to do that. I think the roots of my wish for independence and freedom already developed in those days."[2]

This time of anarchic freedom came to a close in 1948 with two significant developments. Brötzmann's father, having escaped from the Russian prisoner of war camp, returned to Remscheid and resumed his job as a tax officer, bringing a measure of paternal Prussian authority to Peter's life for the first time. And, around the same time, Peter started school, where within a few years, aged about ten, he became interested in "drawing and painting… and making things out of wood."[3]

Brötzmann was around thirteen years old when he first became interested in jazz. At home, he listened to records by Duke Ellington, Louis Armstrong and American blues artists, and attending a concert by soprano saxophonist/clarinettist Sidney Bechet had a profound influence on him. He persuaded his teachers to let him set up a jazz club in the music room at school, where he and similarly jazz-mad youngsters would gather to listen to records and read from *Das Jazzbuch*, the best-selling history of jazz by influential journalist and producer Joachim-Ernst Berendt, originally published in 1952. Brötzmann's horizons were also widened by clandestine, late-night enjoyment of Willis Conover's *Music USA Jazz Hour* radio programs — hour-long shows broadcast at midnight, six nights a week, from January 1955 on the US government–funded Voice of America.

The original Dixieland style of New Orleans–born traditional jazz was, at this time, enjoying a revival in Europe, spearheaded by British musicians such as Chris Barber and Humphrey Lyttleton. German youngsters were not immune to its excitement, and a Dixieland band was formed at Brötzmann's school. When the clarinet player graduated and left the clarinet behind, Brötzmann jumped at the chance to take up the instrument, teaching himself the basics by playing along to records at home. Not long after, he joined a "kind of swing band"[4] — a trio with a drummer and pianist, both somewhat older, with whom he played semi-professionally at local school concerts and fashion shows, and even undertook short tours in northern Germany. These were the first steps on a long, long road.

Brötzmann told Gérard Rouy:

"After a while, the guys in the swing band I was working with started to be more oriented towards bebop and hard bop and they told me, man, you have to get a saxophone. Tenor was the thing. I sold all kinds of things to get some money and I bought a tenor and tried my best to learn. I never had a teacher, there was nobody else around, no other saxophone player, so I just had to teach myself."[5]

Despite this early enthusiasm for music, Brötzmann's main ambition at this time, as a teenager in the late 1950s, was to develop a career as a visual artist. He rented a studio with his friend Gerd Hanebeck and produced drawings, paintings and collages made of old coal sacks, influenced by the assemblages of Kurt Schwitters. Aged seventeen, he took a job in a print shop and learned core skills that would prove useful in later years. By 1959, he and Hanebeck were ready to present their first collaborative exhibitions in Remscheid's Stadttheater (City Theatre) and in Nijmegen, in the Netherlands. That same year, aged eighteen, Brötzmann moved to the nearby city of Wuppertal — an industrial hub famous for its futuristic suspended monorail.[6] Here he attended the local Werkkunstschule (School of Applied Arts), enrolling in a graphic design programme in which he studied printing techniques such as lithography and etching while taking extra art classes in painting and sculpture. His first solo exhibition proper, *Metallbilder & Collagen* ("Metal Pictures & Collages"), was held in February 1961 at the Galerie Schnoor in Bremen, in northern Germany.

Through gallery visits and engagements in Germany and the Netherlands at the beginning of the '60s, Brötzmann met artists such as Jan Schoonhoven and Yoko Ono. But, even during these earliest endeavours, the mannered politics of the art establishment were anathema to the young artist: "What I didn't like was the audience I had around in gallery openings and such — these completely stupid, bourgeois kind of people. I didn't like that."[7]

The stifling atmosphere and pervasive spectre of commodification he encountered in the art world were in stark contrast to the unmediated expressive freedom he'd already sampled in his tentative forays as a fledgling musician:

"What I always liked about music, it's the most direct way to approach somebody. If you are on stage for this one hour, you do it and then it's done. You go on stage with all that you have and, if you're good, it's good. Sometimes you are not so good, but it's done, it's there. It's a thing you can't sell."[8]

By end of the '50s, Brötzmann's burgeoning musical evolution was already causing him to strain against the limitations of Wuppertal's local jazz scene. "I was looking around for some musicians. We had here [in Wuppertal] a couple of clubs with swing, be-bop, hard bop, but, already then, I wanted something else."[9] Brötzmann told musicologist and author Harald Kisiedu how this hunger influenced his listening habits at the time: "When the first... records showed up of Ornette [Coleman] or [Charles] Mingus and, of course, we all listened to Art Blakey and Horace Silver but it was not enough. It was too fixed, too formulaic. I wanted to get away from that."[10]

In 1960, Brötzmann made a personal connection that was to provide a bolt of energy in his development as a musician when he was introduced to Peter Kowald: "Somebody mentioned there is a very young guy who is playing tuba in the school orchestra, and that was Kowald. I was nineteen and he was seventeen or something like that and he was still going to school."[11] Born in 1944 in Masserberg in Central Germany, Kowald had moved to Wuppertal as a very young child just after the end of the war. At school, he'd picked up the tuba and, like Brötzmann, joined a Dixieland band. By the time he crossed paths with the restlessly inquisitive, slightly older art student and saxophone player, Kowald, too, was ready for something new. As Brötzmann recalled:

"He was living around the corner from me with his family so we could meet at least a couple of times in the week and we went to our rehearsal room. I could convince him to change to double bass and he took some lessons with a very serious, very good classical guy we had here in our [Wuppertal] Symphony [Orchestra]."[12]

It was the beginning of an extraordinarily close and long-lasting musical collaboration that was to have a profound influence on both their lives: "Since that, whatever we did in the first years, we did together. We were not only preparing and looking for gigs, we printed our posters, we tried to organise."[13]

"Brötzmann, do your thing"

At the same time as Brötzmann was formulating his own attitudes and aesthetics as a visual artist and musician, he found himself drawn into the orbit of the nascent art phenomenon known as Fluxus. Originating in New York at the end of the 1950s, and reaching Europe by the early 1960s, Fluxus exactly coincided with Brötzmann's early development, and it was to exert a profound influence on the young artist.

Spearheaded by Lithuanian-American artist and designer George Maciunas, Fluxus was a conceptual lightning rod for a trans-national coterie of composers, poets, writers, visual and performing artists and designers from the US, Europe and East Asia who, informed by Dada, Surrealism and John Cage's notions of indeterminacy, organised performances and happenings that foregrounded an interest in the artistic process over the finished artefact. In fact, with the benefit of hindsight, it's remarkable just how many of the attitudes and ideas that defined Fluxus were also adopted as central tenets by Brötzmann as his artistic identity coalesced and developed: spontaneity, improvisation, participation, humour, a multidisciplinary openness and — perhaps most crucially — as Fluxus scholar Owen F. Smith has noted, "internationalism, collectivism, egalitarianism."[14]

In late 1961, Maciunas left New York, on the run from debt collectors, and moved to Wiesbaden, Germany, where he took a job as a graphic designer at the nearby US Air Force base. At this point, he had momentum on his side: earlier that year, he had co-founded the short-lived AG Gallery on New York's Madison Avenue and, during the space's brief existence, curated a series of ground-breaking performances presenting works by John Cage, La Monte Young, Henry Flynt, Yoko Ono and others. Now, transplanted to Germany, he set about organising similar events, beginning with the first Fluxus Festival in Wiesbaden in September 1962. He also initiated a series of touring avant-garde recitals, billed as Fluxconcerts, which during 1962 and 1963 touched down in a number of European cities including Cologne, Düsseldorf, Amsterdam, Paris —and Wuppertal. It was at one of these concerts that Brötzmann witnessed performances by Maciunas, Cage and the influential German artist Joseph Beuys. But it was another participant who was to have the biggest influence on Brötzmann's life: Korean artist Nam June Paik.

Born in Seoul in 1932, Paik studied in Tokyo before relocating to West Germany in 1956 to study music history in Munich. While there, he became acquainted with avant-garde composer Karlheinz Stockhausen, as well as Cage, Maciunas, Beuys and others, and by 1962, he was fully aligned with Fluxus. In March 1963, Paik presented his debut solo exhibition, in Wuppertal at the Galerie Parnasse, which was actually situated in the home of gallery owners Rolf and Anneliese Jährling. Titled *Exposition of Music — Electronic Television*, the show turned the Jährlings' abode into a disorientating environment, filling every available space — including the bathroom, the staircase and the basement — with a dizzying array of objects including twelve modified TVs, record players, audio tape installations and various mechanical sound makers. Visitors were greeted at the entrance of the house by a recently slaughtered and rapidly decomposing cow's head (mistaken by many for the head of a bull), announcing, none too subtly, the killing of artistic sacred cows.

Among the more important objects installed by Paik were four pianos, two of which developed Cage's idea of preparing the strings by inserting objects to transform their timbre. Paik's pianos, which he called *Klavier Intégral,* took this technique to ridiculous extremes. One of his assistants, Tomas Schmit, listed their contents as: "a doll's head, a hand siren, a cow horn, a bunch of feathers, barbed wire, spoons, a little tower of pfennig coins stuck together, all sorts of toys, photos, a bra, an accordion, a tin with an aphrodisiac, a record player arm."[15] When certain keys were struck, hidden devices activated a hot-air fan, a transistor radio, a siren, film projectors and a switch to control the lighting for the whole room. Visitors to the exhibition were encouraged to play the pianos and, at the end of each day, the delicate preparations would need to be reset, a job that was allocated to a team of students recruited from the local Werkkunstschule, which included Brötzmann.

"I had to repair the very fragile constructions he did," Brötzmann recalled.

"The good part was Paik — in opposition to Joseph Beuys, for example, who took himself very, very seriously, a very

German way of taking things seriously — Paik was, when we were sitting after the gallery was closed, with a six-pack and some Korean radish or whatever, when he was talking about things he was doing, he was always laughing."[16]

Brötzmann accompanied Paik as an assistant on a number of trips to European cities, helping to set up his installations and exhibitions. One such sojourn was to the Fluxus Festival, held in Amsterdam in an old cinema building called the Hypokriterion Theatre on 23 June 1963, where Brötzmann took part in a performance of Arthur Köpke's *Reading Work Piece No. 1: music while you work*. A poster for the festival reveals the calibre of the company the twenty-two-year-old Brötzmann was keeping at this time:

FLUXUS
FESTIVAL
THEATRE COMPOSITIONS
STREET COMPOSITIONS
EXHIBITS
ELECTRONIC MUSIC

George Maciunas, Nam June Paik, Tomas Schmit, Emmet Williams, Robert Watts, Dick Higgins, Alison Knowles, Daniel Spoerri, George Brecht, Arthur Koepke, Gyorgy Ligeti, Toshi Ishiyanagi, Jackson Mac Low, Benjamin Patterson, La Monte Young, Richard Maxfield, Ben Vautier, John Cage, Walter de Maria, Bernt Reissmann, Peter Brötzmann, Manfred Laurens Montwé, Willem de Ridder[17]

The same month, Brötzmann was part of a quartet, also including Tomas Schmit, Manfred Montwé and Willem de Ridder, that performed Paik's piece *Piano for All Senses* at de Ridder's Amstel 47 gallery in Amsterdam. Around the same time, Paik introduced Brötzmann to Beuys, a Fluxus heavyweight twenty years his senior: "Paik and Beuys worked together in certain situations and so I was lucky — Paik took me with him to Beuys' atelier a couple of times. We talked, we even exchanged later some letters about music and so on."[18]

Through all these interactions, Brötzmann was brought into direct contact with a network of iconoclastic, anti-establishment artists who expressed disdain for the formal gallery system and the business of art while striving to break away from old norms and create genuinely new forms of expression. It's impossible to overstate the profound influence Paik and his peers had on the young artist. "I learned a lot in the very young years from Nam June Paik," Brötzmann said. "He was a very important man for me. All these guys said, 'Brötzmann, do your thing. Don't care what jazz critics or colleagues say, just do it.' That was, for me, as a very young and naïve guy, very important."[19]

Paik had another hugely important effect on Brötzmann by introducing him to the music of Cage — with all its fascinations with the element of chance — and Stockhausen. Based just sixty kilometres away in Cologne, Stockhausen was extending the possibilities of electronic music through his praxis at the public broadcaster Nordwestdeutscher Rundfunk's Studio for Electronic Music where he had been working since 1953, and of which he became director in 1963. Combined with the rule-breaking imperatives of Fluxus, these influences played a decisive role in helping Brötzmann burst free of the constraints of conventional jazz, encouraging him to renegotiate his conception of what sounds could be considered music and steering him on a course towards the uncharted freedom of total improvisation.

"Living Ball of Fire"

But he still had some dues to pay. By 1962, Brötzmann and Kowald had a regular gig at a local Wuppertal jazz club, playing the music of Ornette Coleman and Charles Mingus in a trio with a succession of temporary drummers. "The drummers were a problem in those days," Brötzmann laughed,

> "because they all wanted to play what everybody wanted in those days — some kind of Art Blakey hard bop stuff. But I had something else in mind. We invited in our area of North Rhine-Westphalia — we had, I think, about twenty million people living in this area — and we spread the news around, we had a club here and we have rehearsals and you're welcome. So, from time to time, some drummers showed up. Not very many of them stayed, I'm afraid. It was a little bit too far out."[20]

The lack of a dependable drummer was not his only concern. Making a living out of art or music still seemed a long way off, and Brötzmann now had responsibilities. In 1962, he married Krista Bolland, and they soon had two children: a son, Caspar, that year, and a daughter, Wendela, the next. With a young family to support, Brötzmann picked up what work he could: helping in his father-in-law's blacksmith shop; assisting his professor at the Werkkunstschule; taking shifts at the local Wicküler brewery; he even put his design studies to use by co-founding a small, independent advertising agency with a fellow student.

Meanwhile, Brötzmann and Kowald continued to operate as musical outliers, largely unrecognised by the rapidly coalescing West German progressive jazz scene. In the mid-60s, this scene was centred on two key hubs of activity. In Frankfurt, the nexus was Albert Mangelsdorff, a trombonist who'd been recording since the early '50s. His debut as a leader, 1963's *Tension,* showcased sophisticated and hard-swinging originals performed by a quintet with an unusual three-horn front line featuring Heinz Sauer on tenor sax and Günter Kronberg on alto. In 1964, the same band released *Now Jazz Ramwong,* which added Asian influences to the mix, from the ersatz orientalism of the title track's theme to an adaptation of music by Ravi Shankar in "Three Jazz Moods." Meanwhile, in Cologne, vibraphonist Gunter Hampel was leading a quintet made up of some considerable young talent: trumpeter Manfred Schoof, pianist Alexander von Schlippenbach, bassist Buschi Niebergall and Dutch drummer Pierre Courbois. Their 1965 debut, *Heartplants,* simmered with a potent mix of urgent energy and noirish cool. While much of the album rides an assured, often deeply swinging melodicism, von Schlippenbach's composition "Iron Perceptions," with its sudden sprints and Schoof's brash trumpet spurts, is the first documented free-jazz piece by a German band.

By this time, however, Brötzmann and Kowald were already approximating a much rawer and more instinctive free jazz that wasn't fully appreciated by these leading West German progressives. "We did some shit that was really far away from the other, let's say, avant-garde bands who were better known at the time," Brötzmann told writer David Keenan. "When Kowald and I showed up somewhere at some little festival, everyone laughed or looked the other way. Like, 'Ach, they can't play.'"[21]

With its Fluxus connections, Wuppertal in the mid-60s was a thriving cultural and artistic hub, and American jazzers in Europe would often pass through. Many, as a result, encountered the enthusiastic young firebrands Brötzmann and Kowald in the natural habitat of their regular jazz club residency. One of these visitors — and an important source of early encouragement — was free-thinking soprano saxophonist Steve Lacy. Originally coming up, like Brötzmann, playing Dixieland as a teenager in the early '50s, Lacy played on pioneering avant-garde pianist Cecil Taylor's debut album, *Jazz Advance,* in 1956, before forming a life-long engagement with the music of Thelonious Monk, recording his first album to feature only Monk's compositions, *Reflections,* in 1958, and serving a brief stint in the pianist's band in 1960. In 1965, Lacy arrived in Europe for the first time, working in a trio with exiled South African musicians, bassist Johnny Dyani and drummer Louis Moholo.*

"Steve was touring in Germany quite a bit," Brötzmann recalled.

"We had a couple of jazz clubs in my town, so he showed up with his trio sometimes and sometimes solo. He was always very open and liked to talk. He was always a guy who you could ask and he would answer. So, we with our bad English in those years were hanging out at night with him and he was very patient. He was very interested in the art that was going

---

* In 2005, Moholo returned to South Africa and adopted the name Louis Moholo-Moholo after the death of his grandfather technically made him clan chief. However, while describing events before that change, this text will continue to refer to him by his previous name of Louis Moholo.

on in Wuppertal — especially the Fluxus movement. I think he was very influenced by it, the way he put his Monk pieces together, or how he wrote and performed his own pieces: it was a kind of intellectual game for him. He was a very intellectual guy."[22]

The fact that Lacy didn't dismiss the duo but actually took them seriously as musicians was hugely encouraging. But Lacy's biggest gift to Brötzmann was undoubtedly the introduction he provided to another peripatetic American avant-gardist — trumpeter Don Cherry, a man who proved to be every bit as important to Brötzmann's artistic development as Nam June Paik had been. Certainly, if Brötzmann had wanted a connection to the source of free jazz, he couldn't have asked for better. Cherry was royalty.

Born in Oklahoma City in 1936, Don Cherry grew up in Los Angeles, and from the mid-50s had a strong musical bond with saxophonist Ornette Coleman. He played on Coleman's earliest albums, widely recognised as the opening salvos of the free-jazz revolution — from 1958's *Something Else!!!!* through to 1960's *Change of the Century*. In 1960, he recorded *The Avant-Garde* with members of Coleman's quartet and John Coltrane, helping to catalyse Coltrane's later immersion in free jazz. Cherry also added avant-garde credentials to Sonny Rollins' music, and travelled to Europe for the first time in 1963 as a member of Rollins' quartet. In the same year, he returned to Europe with the New York Contemporary Five, alongside saxophonists Archie Shepp and John Tchicai, and in 1964 cemented a musical relationship with arguably the most radical and iconoclastic free-jazz pioneer, saxophonist

Albert Ayler, taking part in an Ayler-led recording session that was later used as soundtrack for Michael Snow's experimental film *New York Eye and Ear Control*, and undertaking a tour of Scandinavia with Ayler's quartet.

By the mid-60s, the nomadic Cherry was living — at least part of the time — in Sweden with artist and designer Monika Karlsson, who became his wife and collaborator Moki Cherry. Sweden had proven to be particularly welcoming territory for the new wave of free-jazz musicians: Cecil Taylor had been warmly received when he played at Stockholm's Golden Circle in late 1962, with his trio featuring alto saxophonist Jimmy Lyons and drummer Sunny Murray, joined later by Albert Ayler, who had already been living in Sweden since early 1962. It was here that Cherry first encountered a young German saxophonist who came with a recommendation from none other than Steve Lacy. "My first foreign country I played regularly was Sweden," explained Brötzmann. "Don heard me there with my trios and always supported, got me information and some gigs even."[23] Perhaps Cherry heard something of Ayler's raw intensity and energy in Brötzmann's wild, unschooled roar: he was sufficiently impressed to bestow two nicknames on the young German, as Brötzmann recalled: "One was Machine Gun, the other was Living Ball of Fire."[24] At this time, Cherry was getting regular work on German radio stations, and particularly the Südwestfunk Baden-Baden, where jazz journalist Joachim-Ernst Berendt was a producer. On his long journeys from his home in southern Sweden to Baden-Baden, Cherry regularly visited Brötzmann in Wüppertal:

"He was in his Volkswagen bus, traveling down to southern Germany, and he would pass by my place and stay for a night or two, sometimes with his family, sometimes alone. So we talked a bit and I learned a lot. He was such an open guy, and so curious. He wanted to know everything that had to do with music."[25]

Cherry was among the first American jazz musicians to recognise — and make regular use of — the quality of musicianship in European jazz. By early 1965, he was already leading a Paris-based, multinational quintet (known variously as Togetherness, the Complete Communion Band or the International Quintet), which included German vibraphonist and pianist Karl Berger, French double-bassist Jean-François Jenny-Clark, Italian drummer Aldo Romano and expatriate Argentinian saxophonist Gato Barbieri. In February 1966, Cherry asked Brötzmann to join the group for a series of concerts in Paris:

> "He was playing at Le Chat Qui Peche — *the* jazz place in Paris in the middle of the '60s — and he said, 'Why don't you come over for a weekend and play with us?' That was, of course, a very, very important weekend for me. There was a time when I was not really accepted by anyone here in Germany and this changed when I came back from Paris. I could tell the guys, 'Man, I played with Don's band at the weekend.' It helped me a lot to get more accepted."[26]

Brötzmann wasn't the only young German jazz musician who drew inspiration from the mercurial presence of Don Cherry. Gunter Hampel's quintet encountered Cherry in the summer of 1965 while playing a residency at the Blue Note club in Paris, at the same time that Cherry's International Quintet were installed at Le Chat Qui Peche. At the time, Cherry's live sets took the form of uninterrupted suites that melded composed themes with individual solos and bursts of collective improvisation

— an approach that he crystallised on his Blue Note albums *Complete Communion* (1966) and *Symphony for Improvisers* (1967), both of which featured just one long piece on each side. In the liner notes for *Symphony for Improvisers,* Cherry told A.B. Spellman: "We improvised from the flavour of the tune, from the mode, and the themes come back from time to time, so that it's definitely one thing that we made, not eight."[27] Hampel's group quickly saw the possibilities in this technique and began to structure their own performances in a similar way.

The explicit fluidity and freedom experienced in Cherry's aesthetic was also a spur to a key defection of major significance for the development of German free jazz. In October 1965, Schoof, von Schlippenbach and bassist Buschi Niebergall left Hampel's employ and formed the Manfred Schoof Quintet with drummer Jaki Liebezeit and saxophonist Gerd Dudek. Recorded on 2 May 1966, their debut album, *Voices,* revealed a unit determined to strike out further than Hampel had ever done: thematic fanfares with echoes of Cherry's mid-60s work give way to fierce and turbulent group improvisations powered by Liebezeit's powerfully roiling drums, while von Schlippenbach's percussive stabs and splashes signal the influence of Cecil Taylor's epochal 1966 album *Unit Structures,* and Dudek's hoarse cry summons the spirit of Albert Ayler.

"Admirable discipline and utmost exertion"

The day before Schoof's quintet recorded *Voices,* on 1 May 1966, an event took place that proved to be both a decisive rallying point and a life-changing quickening of energies: the tenth German Jazz Festival in Frankfurt. The festival was notable for being the first time a major American artist had taken part — in the form of Don Cherry leading his

International Quintet — and also featured the vanguard of European progressives: the Gunter Hampel Quintet, the Manfred Schoof Quintet featuring von Schlippenbach, plus two trios, one led by German pianist Wolfgang Dauner and another by Swiss pianist Irène Schweizer. In the wake of their recent seal of approval from Cherry, it was also the first time Brötzmann and Kowald were asked to play a major German festival, for which they formed a trio with Hampel's Dutch drummer, Pierre Courbois. "I had met him in Holland a couple of times and we played a little bit," Brötzmann recalls. "He was interested in what we were doing. To have him play with us at the festival was a very sensational thing for us."[28]

In the event, the trio played for less than fifteen minutes (released in full on CD in 2010 with the title *Mayday*, credited to the Peter Brötzmann Trio) before the plug was pulled on them, provoking not a little consternation among audience and critics not yet attuned to Brötzmann's harsh freedom. But the occasion also afforded him some much-needed validation from an unlikely source: American alto saxophonist Lee Konitz — a major figure in the cool jazz movement of the late '40s and early '50s, recognised by Brötzmann as "a guy who you wouldn't expect would actually like my music."[29] Brötzmann recalled: "The press wrote, 'Oh, Brötzmann, that's no jazz, no music,' but Konitz came afterwards backstage and said, 'Don't worry, just do your thing and play.' That was very important for me."[30]

The festival was Brötzmann and Kowald's first taste of national exposure, and was quickly followed by another high-profile opportunity when American pianist and composer Carla Bley invited them to tour Europe as part of her band. Born in 1936, Bley was a hugely influential figure in New York's free-jazz community who had started out composing fiercely imaginative pieces for her husband, pianist Paul Bley, before becoming known as a pianist in her own right. In 1964, trumpeter Bill Dixon invited her to be a charter member of the Jazz Composers Guild — an organisation dedicated to independently promoting free-jazz performances in the city — alongside Archie Shepp, John Tchicai and Cecil Taylor. Bley took a leading role, and together with trumpeter (and second husband) Michael Mantler, in the autumn of 1964 she formed an associated ensemble, the Jazz Composers Guild Orchestra, which evolved into the Jazz Composers Orchestra after the guild quickly dissolved. For Brötzmann and Kowald, she was another clear connection to the source.

In fact, Brötzmann's first encounter with Bley had taken place in Wuppertal in 1965, thanks to an introduction from Steve Lacy.

"Steve was touring with Carla Bley — Kent Carter was the bassist and Aldo Romano was the drummer. He said, 'I am coming with Carla, come to the club, show up and bring your sax.' So, I did that and, at the end of the show, I really with shaking knees went on stage and just played my arse off and it ended really so crazy. Aldo couldn't believe it; he was throwing his cymbals around and the band turned really crazy. I thought, 'OK, now you make one more mistake!' But, half a year later, I got a letter from Carla inviting me for her next European tour."[31]

When the invitation arrived, Bley, Mantler, Lacy, Carter and Romano had just recorded the album *Jazz Realities*, and Brötzmann and Kowald joined the tour replacing Lacy and Carter. No official recordings were made of the quintet, but a widely circulated bootleg, reportedly recorded in Rome in November 1966, captures a ferociously energetic ensemble, with Brötzmann squealing high and free and Kowald sawing a wild arco.[32] If the tour was a welcome opportunity for Brötzmann and Kowald to engage with new audiences, it was nevertheless not without its challenges. On the last night, at a concert at the Galerie Hammer in Berlin, the two of them were the only band members to show up, leaving them no choice but to perform as a duo in front of a phalanx of German and international journalists and photographers.

After the tour, back in Wuppertal, there was another setback. The trio with Pierre Courbois that had ruffled feathers at the Frankfurt Jazz Festival turned out to be only a temporary solution to the search for a suitable drummer: "Gunter Hampel insisted Courbois should stay with him," Brötzmann remembered. "I started again to play with various drummers here from the area. Then, very soon after that, we met, in Brussels, Sven Åke Johansson, who was alone, travelling around Europe at that time."[33] In conversation with Markus Müller, Brötzmann elaborated on how he and Kowald initially encountered Johansson "in some park in Brussels. You know those Swedish bicycles that have a box in the front? A little man was sitting there on a big bicycle with a drum set piled up in front of him, riding through the park."[34]

It was a highly fortuitous meeting. Born in Mariestad, in southern Sweden, in 1943, Johansson had come up playing be-bop but, by the time he ran into Brötzmann and Kowald, he, too, was beginning to strip away inherited form, striving for a more personal, more immediate form of expression. The two Germans knew right away they had finally found a percussionist who understood what they were trying to achieve. At the time of their meeting, Johansson had just finished a European tour with American pianist Ran Blake and found himself at a loose end, stranded and alone. "We convinced him to come over to Wuppertal,"[35] Brötzmann recalled. "And so he rode his bicycle over the autobahn to Wuppertal and showed up there one evening. He had to sneak his way over the border on side roads, of course, but he made it."[36] It was the beginning of a long and fruitful association. "We found him a place to stay and so he stayed with us for quite some years."[37]

Johansson later remembered the great freedom — in all senses — he enjoyed during his time on the road with Brötzmann's youthful first trio:

> "It was with Peter Kowald as driver and his mid-range car, a Borgward Isabella, a German make no longer being manufactured at the time… and thus it could be brought quite cheaply — endless journeys across Europe on the autobahns, with Brötzmann in front, his baritone saxophone between his legs, me in the back between the drums and the neck of the bass. In those early years… everything was new: sound — overtones from the sax and the bowed bass with free figuration on the drums, plus Brötzmann's tremendous forward momentum, often mixed up with lots of beer in those days."[38]

Around this time, Brötzmann and several others on the scene took the first tentative steps towards self-organisation, an urge that would become increasingly important in the next few years.

In May 1966, just after the tour with Carla Bley, Brötzmann and Kowald, together with jazz journalist and critic Rainer Blome, founded the New Jazz Artists' Guild. Presumably inspired by the Jazz Composers Guild that Bley had helped establish in New York a couple of years earlier, the Germans' guild sought to encourage solidarity among free-jazz musicians and find a wider audience for the music. Bley and Mantler were, in fact, present at the guild's first meeting, and discussed the possibility of international cooperation in promoting the music, an idea that was soon dropped in the face of seemingly insurmountable obstacles.

Instead, Brötzmann, Kowald and Blome focussed their energies on an issue closer to home: the establishment of a new German music magazine to champion the new home-grown music. In this respect, it was conceived as an alternative to the well-established *Jazz Podium* periodical, which had rigidly focused on covering American artists — an editorial policy that had only begun to loosen somewhat the previous year.

The guild's first initiative to this end was to arrange a tour of West Germany and the Netherlands by the Don Cherry Quintet, putting their fee as managers of the tour towards establishing the new magazine. Following this, between July and October, the guild staged a series of concerts by the Peter Brötzmann Trio, the Gunter Hampel Quintet, the Manfred Schoof Quintet, the Irène Schweizer Trio and a quintet led by East German brothers Rolf Kühn, saxophonist, and Joachim Kühn, pianist. The shows also featured American comrades-in-arms the Paul Bley Trio and Carla Bley's Jazz Realities quintet. The series kicked off with a benefit concert in Aachen, near the borders with Belgium and the Netherlands, all the proceeds of which were ploughed into jump-starting the embryonic magazine.

The plan came to fruition in late 1966, with the publication of the first issue of *Sounds* magazine. Blome assumed the role of editor, single-handedly typing and assembling the magazine from his home in the city of Solingen, nineteen kilometres from Wuppertal. He also ensured that, from the start, the publication pursued an editorial slant that proudly foregrounded the avant-garde. The masthead proclaimed its arrival as "the Journal for New Jazz,"[39] while an opening epigram revealed that the magazine's title was derived from a quote attributed to Albert Ayler: "Our music is no longer about notes, it's about sounds."[40]

(While this dictum's origins are unclear and possibly apocryphal, it chimes with a similar sentiment Ayler expressed in a 1965 interview, in which he stated: "You have to really play your instrument to escape from notes to sounds."[41]) To emphasise the explicit connections being made between the American New Thing and German free jazz, the front cover of the first issue was emblazoned with a photograph of Brötzmann in stark monochrome and extreme close-up, saxophone in mouth, eyes screwed shut in intense concentration.[42]

While it's been suggested that Blome's primary inspiration was countercultural underground newspapers such as London's *International Times* and New York's *East Village Other*,[43] it's startling just how much *Sounds* stands as a clear precursor to a short-lived, later American periodical *The Cricket*, which ran for four issues in 1968 and 1969. Founded and edited by African American poets/critics Amiri Baraka, A.B. Spellman and Larry Neal, *The Cricket* was a defiantly lo-fi, no-budget bulletin, mimeographed in Baraka's Newark basement in runs of around five hundred per issue. At the heart of this was an appreciation of jazz, and particularly free jazz — referred to throughout as "the New Black Music." While this was revolutionary music for revolutionary times, the writing in *The Cricket* was equally restless, combining politics, poetry and the vernacular of the streets in an effort to strike out from and challenge the overwhelmingly white critical establishment. *The Cricket* was full of impressionistic album reviews of Ornette Coleman, Albert Ayler, Pharoah Sanders and others, scene updates from L.A, Detroit, Newark and elsewhere, as well as ear-to-the-ground gossip and more scholarly essays, all written with a hip, often combative urgency. Musicians contributed too: Sun Ra preached his mystical philosophy in several poems, Milford Graves wrote about the need for self-organisation in Black musical communities, and Albert Ayler offered an apocalyptic vision conflating alien abduction with the Book of Revelation.

Sounds' opening salvo offered a similar aesthetic, offering a mix of articles, reviews and poems by Blome and others. One notable contributor was the American poet, writer, activist and later founder of the White Panther Party, John Sinclair, who contributed a poem and a piece on pianist Andrew Hill to the first issue. It also contained an article by Pierre Courbois on the role of rhythm in the New Jazz, interviews with Coleman, Schoof and Joachim Kühn, as well as US pianist Ran Blake taking the "ESP RECORDS ARTISTS' QUESTIONNAIRE."[44] Again, it's easy to discern an internationalist agenda that sought to raise the profile of German free jazz and cement its position in the wider global scene. Over the years, *Sounds* moved away from jazz, widening its scope to cover rock, then punk and new wave, before folding in 1983 — but there's no denying it played a crucial role in the early establishment of German free jazz.

Autumn 1966 saw another key collaborative development in Brötzmann's early career, which was to have lasting reverberations in the years ahead. It sprang from the quixotic imagination of the ubiquitously influential producer and journalist Joachim-Ernst Berendt — colloquially known as the "Jazz Pope" by musicians.[45] As artistic director of the Berlin Jazz Days festival, Berendt was keen to commission a meeting between jazz and contemporary classical for the 1966 festival's opening concert. He was sufficiently switched on to Germany's nascent progressive jazz scene to know there were a few obvious, classically trained candidates.

A Berliner born in 1938, Alexander von Schlippenbach had received academic training in the late '50s at the Cologne

Musikhochschule, where he studied composition under the
tutelage of composer Bernd Alois Zimmerman and attended
Germany's first post-war jazz program, run by big band leader
Kurt Edelhagen. Here, he'd first met trumpeter Manfred Schoof,
a couple of years older, who had already studied trumpet at the
Academy of Music in Kassel before relocating to Cologne (where
he was soon followed by drummer Jaki Liebezeit and bassist
Buschi Niebergall). Berendt reached out to von Schlippenbach,
attempting to commission him to produce a work in collaboration
with composer Boris Blacher, with financial backing from RIAS,
a Berlin-based TV and radio network and major sponsor of
Berlin Jazz Days. Von Schlippenbach, however, had another,
more radical idea, and suggested writing and performing a piece
for a specially convened free-jazz orchestra. "Since the beginning
of the free-jazz era in 1960," he explained, "we played almost
exclusively in small groups. I was fascinated by the idea of playing
our new music with a large ensemble."[46]

With Berendt's approval — and with Brötzmann's performance
at the Frankfurt festival earlier that year still ringing in his ears —
von Schlippenbach assembled a thirteen-piece ensemble with,
at its core, a "double nucleus"[47] formed by merging two existing
units: the Manfred Schoof Quintet (Schoof, von Schlippenbach,
Niebergall, Liebezeit and Dudek) and the Peter Brötzmann Trio
(Brötzmann, Kowald and drummer Mani Neumeier*), with the
addition of Gunter Hampel, tuba player Willi Lietzmann, Dutch
saxophonists Willem Breuker and Kris Wanders, and Belgian
trumpeter Claude Deron. The group rehearsed for three days, and

---

* Some accounts, including Brötzmann's recollections, suggest the trio
at the time was Brötzmann, Kowald and Johansson. However, this
appears to have been at a time when the classic trio had yet to coalesce
and other drummers such as Neumeier were still being used.

41

on 3 November 1966, performed von Schlippenbach's piece "Globe Unity" at the Philharmonie in Berlin under the name Globe Unity Orchestra. As von Schlippenbach recalled, the performance "was a sensational success, because the press outdid themselves equally in extravagant praise and hysterical vituperation."[48] Crucially, it also marked the first public performance of a pan-European avant-garde jazz ensemble, an idea that Brötzmann was to revisit with career-defining vigour within a couple of years.

Just over a month later, on 6 December 1966, the same personnel went into the studio in Cologne and recorded a twenty-minute version of the piece, which occupied one side of the album *Globe Unity*, released under von Schlippenbach's name the following year. From the outset, it's a huge, tumultuous sound, with massed horns and percussion swirling and churning while squalling, altissimo solos ride the fierce group energy. The impression of chaos is neatly brushed aside by dramatically ascending horn charts intersecting with plunging, depth-charge piano chords and punctuating tubular bells — structural gambits in which it's possible to detect the influences of both von Schlippenbach's studies in new music and Don Cherry's innovative extended suites. Reflecting on the performance — and "Sun" on the record's B-side, which features the same ensemble plus vibraphonist Karl Berger — von Schlippenbach wrote in the sleeve notes:

"Fourteen European musicians of the last jazz generation have realised with admirable discipline and utmost exertion the idea of playing free-tone jazz with a big orchestra. By their reaction to the scores, which consisted almost exclusively of directions for improvisations derived from certain principles and ciphers, they demonstrated the finest intuitive grasp of music. They were attuned to the new sounds and illuminated their dynamic properties. By their ability to grasp graphically drawn structures, to improvise with available groups of notes and interval dispositions, as well as to play strictly written phrases absolutely freely, they opened up a world of fascinating possibilities for such orchestras."[49]

Of course, as these notes suggest, von Schlippenbach's experiments with graphic and freely interpreted scores weren't operating in a vacuum. He was one of several composers working in free jazz who were, around this time, using unusual techniques to write for larger ensembles. In February 1966, Impulse! released John Coltrane's world-shaking *Ascension*, featuring eleven musicians creating huge gusts of collective improvisation hung on the most slender of motivic fanfares. On *The Magic City*, also released in 1966, Sun Ra used gestural conduction to guide a 15-piece Arkestra through raucous swells and abrupt abstractions. Recorded at the end of 1964, Carla Bley's "Roast" — which took up almost a whole side of The Jazz Composer's Orchestra's 1966 debut album, *Communication* — melded sly themes and interludes of freedom, imposing remarkable structural discipline on an eleven-piece ensemble of leading New Thing practitioners.

Of these peers and influences, von Schlippenbach's concepts were closest to Bley's in their complexity and detail. They were also a far cry from Brötzmann's unfettered, spontaneous aesthetic, as Brötzmann readily acknowledged:

"When the Berlin festival asked him to write that piece for larger ensemble, he wrote a very sophisticated piece of... you could even call it contemporary music. Kowald and I, we had a much more open vision for the music, more of an idea of just let the band improvise and get it as open as possible — and so we tried to combine that."[50]

If there's a sense, then, that Brötzmann's association with the Globe Unity Orchestra necessitated a partial subsuming of his own musical identity, he and Kowald also knowingly brought a feral quality to von Schlippenbach's pieces, which the composer encouraged and incorporated in much the same way that Duke Ellington had written his big band scores with individual instrumentalists in mind. Listen to contemporaneous recordings of the Globe Unity Orchestra — such as the radio commission recorded in October 1967 at the Donaueschinger Festival for New Music (and released in 2001 as half of *Globe Unity 67/70*) — and there's no mistaking the gleeful ferocity of Brötzmann's savage irruptions.

"The concept of total improvisation"

By 1967, the time was right for Brötzmann to present his own vision for the first time in its most pure and uncompromised form. In June, he went into the studio with Peter Kowald and Sven Åke Johansson and recorded the music that became his first album, *For Adolphe Sax*. Named for the Belgian musician and inventor who had created the saxophone in the early 1840s, its title is at once a dedication of thanks and a wryly irreverent comment on Brötzmann's rebellious subversion of the instrument's commonly agreed capabilities. This music clearly didn't belong to any tradition at all. Its three tracks — the nineteen-minute title piece taking up the whole of side A, with the nearly five-minute "Sanity" and the sixteen-minute "Morning Glory" on side B — are wholly improvised, jettisoning tempo and melody in favour of fierce energy and harsh timbre. From the outset, Brötzmann's tenor is doggedly lodged in a high, keening shriek, save for a few brief moments of guttural mutter and growl. Scornfully disregarding any of the sounds Monsieur Sax intended his brainchild to be capable of, Brötzmann explodes its conventional usage in search of more painfully expressive possibilities. Meanwhile, Kowald alternates between a frenzied arco sawing and belligerent plucking, while Johansson deals pulsating rolls on the snare and toms, supported by a constantly hammering kick pedal. Relentlessly raw and savagely confrontational, it's the sound of three impetuous young warriors emerging fully formed and ready for battle.

Over half a century after it was recorded, the album retains a revolutionary significance as one of the first recorded examples of European free improvisation. In London, Spontaneous Music Ensemble had already released its debut album, *Challenge*, in 1966, revealing an aesthetic that was clearly still indebted to an American free jazz that, in turn, had its roots in hard bop. Tracks like Trevor Watts' "E.D.'s Message" opened with conventionally written head arrangements, with drummer John Stevens laying down bullish swing rhythms for the horns to improvise over. By contrast, Brötzmann's trio were free of any formal metric or harmonic constraints, diving head first into truly free, instantaneous composition. London's AMM were, by then, pursuing something related, as documented on their first album, *AMMMusic*, recorded in June 1966 and released in 1967. But, while AMM were largely concerned with heavily amplified, long-form tones and drones in which the individual musicians' personalities were all but obliterated, the Brötzmann Trio were operating in a spare and intimate setting in which it's possible to hear three keen intelligences and distinct voices at work, creating a new sound with a subtlety and responsiveness somewhat belied by the music's ferocity. Influential German musicologist Ekkehard Jost described *For Adolphe Sax* as "the first German, probably even the first European jazz record, which consequently pursued the concept of total improvisation."[51]

The music wasn't the only radical thing about *For Adolphe Sax*. Brötzmann released the album on BRÖ, an independent label that he set up himself, funded by his work as a freelance graphic designer. It's possible to see this as part of the venerable jazz tradition of the artist-run record label, which stretches back as far as 1921, when brothers John and Reb Spikes founded the California-based Sunshine Records. More famously, in 1952, bassist Charles Mingus, his wife Celia and drummer Max Roach founded Debut Records, which focused on releasing music by emerging artists until it folded in 1957 — the same year Sun Ra and his business partner Alton Abraham established El Saturn records in Chicago, primarily as a vehicle for disseminating Ra's intergalactic missives. While the endeavours of Mingus, Roach and Ra were obviously statements of African American self-determination entirely emblematic of the civil rights era, Brötzmann's founding of BRÖ at least shared their urge to seize control of artistic output and the means of its production. It was, by definition, a revolutionary act. Describing his aims in setting up BRÖ, Brötzmann told David Dacks: "We were all reading our Karl Marx and he says the tools have to be in the hands of the guys doing the work, and so we tried to keep the fabrication and the distribution in the same hands."[52]

For Adolphe Sax was released in 1967, in a very limited private run, with a silkscreened cover designed by Brötzmann (the first of many examples of the artist using his graphic training to create a full package of sound and visuals). The cover photograph shows a young Brötzmann captured in profile, all but obscured by a huge baritone saxophone, emerging from a black void at his back, pointing the way forward with his right hand towards a bright glow of dawning possibilities.

Machine Gun

"You know what kind of pigs we're up against"

In the 1960s, a whole generation of young Germans felt as though they were emerging from dark shadows. This was a generation born into the rubble of World War II who, as young adults, were beginning to grapple with the horrors perpetrated in the name of Nazi Germany. "It's a shame that follows you all your life," Brötzmann confided. "It's not guilt. It's a shame."[1] While young searchers like Brötzmann struggled to comprehend the atrocities carried out by their parents' generation, crimes that loomed over them like a poisonous cloud, many found that explanations were unforthcoming, even — perhaps especially — from those who had been there to witness them.

> "I never talked with my father," he recalled. "My father did his job and didn't want to talk about politics, he didn't want to talk about the war. He was just a small soldier, nothing special. No, he just wanted to make his family happy, building a house and have a job. There was nothing else. Of course, If you start to think about things when you are fourteen or so, you want answers — answers about how could this happen? We didn't get answers, so I had to look for answers somewhere else. My town is just 150 kilometres away from the Dutch border, so it was the first country I visited as a kid — I was about fourteen, fifteen — and it was always so good to cross a border. You felt

it was another air. It was easier to breathe, much more open. My first time in Holland, I met Jewish people and they were very kind to me. But there I was confronted directly with it, when you see the guys with numbers on their arms."[2]

It's little wonder that many German youths, disgusted by the sickening evidence of Auschwitz, Dachau and Buchenwald, vehemently rejected adult society, choosing instead to create their own alternative lifestyles on the fringes of the straight world. In late 1966, the London-based countercultural newspaper *International Times* ran a report by Alex Gross entitled "Beatniks of Berlin," which shone a spotlight on underground youth culture in West Berlin. "The German beatniks have made some progress in achieving a style of their own," Gross observed. "Their name for instance — they are called, and call themselves, not beatniks, but Gammlers (without the 's' in German), a word that could hardly be more German, coming from a disused word for garbage and meaning perhaps scrounges or scroungers." Gross went on to describe how these self-marginalised young Berliners were attracting the opprobrium of their elders: "The Gammlers sometimes engaged in public displays of affection... they were smoking marijuana in public... it might also happen that you would see a beatnik flattened onto the pavement by a policeman."[3]

Of course, this wasn't a specifically German phenomenon. All over the world — in New York and San Francisco, London and Paris, Istanbul and Tokyo — the growing post-war youth movement was fomenting an enormous upsurge of anti-establishment, refusenik energy. But there was a chilling extra dimension fuelling the angry rebellion of German youngsters. As Gross wryly observed in the same report: "A few hundred miles away in Bonn an ex-Nazi was about to become Reichs-Chancellor."[4]

The politician in question, Kurt Georg Kiesinger, had joined the Nazi Party in 1933, served as assistant director of the radio propaganda department in the foreign ministry during the war, and was interned by US forces when hostilities ended. For young Germans, his accession in 1966 to the highest office in West Germany was a brazen confirmation of the lingering — and largely unaddressed — continuities between the Nazi regime and the post-war administration of the Federal Republic. It was an accusation that had been angrily simmering ever since the formation of the Republic in 1949 and Chancellor Konrad Adenauer's swift move away from robust denazification in order to concentrate on economic recovery. The narrative propagated by the new West German establishment was that Nazis had been a minority, and that those associated with the former regime had already been properly punished. While certainly a useful expedient for a country intent on building new stability and prosperity, for many it shone an uncomfortable spotlight on the parent generation's unwillingness to confront the recent past and accept blame. Young West Germans found themselves living in a world where ex-Nazis still held positions of authority — whether as parents, teachers or politicians — and were actively engaged in erasing their own complicity. Naturally, the youth wanted no part in what they saw as a sick, wilfully amnesiac society.

Tensions came to a head in early summer 1967, when the Shah of Iran, Mohammad Reza Pahlavi, and his wife, the Empress Farah Diba, arrived in West Berlin for a state visit. The dictator's official welcome was strongly opposed by both anti-Shah Iranian students resident in the city and sympathetic

West German students affiliated with the Socialist German Students' Union (SDS), and on 2 June, several thousand protestors gathered outside the Opera House, where the Shah was attending a performance. During violent clashes with police, a twenty-six-year-old student, Benn Ohnesborg, was shot in the head and killed by a plainclothes policeman. Later that night, at the headquarters of the SDS, a student by the name of Gudrun Ensslin issued the following provocative statement: "They'll kill us all. You know what kind of pigs we're up against. The is the Auschwitz generation. You can't argue with the people who made Auschwitz. They have weapons and we haven't. We must arm ourselves."[5]

Ensslin's words were a warning of things to come. During the following few years, fuelled by anger over the US war in Vietnam and the authorities' heavy-handed policing of demonstrations, West German youths became increasingly militant in their protests, as youthful idealism hardened into more violent forms of dissent. In May 1970, Ensslin, together with Andreas Baader and Ulrike Meinhof, founded the notorious far-left terrorist organisation the Red Army Faction, which went on to wage a campaign of bombings, bank robberies, assassinations and kidnappings in angry opposition to a West German political establishment that they perceived as still stubbornly unwilling to address Germany's Nazi past.

Inevitably, this anger and impatience was also expressed through youthful artistic endeavours, and it's worth taking a moment to consider the extent to which the playing of jazz was an implicit rejection of the parent generation's nefarious history. The Nazis had harboured a deep loathing and intolerance for jazz, in part because it was created and performed by Black and, to a lesser degree, Jewish musicians, and partly because the music very clearly enunciated a visceral cry for personal freedom that did not sit well with jackboot fascist ideology. During the 1930s and '40s, the Nazi regime had enacted a series of ever more repressive prohibitions against the music — which it called *entartete Kunst* (degenerate art) — beginning with a ban on its broadcast on German radio and finally forbidding its performance entirely at the beginning of the war.

This repression had even resulted in the blossoming of a defiant teenaged counterculture known as the *Swingjugend* (Swing Youth), the name a clear parody of Nazi-affiliated groups such as the *Hitlerjugend* (Hitler Youth). The Swingjugend followed American clothing and dance fashions and were passionate about swing and jazz music. Even when several of the movement's young leaders were rounded up and sent to concentration camps, the Swingjugend continued to run clandestine swing clubs and dances in Hamburg and Berlin. For young musicians coming of age in post-war Germany, the act of playing jazz, though infinitely less risky, was still charged with some of the same rebellious glamour, the same spirited rejection of Nazism's deathly cultural torpor. Moreover, for those involved in the rumblings of the nascent German free-jazz community, the music held even more revolutionary connotations.

"We have to change it"

In the US, free jazz had been an explicitly revolutionary art form almost since its inception. The four-day festival widely seen as announcing the arrival of the so-called New Thing in jazz — organised in October 1964 by trumpeter Bill Dixon at the Cellar Café in New York City and featuring the likes of Paul Bley, Sun Ra and Alan Silva — had been billed as the October Revolution In Jazz, a title that consciously echoed the historical name given to the Bolsheviks' socialist power grab in Russia some forty-seven years earlier.

For African American artists like Dixon, associated with the rise of the New Thing free-jazz aesthetic in the 1960s, the revolutionary energies that powered the music were inextricably linked to broader socio-political concerns, and particularly the civil rights movement, anti-racism and anti-colonialism. Poet, playwright and jazz critic LeRoi Jones (later known as Amiri Baraka) sought to foreground this element of racial rebellion by suggesting the music created by Sun Ra, John Coltrane, Cecil Taylor and others be known not as the New Thing or free jazz but simply as the "New Black Music."[6] He went on to suggest that the music was chiefly characterised by "a newness and a defiance, a demand for freedom, politically and creatively, it was all connected."[7] Moreover, as the outspoken Marxist jazz critic Frank Kofsky elucidated, the music's very form — or perceived lack thereof — was an explicit embodiment of this rebellion. As Kofsky explained, "The New Black Music's... rejection of Western musical conventions... mirrors the larger decision of the Negro ghetto to turn its back on an exploitative and inhumane white American society."[8] Writing in the mid-60s, Kofsky argued that "today's avant-garde movement in jazz is a musical representation of the ghetto's vote of 'no confidence' in Western civilisation and the American Dream — that Negro avant-garde intransigents, in other words, are saying through their horns, as LeRoi Jones would have it, 'Up your ass, feeble-minded ofays!'"[9]

Drummer Milford Graves, who performed with the New York Art Quartet at the October Revolution in Jazz and went on to play with Albert Ayler, stated in a 1998 magazine interview:

"Free music at that particular time was dealing with major change in this country. When you say it was mostly the Black Americans that were playing free music, it was because of this great desire for freedom. That's what was coming out in the music. It was tearing down all those structures. You would almost reject anything that came from a racist, oppressive element in this country."[10]

Of all the American free-jazz protagonists, the most forthright and articulate in communicating these concerns was tenor saxophonist and playwright Archie Shepp. Moreover, he went further than most in looking beyond immediate racial issues to expose the left-wing political convictions that underlined the music's revolutionary impetus. In his controversial essay, "The Artist Speaks Bluntly," published in *Down Beat* magazine in December 1965, he baldly stated: "I am an antifascist artist."[11] The following year, in the same magazine, he claimed: "[Jazz] is anti-war; it is opposed to Vietnam; it is for Cuba; it is for the liberation of all people."[12]

Shepp's commitment to the cause wasn't just reserved for the pages of American jazz publications. In summer 1962, he and Dixon had travelled to Helsinki to take part in the eighth World Festival of Youth and Students, a huge cultural event backed by the Soviet Union at which more than fifteen thousand delegates from all over the world gathered to witness discussions and performances celebrating left-wing engagement with the struggle for peace, decolonisation and global liberation movements. For Shepp and Dixon, it was a risky move, and not just because openly aligning oneself with communist politics could attract unwelcome attention at the height of the Cold War. For their first ever shows outside of New York City, the Shepp-Dixon Quartet — featuring Shepp on saxophone, Dixon on trumpet, Don Moore on bass and Howard McRae on drums, and temporarily joined by clarinettist Perry Robinson — played two concerts, one in a concert hall and another in an open-air stadium, to an audience of youngsters who had probably heard very little of the burgeoning avant-garde jazz sound. In the event, the group's mix of chord-based jazz, modal improvisation and more experimental flights of free jazz was rapturously received, providing a highlight of the entire festival and an emblematic congruence of political and musical radicalism.

Yet, if European jazzers were, on the whole, perhaps less well informed about the intertwined conceptual breakthroughs and left-wing ideas proposed by free jazz, many had already been enthusiastically waging a committed, albeit somewhat less forward-thinking, musical revolution of their own.

In the middle of the 1950s, a schism had taken place among young European jazz musicians with the arrival of be-bop. While some embraced this new, ultra-modern style, others reacted by throwing themselves wholeheartedly into replicating the earlier sounds of Dixieland or "traditional" New Orleans jazz. In the UK, bands led by the likes of trumpeters Ken Collyer and Humphrey Lyttleton and trombonist Chris Barber sparked the so-called Trad Boom, with countless amateur jazz revivalists springing up to play this carefully preserved sound. Curiously, while be-bop was the more musically radical aesthetic, its proponents were largely unconcerned with politics, while the Trad jazz fanatics passionately espoused left-wing politics. The phenomenon was authoritatively documented by the British Marxist historian Eric Hobsbawm, who from 1955 to 1965 wrote a monthly column of jazz reviews for the left-wing magazine *New Statesman* using the pen-name Francis Newton (actually the name of a communist trumpeter who had played on Billie Holiday's famous recording of the anti-racist lament "Strange Fruit"). In his definitive 1959 study of British jazz, *The Jazz Scene,* Hobsbawm (writing as Newton) noted that Trad jazzers in the UK had "maintained links with the political left," pointing out that "world youth festivals, anti-nuclear marches, May Day demonstrations, or other expressions of hostility to the social *status quo* have rarely lacked their quota of imitation New Orleans jazz players."[13]

Of course, the Trad Boom wasn't just confined to the UK. As a teenager in the 1950s, Brötzmann had owned and played along to records by Barber and Lyttleton, and both he and Peter Kowald had started out playing in Dixieland bands. Kowald told writer Mike Heffley: "When I grew up in the '50s, as a boy — more consciously, after the early '60s — I had a broken tradition, because all of German culture had been abused by the fascism of Hitler. So I didn't want to sing any German songs. All of us felt that way."[14] Brötzmann, for his part, was, from a young age, keen to embrace the leftist ideology that permeated jazz:

"For me, jazz had a kind of political meaning, because in my very early youth I was already very left wing, and connected to the Communist Party — naïve, of course, but genuine. Then Vietnam started up; Korea was just over, and to deal with jazz music was a way to be on the right side in the war between the poor and rich, the black and white — well, we didn't have that particular problem, but, you know, the worldwide class struggle and so on."[15]

For musicians like Brötzmann and Kowald, coming out of the left-wing milieu of the Dixieland scene and conscious of the emancipatory promise of jazz, the advent of free jazz was a major revelation. Not only was it daringly new and artistically challenging, its most vociferous proponents, such as Shepp, also embodied an attitude of angry dissent that resonated profoundly with a German youth who were, in their own way, every bit as anxious to turn their backs on an inhuman mainstream society as their African American heroes were. Put simply, for Brötzmann and his peers, to play free jazz was to mark oneself as an outlaw desperate to dissociate oneself from the shame of Germany's racist past. "For us, it was really something that we could use to free ourselves from all of that that was behind us," Brötzmann explained. "In that connection, the word 'free' had a different meaning from just a kind of aesthetic process."[16]

There's certainly no doubting Brötzmann's commitment to the notion of liberation — in all its forms — during these years. Like many young West German leftists and radical thinkers, he found himself increasingly sympathetic towards the aims of the African American black power movement. As Harald Kisiedu points out, Brötzmann recognised a growing sense of solidarity with what he thought of as "our black comrades in the States," instinctively understanding that they had "different problems but the same way of 'we have to change it.'"[17]

In fact, just a few years later, in 1971, Brötzmann put these convictions into practice by briefly providing shelter in his home for an African American G.I. who had gone AWOL in a desperate attempt to avoid service in Vietnam. At the time, Brötzmann was known to a network of radicals as a potential anti-war ally, so he was unfazed when the American — known only as Nolan — appeared at his door one day seeking shelter.

"He was a nice guy but kind of spaced," Brötzmann told me. "This was the days of acid and all that. He was a kind of a drummer and we even played together once."[18] Brötzmann recounts how he subsequently found Nolan some basic accommodation nearby, "with water and a toilet." However, things took a sinister turn when Brötzmann returned home one afternoon to find Nolan holding his wife and children captive, sitting on the sofa, at gunpoint — "like a movie," he recalled. "He was confused. By the time I talked him into putting down the gun, it was dark." When, a couple of weeks later, Brötzmann went to check on Nolan's digs, he discovered that the American had disappeared. "I paid a couple of weeks' rent on the place," Brötzmann chuckled, without regret.

Yet, despite his obvious dedication to the cause, by the second half of the '60s Brötzmann was already beginning to feel disillusioned with aspects of the organised left. "I was involved," he admitted. "Of course, it went together with our musical intention to change society, to change people, to change the way of life in a way... I always was... let's call it a socialist or whatever... On the other hand, I would say I had always quite a good nose for not getting involved in this kind of nonsense because, when you look closer and closer into these party-like organisations, man, then you better give up."[19] Perhaps inevitably, Brötzmann's dissatisfaction with the left was exacerbated by musical differences, as he found himself increasingly at odds with a cohort of his peers whose tastes reached only as far as "Joan Baez, some American bullshit, some softy guitar music."[20]

"At that time, we played quite a bit in German Universities," he recalled, "and I remember one concert in the Freie Universität Berlin, all these left-wing political guys were sitting there throwing tomatoes, beer cans and shit, and even some of them tried to get on the stage to fight, because our music, to them, was very elitist."[21] For Brötzmann, this rejection signalled not only a lack of imagination, but an unforgivable intellectual deficiency: "This music was not allowed. That was one of the first times you started to think about what kind of bullshit was going on. If they don't understand, they must be as stupid as the rest." (It should be noted that not all of his fellow jazz-heads felt such antipathy towards "softy" music. In 1969, Albert Mangelsdorff and tenor saxophonist Joki Freund recorded the album *Wild Goose* with British folk singers Colin Wilkie and Shirley Hart — a somewhat perplexing date on which jaunty, acoustic guitar–driven folk ditties with mythic themes and yearning harmonies are riven by sudden, savage intrusions of wailing free jazz.)

At the same time, several members of the avant-garde community were turning away from their jazz roots and helping to birth new musical forms in step with the times. In 1968 alone, three noted improvising drummers helped lay the foundations for key units in the nascent West German rock scene: Jaki Liebezeit left Manfred Schoof's employ to co-found Can; Mani Neumeier, who had passed through Brötzmann's trio in the mid-60s, launched Guru Guru; and drummer Paul Lovens, who later worked with Brötzmann and Alexander von Schlippenbach, played in an early, acoustic incarnation of Kraftwerk.

Brötzmann himself dallied with some of these emerging forms, playing with underground musicians including the earliest line up of Edgar Froese's pioneering *kosmische* outfit Tangerine Dream. "We all listened to each other," he mused. "It was a wide-open field and everything was possible."[22] In fact, the psychedelic rock bands coming up in West Germany were just as committed to improvisation as those on the jazz scene. Lutz Graf-Ulbrich, guitarist and founding member of

Berlin-based group Agitation Free, told me: "Looking for new sounds, that was very important, and breaking all the rules, not playing songs with verse and chorus but open up and improvise and see what's happening, to be free and express your feelings."[23]

Even so, Brötzmann drew the line at some of the new groups' more radically countercultural stances — and particularly the communal living arrangements experimented with by bands such as Guru Guru and Amon Düül. Underlying many of these alternative models of habitation was an explicit left-wing agenda, as in the West Berlin urban community Kommune 1, which existed from the beginning of 1967 to the end of 1969. Graf-Ulbrich of Agitation Free remembers: "Our guitar player was living there. They were twenty people living in one room, with [author] Uwe Johnson and Uschi Obermaier, a model — she was earning the money, actually — and we were rehearsing there so we were in this political scene. We played for the left students, we played quite a lot at the university for the revolution."[24]

"I always hated that," Brötzmann told me, speaking of the vogue for shared living spaces.

"Some gigs were organised by commune people, so you had to be there. But I was always too individual-orientated. If you are busy with your own stuff so intensively, you don't need it. I had my family, and our house was always full of people travelling through or working with me, so it was an active commune anyway — but to make a kind of principle out of that lifestyle, was not for me."[25]

Despite this somewhat gruff refusal to romanticise the situation, Brötzmann could, when the mood struck, indulge in a more wistful nostalgia. In 2013 he told me:

"In these times, in the '60s, when we all wanted to change the music, even to change the world, we were all working together without talking too much, drinking together, living together. I was living with my wife and two kids in a small flat, but sometimes we had ten musicians, in any corner on some mattress. There was no money in the casa but there was always a soup on the table. I don't want to glorify this kind of thing, because it was hard times. I had to work my daily job, I had to make some money for the family, because there was none from the music. Wherever I could work something, I did. But, on the other hand, people were passing by and stayed for weeks — even sometimes people I didn't know passed by. It was really a different time. We all played together. It was really a completely different way of life."[26]

Crucially, while many of the rock bands that grew out of the burgeoning West German hippie scene sought domestic fraternity, improvising free-jazz musicians like Brötzmann found an explicitly idealistic intimation of utopia in the music itself — a music without leaders, in which every participant was engaged in a collective, communal endeavour. Belgian pianist Fred Van Hove explained:

"In jazz, there was a rhythm section — the piano played the chords, the bass played the bass notes and the drummer did the rhythm and the timing — and then there were the wind instruments, they were the soloists. So the rhythm section was just there to help the soloists do solos. Now, when we came to improvised music, this order was completely gone, because now we knew that every instrument is equal to the other one. There's no such thing as a rhythm section and a soloist. Every instrument has his own right."[27]

It's a crucial distinction that strikes at the heart of Brötzmann's whole approach to music and, indeed, to life: "In all my ensembles I've tried to involve the members of the band in the process of decisions and the process of music," he claimed. "I never was the guy who said, 'OK, here's your solo, play your arse off.' No, no, I want to get, you can call it a kind of democratic process. That's what the music is, that's what human society should be."[28]

"We wanted to play with the musicians we could meet"

As Van Hove's observation reveals, the gathering European free-jazz revolution was not only taking place in Germany. By now, Brötzmann and his associates were aware of a febrile, international network of like-minded improvisers.

In fact, Brötzmann's first encounter with progressive jazz musicians in neighbouring countries had taken place several years earlier, in the mid-60s, during one of his trips to Amsterdam as part of a "Fluxus band" featuring the likes of George Brett and Emmett Williams. "That's where I first met Misha Mengelberg," he recalled, "he was in the audience and we talked a bit."[29] Five years Brötzmann's senior and with a similar background in Fluxus, Mengelberg was, by this time, already carving out a reputation as a pianist in the vein of Thelonious Monk, at the vanguard of Dutch jazz. "A bit later, I heard Misha for the first time in a place called Sheherazade, in a side street off the Rembrandtplein. He was playing with Piet Noordijk, the sax player, Cees Slinger, I think, on the drums and I think Ruud Jacobs was the bass player. Misha's quartet was quite impressive, very much Monk-influenced and already quite avant-garde."[30] Around this time, Brötzmann's frequent trips to Amsterdam meant that he was renting a small room in the city's Jewish quarter and meeting other young jazz musicians, most notably saxophonist Willem Breuker and drummer Han Bennink, both of whom would go on to play key roles in Brötzmann's musical path.

Kowald, too, was busy making international connections. "I had a family already and had to make money," said Brötzmann, "but Kowald was studying, so he was a bit more flexible and could travel a bit more."[31] As early as 1967, Kowald struck up a working relationship with a cadre of London-based improvisers, foremost among them the members of Spontaneous Music Ensemble — drummer John Stevens (born 1940), saxophonist Trevor Watts (1939) and trombonist Paul Rutherford (1940). The three had met in 1959, arriving together at the RAF Music School in Uxbridge to begin their National Service in the form of training as members of Her Majesty's Royal Air Force Band, and immediately discovered a shared love of jazz. Playing together as much as they could in their spare time, the three friends quickly became known around barracks as "the jazzers," and when, shortly after, Watts was posted to the 2nd Tactical Air Force Band at RAF Butzweilerhof near Cologne, West Germany, Stevens and Rutherford requested the same assignment. During the next few years, they played regularly at a Cologne cellar club alongside young local musicians including Manfred Schoof, Buschi Niebergall and Alexander von Schlippenbach.

Out of the RAF and back in London in 1964, Stevens quickly worked his way into the capital's modern jazz scene, earning a living playing regularly at Ronnie Scott's Club in Soho and forming a septet including saxophonist Alan Skidmore, expatriate Canadian trumpeter Kenny Wheeler and others. Meanwhile, Watts and Rutherford carried on rehearsing together as a duo and, by the end of 1965, had formed a quintet playing original free-jazz compositions, a repertoire that they eventually got the chance to try out on stage at the Peanuts Club, a candle-lit underground poetry and jazz haunt on Liverpool Street. Stevens, who was working nearby at Ronnie Scott's, came to hear his old forces pals in action and experienced something of an epiphany, deciding then and there to turn away from the more straight-ahead sounds he'd been involved with and become the drummer of the Watts-Rutherford Quintet. In September that year, invoking the excitement and sense of possibility the collective found in their new identity, Stevens suggested renaming the group the Spontaneous Music Ensemble (SME).

From the beginning of 1966, SME began playing improvised music six nights a week in a venue known as the Little Theatre Club: a tiny room up four flights of stairs in the heart of London's West End theatre district, which the manager, Jean Pritchard, was willing to turn over to the young musicians every night after the evening's play was finished. Its atmosphere of intense experimentation served as a lightning rod to a rapidly coalescing community of fellow musical searchers, including Kenny Wheeler, pianist Howard Riley, bassists Barry Guy and Dave Holland, and others.

While SME's debut album, *Challenge* — recorded in March 1966 by Stevens, Watts and Rutherford, with Bruce Cale and Jeff Clyne taking turns on bass — bore vestigial traces of the American New Thing, the music they were making just a year later had undergone radical change. Recorded in March 1967, but unreleased until thirty years later, *Withdrawal* was conceived as the soundtrack to an aborted thirty-five-minute film of the same name based on the experiences of a young drug addict (analogous to Shirley Clarke's 1962 movie *The Connection*, soundtracked by US hard-bop alto saxophonist Jackie McLean). Here, the group's bluster and macho, shoulder-barging solos have been jettisoned to make room for a diffident consideration of space and close attention. While much of this transformation was due to Stevens' leadership — and particularly his growing fascination with the spectral atonalities of Austrian composer Anton Webern — *Withdrawal* also benefits from the addition of two compelling voices supplied by fellow Little Theatre habitués: young saxophonist Evan Parker (born 1944) and guitarist Derek Bailey.

Born in Sheffield in 1930 — and characterised by Brötzmann as "the grand old man"[32] — Bailey had been a working musician since the beginning of the 1950s. and throughout his early adult life earned a living in a bewildering array of "straight" contexts, from restaurants and night clubs to dance halls and music hall orchestras accompanying light entertainers such as comedians Morecombe and Wise and Bob Monkhouse. But he showed an interest in free improvisation from an early age, and was among the first British musicians to pursue it as a serious practice. Though he claimed, in conversation with Ben Watson, to have first taken part in free playing as early as 1953, with two guitarists in a flat in Glasgow, and again around 1954 sitting in with a jazz piano trio led by Eddie Barton,[33] his first major contribution to free music came in 1963 when he co-founded (along with fellow Yorkshiremen drummer Tony Oxley and bassist Gavin Bryars) a unit somewhat jokingly named the Joseph Holbrooke Trio. Named after an obscure British composer (whose works they never performed), the trio started out playing more or less conventional jazz but gravitated closer and closer to free-form playing during their three-year existence, until Bailey relocated to London in 1966 and quickly fell into the orbit of the Little Theatre Club. Here, he was free to develop daring stylistic gambits — like Stevens, influenced by Webern — which included brittle, atonal clusters, ringing harmonics and jarring intervallic leaps.

It should be noted that the British improvisers Kowald encountered weren't just musically aligned with the German scene but shared many organisational and socio-political concerns too. Though Stevens was undoubtedly SME's driving force, he, like Brötzmann, espoused a non-hierarchical, leaderless music that rejected the tradition of solos with accompaniment and placed a premium on collective playing. As noted by critic Brian Olewnick, he stipulated that all group improvisations should adhere to two strict tenets, later summarised by Evan Parker as: "(1) If you can't hear another musician, you're playing too loud, and (2) if the music you're producing doesn't regularly relate to what you're hearing others create, why be in the group?"[34]

At the same time, many of the UK improvisers were avowed leftists of one sort or another. Evan Parker told Mike Heffley that "having been introduced to anarchist-socialist philosophies as a student," he was "always more interested in the anarchist-socialist life than the Marxist one."[35] Paul Rutherford, on the other hand, was a card-carrying communist. This political affiliation was made explicitly clear by the 1972 release of a self-titled album by Iskra 1903, the trio of Rutherford, Bailey and Barry Guy. Both album and trio were named after a political newspaper founded in 1903 by Vladimir Lenin as the official organ of the Russian Social Democratic Labour Party to champion the cause of socialist revolution. Writing of the album in his detailed and entertaining biography of Bailey, Ben Watson observes: "It intimates what a world might be like in which everything was as resonant and responsive as these squeaks and squeals and bongs: the socialist vision of human activity as an end in itself, rather than merely a means to accumulate capital."[36]

Kowald's travels also brought him into contact with Fred Van Hove (born 1937), the Belgian pianist who half-seriously claimed to have been less influenced by Cecil Taylor than by the bells of Antwerp Cathedral, but who, nevertheless, had developed a highly kinetic style that owed much to Taylor's percussive innovations. Speaking of the improvising scene in '60s Antwerp, Van Hove told Gerard Rouy:

> "We thought we were the first ones to improvise in music, that we invented it, which in a way was true. At that time, we didn't have much contact with countries around and it was quite a surprise to discover that people were doing the same thing in Holland, in Germany, later we discovered that we were lots of people doing the same in Europe. We tried to meet the other people who were doing the same thing. For example, when I heard that Han Bennink was playing with Willem Breuker, I went to Amsterdam by car to listen to them, they asked me to join in for the second set. We wanted to play with the musicians we could meet."[37]

Clearly, for Van Hove, the discovery of fellow improvisers beyond his immediate milieu was nothing short of an epiphany. For Brötzmann, these new connections with kindred spirits in Britain, Belgium and the Netherlands were both a vindication of the radical path he had chosen and an unmistakable gathering of the tribes.

"It was really a very special connection"

Yet, of all these newly revealed artistic outposts, it was undoubtedly the Dutch improvising community with whom Brötzmann felt the most significant affinity.

That scene was centred around Instant Composers Pool (ICP), a collective founded in 1967 (just a few months after the release of Brötzmann's *For Adolphe Sax*) by Mengelberg, Bennink and Breuker. It arose at a time when musicians on the more experimental fringes of jazz and improvised music were recognising the strength to be gained through solidarity. Much like the Jazz Composers Guild, formed in New York in 1964, and the Association for the Advancement of Creative Musicians (AACM), formed in Chicago in 1965, it offered members an element of self-determination in organising their own performance opportunities outside of the restrictive and largely uninterested world of commercial jazz clubs and festivals. Moreover, as the name, coined by Mengelberg, suggested, ICP sought to confer a certain legitimacy on the practice of free improvisation by maintaining that improvisers were, in fact, composing their works at the moment of creation.

From the start, it wasn't just an umbrella for Dutch improvisers but also actively welcomed international artists. An important member from its inception was John Tchicai, the Danish saxophonist who had made key contributions to the birth of the American free-jazz New Thing during a four-year sojourn in the US, participating in Bill Dixon's October Revolution in Jazz, co-founding the New York Contemporary Five (with Archie Shepp, Don Cherry, bassist Don Moore and drummer J.C. Moses) and the New York Art Quartet (with trombonist Roswell Rudd, drummer Milford Graves and bassist Lewis Worrell), and playing on John Coltrane's

Ascension, before returning to Europe in 1966. Moreover, in the years following its formation, ICP enthusiastically embraced the gathering tribes of European improvisers. Bennink recalled: "We wanted to be a collective where there would be room for other Dutch improvisers but also internationals like Peter Brötzmann, Derek Bailey, Evan Parker, Paul Rutherford, etc. Everybody playing with us was part of the pool."[38]

Crucially, ICP also operated as a cooperative record label devoted to documenting the work of its members, beginning with *New Acoustic Swing Duo* by the duo of Breuker and Bennink, recorded and released in late 1967, and *Instant Composers Pool* by Mengelberg, Bennink and Tchicai, from the following year. While the label's activities were certainly informed by the same revolutionary urge to seize control of the music's ownership and production that spawned Brötzmann's BRÖ imprint, it was also born of DIY pragmatism. "We wanted to have control over our own recordings," Bennink confirmed. "Nobody was interested in releasing them so we didn't have another choice [than] to do that ourselves."[39] Also like BRÖ, this artistic control extended to the LPs' cover art. With echoes of the hand-drawn album art Sun Ra famously created for releases on his El Saturn label, ICP covers were overseen and crafted by ex-art student Bennink. "The covers also have their own character, designed by me," he explained, "beginning with *New Acoustic Swing Duo*, making around 3,000 original covers by hand for each LP, to make the production as cheap as possible at the lowest sales price for the public."[40]

While ICP was clearly a serious endeavour, the music its Dutch members made was often characterised by an openness to the intrusion of absurdist theatricality and humour, influenced by surrealism and Dada, which, to a certain extent, set it apart from the intensely furrowed brows of many of the German improvisers. "We were interested in Dada and Kurt Schwitters," Bennink said. "Humour just happens when it happens. It was never agreed upon before the concert, it was part of the improvisation."[41] Despite Bennink's attempts to downplay its significance and centrality, much of this humour was very deliberately directed by Mengelberg's impish intellect. See, for instance, the duet he recorded with his pet grey red-tail parrot, Eeko, in 1972, entitled "Instant Composition 5/VI/'72" (and released on the 1974 album *Epistrophy*), on which the bird's contributions are listed as "whistling, speaking and clacking." It's a prime example of Mengelberg's penchant for musical games and ludic devices.

Brötzmann, for all his perceived seriousness, recognised and appreciated in Mengelberg's humorous experiments the powerful influence of Fluxus, not least its proponents' ability to operate at an ironic distance from their art. He told Gerard Rouy: "I always like people, in the field of music or the arts, who are working hard and are taking what they are doing, when they are doing it, very seriously but also at the same time being able to look at the thing from a distance and with a humour too. That's what Misha had in common with Nam June Paik, for example."[42] In Mengelberg's pieces, this often took the form of comic self-interrogation. "Misha was always reflecting things and taking things apart," Brötzmann recalled. "He took melodies out of the Dutch folk music, and his greatest thing was to turn things around and make some fun out of them."[43] For Brötzmann, Mengelberg's mischievous ruptures were intimately connected to the same rule-breaking imperative Paik had instilled in him at an early age: "I liked [Mengelberg's] way of performing, sometimes just doing something very beautiful, and the next second questioning it with other kinds of actions, destroying it or leaving and then going in a completely different direction."[44]

For ICP, much of this ongoing interrogation was bound up in a self-reflexive attitude to their source material, and particularly a simultaneously respectful yet irreverent relationship with American jazz. On the one hand, unlike their German and British counterparts, ICP musicians were happy to incorporate earlier forms of jazz, from Duke Ellington compositions to blues and ballads. "We were being very Dutch," agreed Bennink. "We could still play a blues but, in Germany and England at that time, it was absolutely forbidden. We were doing another thing."[45] Yet, at the same time, these traditional American jazz paradigms were frequently used as springboards to deconstruction via improvisation, where all the certainties of form would melt away into loose and unpredictable variations, presenting a concerted investigation of the tension between composition and improvisation that has remained a central concern of improvisers well into the twenty-first century.

Perhaps because of his immersion in the music of ICP, Brötzmann, for his part, resisted any superficial cataloguing of the differences between the approaches used by improvisers of different nationalities: "I'm not such a friend of saying, 'OK, there is an English way, there is a Dutch way, there is a German way,'" he averred. "I think it always depends on one or the other guys who is doing that."[46] Nevertheless, as Mike Heffley has noted,[47] it is possible to map some of the major traits of the different national scenes that were distinct enough to become persistent stereotypes. The Dutch were bold, anarchic tricksters incorporating elements of Fluxus, theatre and folk tradition to create accessibly humorous deconstructions. The English were what Heffley calls "sound researchers," engaged in non-hierarchical and often quietly introverted experiments. The Germans, by contrast, were the "energy" players, more obviously following the intense and loudly ecstatic example of American free jazz.

As much as Brötzmann may have downplayed these differences, he readily suggested that the extremities reached for by the young Germans were a direct reaction to the shame and trauma they felt as a result of Germany's all too recent Nazi past. "It was really a very strong problem inside of us," he stated, "to find some way to deal with that. We all felt the same. We had so much to fight against. That's why, maybe, our music in those days was much more aggressive, much more violent than, for example, the English music or the Dutch music, because they didn't have our problems."[48]

Despite Brötzmann's deep respect for Mengelberg, his strongest bonds on the Dutch scene were made with two key players slightly closer to his own age, beginning with Willem Breuker (born in Amsterdam,1944), with whom he struck up a convivial rapport that wasn't just limited to the bandstand. "Willem was my first real friend in Holland," he remembered. "Jenever [Dutch gin] and Pils [beer] — that's why we understood each other so well."

Not just a drinking buddy, Breuker was a fellow tenor man who also had a background in interdisciplinary art. In October 1966, he'd collaborated with Australian visual artist Jeffrey Shaw and Dutch sculptor and performance artist Tjebbe van Tijen on a Fluxus-like happening at Better Books in London. This was the legendary independent book shop and countercultural hub where, during the mid-to-late '60s, Beat luminaries including Allen Ginsberg, William

S. Burroughs and Alexander Trocchi gave readings, where visionary artist-activists such as Jeff Nuttal and Gustav Metzger staged installations, and where the new London free-improvisers regularly performed. (The cover of SME's CD *Withdrawal* carries a black and white photo of a sextet version of the group, including Bailey and Parker, assembled in Better Books' dank basement performance space in March 1967.) The event that Breuker, Shaw and van Tijen staged there was an early version of a cinematic performance work entitled *Emergences of Continuous Forms*, which involved rapidly changing visuals containing subliminal images projected through translucent screens and balloons onto spectators, with a live improvised soundtrack by Breuker that gradually transformed the happening into a parade out of the basement and onto the pavement outside the shop.

It was through Breuker that Brötzmann was first alerted to the prodigious talents of Han Bennink. "Willem at that time was working with Gunter Hampel a lot in Germany," Bennink recalled. "He said to Brötzmann, 'If you want a drummer, you should try Han Bennink.'"[49]

Bennink (born 1942), had been playing progressive jazz with Mengelberg since 1961, and the two had gained some attention, together with bassist Jacques Schols, as a trio accompanying iconoclastic American multi-instrumentalist and former Coltrane associate Eric Dolphy on a June 1964 date recorded in Hilversum, North Holland (not far from Bennink's birthplace of Zaandam) just a few weeks before Dolphy's untimely death due to diabetes. The session, which was posthumously released under Dolphy's name the following year as the album *Last Date*, found Mengelberg and Bennink firmly at home backing Dolphy's squawking bass clarinet and loquacious alto sax on off-kilter tracks such as Thelonious

Monk's "Epistrophy." Dolphy had been so pleased with the quartet that he arranged for them to appear at Copenhagen's famous Café Montmartre jazz club — notification of which Bennink received in a letter from Dolphy two days after his death.

In May 1965, the trio of Bennink and brothers Pim Jacobs (piano) and Ruud Jacobs (bass) accompanied American guitarist Wes Montgomery for a Dutch TV special, footage of which[50] reveals the young Bennink deep in the pocket of breezy swing with a crisp snare attack, taking brief "fours" solo spots that elicit grins of appreciation from Montgomery. In fact, Bennink and Ruud Jacobs became the go-to rhythm section for visiting American jazz veterans, also playing with Johnny Griffin and Ben Webster — but Bennink's ears were becoming attuned to the more challenging sounds emanating from across the Atlantic: "When I heard Albert Ayler and Milford Graves, my interest in improvised music began."[51]

Even so, as late as 1967, Bennink and Jacobs were still providing the back line for touring Americans, most notably Sonny Rollins, with whom they performed a number of live shows and Dutch radio broadcasts that summer (unearthed and released as *Rollins in Holland: The 1967 Studio and Live Recordings* in 2020). On tunes like the standard "Tune Up" (generally credited to Miles Davis), Bennink can be heard crashing ahead with up-tempo verve, heavy on the ride cymbal, while still finding room to add unusual tactile patters to his brief solo. "Ruud Jacobs was the bass player of choice for anybody that came through Holland," Rollins recalled. "Han Bennink was known as the more avant-garde guy. I was told they had distinct styles, but I didn't think about that at all, because I could play with both of them. And they both knew something about me. So, it was wonderful to have them play together. I was very happy to have them there as my backup trio."[52] Bennink, for his part, saw no conflict at all with his growing interest in free improvisation, embracing Rollins' hard-bop milieu with the same serious determination he would later apply to Mengelberg's daft polkas and deconstructed blues. "I know what you mean by free improvisation," he told me, "but I hate the term 'free.' Improvisation is always free for me."[53]

It was around this time that, on a visit to Wuppertal, Bennink was introduced to Brötzmann:

> "I remember that I was going in my Deux Cheveux with Willem Breuker to see where Brötzmann lived, and when I came to the house, I really liked it immediately. I liked his wife, she was very, very nice; the kids were young; there were lots of cats around. There was, hanging on the walls, very interesting art that Peter did and we were playing table tennis in the room. It was just great."[54]

Brötzmann, too, instantly recognised a kindred spirit in Bennink, not just as a fearless improviser but also as a practicing visual artist with an interest in design that extended to creating distinctive album covers: "For me, with Han, it was really a very special connection because we both came from art, we both went to art school, we always did our things on the side."[55]

"It was protest music"

For idealistic young artists like Brötzmann and Bennink, the turbulent late '60s were alive with possibility. "That was a very important time," Brötzmann confirmed. "It was such a fantastic exchange of music, musicians, ideas and, of course, it was a very interesting political time too."[56] These simmering energies took on urgent form with the release of Brötzmann's second album, *Machine Gun*, in 1968.

The album's origins can be traced to a suggestion made to Brötzmann in 1967 by concert promoter Horst Lippmann, co-producer of the German Jazz Festival in Frankfurt. Perhaps hoping to repeat the success von Schlippenbach's Globe Unity Orchestra had had at the festival the previous year, he asked Brötzmann to assemble a large band to play the eleventh edition of the festival in 1968. Brötzmann, of course, already had some experience with expanded ensembles, having worked in Globe Unity Orchestra, and even before that, as early as July 1966, his own trio had occasionally merged with Manfred Schoof's quintet to form an octet.

The new nine-piece band he formed in early 1968 was similar in scope, drawing on the same pan-European pool of young improvisers von Schlippenbach had used for Globe Unity. Claiming to be influenced by the Lionel Hampton Big Band, which boasted a heavyweight, four-tenor front line, Brötzmann recruited fellow tenor-men Evan Parker, Willem Breuker and Gerd Dudek. Fred Van Hove played piano, and a substantial double rhythm section included Peter Kowald and Buschi Niebergall on bass, with both Han Bennink and Sven-Åke Johansson on drums. In March 1968, this bulky nonet performed at German music festivals including the German Jazz Festival in Frankfurt and the Jazz Ost-West Festival in Nuremberg. A recording of the Frankfurt performance, released on the CD *Fuck De Boere* in 2001, captures the ensemble brandishing a raggedly implacable power and energy as it blasts through a monolithic composition Brötzmann called "Machine Gun." Its title recalled the nickname bestowed on him by Don Cherry, who also performed at Frankfurt on the same night as Brötzmann's nonet, leading an international quintet called New York Total Music Company featuring bassist Kent Carter, French drummer Jacques Thollot, German pianist/vibraphonist Karl Berger and, on soprano sax, Brötzmann's other former mentor, Steve Lacy.

With the proceeds of these gigs, plus the money trickling into his BRÖ label following the release of *For Adolphe Sax*, Brötzmann arranged a recording session in May at Lila Eule, a club in Bremen in the north of Germany, where his trio had regularly played. As Harald Kisiedu has pointed out,[57] Lila Eule was well known as a radical political hub, and played an important role in organising local protests against the American war in Vietnam. The octet that Brötzmann convened there — with the same personnel as the nonet, minus Gerd Dudek — was, in its own way, every bit as radical and subversive as the club's political actions. "It was a crazy time," Brötzmann recalled, "in all ways — in political ways, the arts were really trying everything that was possible, and we needed to find some other ways to play music. That [session at Lila Eule] was the first meeting of all the west European guys — that means Belgian, Dutch, English — and the first recording of that."[58] Indeed, at more than half a century's remove, it's easy to forget just how progressive this pan-Euro summit was, bringing together young idealists to cooperate as fellow Europeans less than twenty-five years after the end of World War II.

"Right at the beginning, I was the first English person to play with Brötzmann," Evan Parker told me. [59] Moreover, as he told Mike Heffley, Parker found his interaction with Brötzmann's unflagging energy enormously inspiring and something of a catalyst in his own musical development:

"I was playing then in a more English kind of way, but it just didn't hold up to that level of intensity and physical commitment, of acoustic strength and robustness, of the *Machine Gun* record. Peter was important in all kinds of different ways. I was hugely encouraged by his total commitment. He was doing everything that I wanted to do: playing full time, making records, dealing with the problems."[60]

Ever the contrarian, Bennink's memories of the *Machine Gun* recording session are less edifying. "*Machine Gun* is one of my worst musical memories and I don't understand why I am asked so often about that."[61] Things didn't get off to a great start when, after playing a show in Lila Eule, he and Breuker almost got into a fight with a drunken German who was singing Nazi songs. Once the club was cleared, recording could begin. "It was one o'clock in the night and they turned the whole club into a sort of Korean yurt, made by blankets, to damp the sound. I was sitting under blankets, without headphones and I couldn't hear anything. The session was until five o'clock in the morning. I was falling asleep behind my drums. I was so fucking tired."[62]

"There's no question that the political element was there," claimed Parker. "It's explicit in *Machine Gun*. It was protest music."[63]

"At that time it was, for me, a political statement,"[64] agreed Brötzmann. At the moment *Machine Gun* was being recorded, in May 1968, revolutionary fervour was sweeping the world. Anti-Vietnam War protests in Europe and America were becoming more and more strident. Washington, DC, and Detroit were recovering from major riots following the assassination of Dr Martin Luther King. Czechoslovakia was struggling to throw off the Soviet occupation of Prague. Just four hundred miles away from Bremen, anti-capitalist students and sympathetic workers were manning the barricades in Paris, violently clashing with police and bringing the country perilously close to civil war. "That all came together," Brötzmann continued, "and, stupid or maybe naïve as we were at that time, we thought we would be able to change the world. I think, as a young man, you have a right to think like that and to see like that."[65] Van Hove concurred: "In the '60s — May '68 — we were going to renew the world or something like that. I don't say it was a success, but there was a very strong move to go to more freedom. So it was also in the music. Improvisation was already [happening] a bit before May '68 but when these things came we were partners in crime, partners in revolution."[66]

If *Machine Gun*'s title was perceived as a provocation, Brötzmann's cover design was every bit as incendiary: a Day-Glo orange illustration of soldiers manning a gun emplacement above a typewritten dictionary definition: "machine gun — automatic gun for fast, continuous firing."[67] With its obvious echoes of the war in Vietnam, it also closely resembled the Situationist posters and slogans appearing on walls all over Paris. The second (and final) release on Brötzmann's BRÖ label, it maintained Brötzmann's leftist urge to retain the means of production as well as the ownership of his art. At the same time, with its pan-European personnel and defiant critique of American imperialism, it was seen by many as the most powerful example so far of a movement among young European (especially German) improvisers to throw off the influence of US jazz and create an explicitly European form of improvised music.

Needless to say, the music it contains is equally confrontational and revolutionary. John Coltrane's *Ascension*, recorded three year earlier, had provided a template of high-energy horns raised in mass communion, but where Coltrane's cry was one of intense spiritual yearning, Brötzmann gives voice to altogether more earthly concerns. The opening moments of the title track remain one of the most powerful and shocking opening salvos ever recorded: three saxophones exploding in a low, menacing assault of aggressively snarling blasts, signalling the arrival of intense young men with urgent opinions.

Throughout, the octet revels in loud, blustering outbursts of ragged group improvisation, providing an explicit reiteration and update of the left-wing Dixieland tradition Brötzmann had come up in. Yet, the piece also sits within a deceptively tight overall compositional structure (as can be heard in the structural similarities revealed in takes two and three included on the CD reissue in 2000). Brötzmann himself has explained that the structure was partly necessitated by the fact that the group had not yet had a chance to play together very much: "We were all quite new to each other. I had to find a way to organize the most freedom possible, but to give some structure to hold onto… I got some paper and wrote and drew some things. It's a very conventional, simply structured piece… It's a Charles Ives thing: solo, solo background, solo."[68] Indeed, as Harald Kisiedu has noted, throughout "Machine Gun," Brötzmann repeatedly quotes from *Central Park in The Dark,* the 1906 composition by American experimental composer Ives. Parker has also revealed that Brötzmann originally intended to include a reference to the 1940s tune "Flying Home" by US tenor thumper Illinois Jacquet, seen by many as the quintessential proto-rock and roll stormer: "He wanted us to memorise the chorus. I said, 'I don't think I can do it in time.' I forget how many days he gave us but it wasn't very long. He could approximate it himself. I said if it was written I'd probably be alright with it, but just to memorise it in that space of time, I couldn't do it, so that got dropped."[69]

After the initial saxophone bombardment, further sporadic shrieks mimic missile strikes and air raid sirens, while twin basses scrape and fidget, Bennink adds metallic, staccato gunshots and Van Hove flits in the background like a ghost consigned for eternity to some infernal cocktail bar. Brötzmann's final solo darts from guttural expectorations to Ayler-esque altissimo squeals — like tracer rounds firing into the night — even as the ensemble launches into a cornball R&B riff (presumably where Brötzmann originally intended the "Flying Home" chorus to sit).

Taking up all of the first side of the LP, the title track tends to overshadow the two tracks on the B side, but they, too, contain some thrilling moments, and as with the Situationists, subversive humour lurks in the darkest corners. In Van Hove's "Responsible," a lilting salsa rhythm, nudged in by Bennink, seems ridiculously jaunty after the preceding firestorm. And Breuker's "Music for Han Bennink" captures a performance of such ferocity that much of the recording bleeds into a bleary in-the-red max-out.

Given its uncompromising ferocity, one of the most surprising things about *Machine Gun* was its success, which instantly elevated Brötzmann to a position of underground stardom. Certainly, Bennink has remained mystified as to why it was so celebrated: "There are much more interesting recordings," he maintained. "I think it has to do with the upcoming pop culture and it is in the same line as Captain Beefheart."[70] As Bennink has rightly identified, the album was enthusiastically embraced by a hippie counterculture that was much more attuned to rock music, but which was nevertheless happy to listen to *Machine Gun* alongside and in the same spirit as heavy blues-rock experimentalists such as Jimi Hendrix and Cream. This was due, in part, to a rapturous review written by Barry Miles that appeared in the British underground newspaper *International Times* in September 1968, and which, according to Parker, "brought it to the attention of a wider audience than the straightforward, quite small audience for free jazz in those days."[71] For an indication of the delirious praise *Machine Gun* received, it's worth including that review here in full:

"The nine hundred finger chords/screams fall like huge building blocks — sealing different sections of the time (space) continuum of the music. Like the giant stones the Egyptians used to seal the passageways in pyramids.

The chords come like these in Ornette's 'Free Jazz' album but the texture of the music is very different. The depths and spaces and colours here are like those of the painter Matta, strange coloured mists drifting among machine-structures, grids and girders in an endless space.

The endless aspect of this piece comes from its lack of time reference points. No obvious beginning, middle and end — the music extends into the past and future beyond the time-span of the album. Matta's paintings are not contained within the frame — they extend indefinitely in all directions.

Peter Brötzmann's octet have been and will be playing forever. The only facet of time recognised is velocity. Sometimes the blocks shriek, get faster, indicating acceleration. Sometimes a scale progression begins but the image-overload of previous musical situations and references of these notes over-ride any nostalgic time feelings. The human is there, of course, very much so, this is not space music. Sometimes it sounds like a chicken (much of the time it sounds like a European Albert Ayler), other times a battle from an unknown dimension with music/noise bullets coming from the very real machine guns of the pit of the stomach.

Much of the new music (ESP-type) from America is the angry shriek of the American black musician against the system, slums, poverty and his situation. Though similar, this music has a different source. Musical parodies indicating love instead of anger (or sympathy or compassion as much US music) occur.

The music stems from the musical roots steeped in the age-old rocks of Europe. Machine-gun is about machine-guns in a sense of word America does not yet know. Europe with its bomb-sights, concentration camp museums, war-scarred people and buildings and its Berlin wall and occupied Prague. The music is free, much wider open than [SME's 1968 album] Karyobin for instance. Humorous old jazz/swing breaks come through. Though timeless, it has for the most part a beat (rock and roll, even Samba at one point). it can make you sweat, shake, or shout aloud with joy at the 'rightness' or humour of it."[72]

Miles' mention of Albert Ayler reminds us that the European hippie counterculture was perhaps more receptive of free jazz than is generally recognised (a photo of Ayler's quintet graced the cover of *International Times* in 1966, and Paul McCartney was said to be a fan of his music). Certainly, after the tumultuous events of May 1968, music like Ayler's (and, by extension, Brötzmann's) seemed to make more sense to a recently radicalised youth movement.

French journalist Daniel Caux has described the marked differences in the reaction of young French audiences to performances there by Ayler less than two years apart: in November 1966, fights broke out between a small group of admirers and a much larger cohort of audience members angered by Ayler's barrages of sound energy and stratospheric altissimo squeals; while, in July 1970, he enjoyed a triumphant residency at the Fondation Maeght, a prestigious cultural institution in Southern France. "With the student riots of May 1968, a lot of things changed in France as regards the perception of new artistic forms," Caux explained. "In its extreme radicalism and its blatant rejection of show business, the 'free jazz' played by African-Americans became a musical banner for young French protestors almost overnight. This is the reason why Albert Ayler — to his big surprise — was welcomed as a hero by the public who came to see him at the Maeght Foundation in 1970."[73]

Improvising trombonist, composer and academic George E. Lewis has also written about the correlation between post-'68 political radicalism and a growing appreciation of free jazz, claiming that the music's "abandonment of metric regularity... seemed to parallel developments in May 1968 that abandoned accommodation with existing structures of authority." Moreover, he has drawn attention to sociologist Alfred Willener's bold claim that "May [1968] seemed, in turn, to explain Dada, Surrealism, Free Jazz, etc." [74]

For the members of Brötzmann's octet, these radical conjunctions could be a lived reality. Evan Parker told me about attending one of the major demonstrations against the Vietnam War in London, which ended with protestors clashing with mounted police in Grosvenor Square. "At about four o'clock, I looked at my watch and thought, 'I've got to go now,'" he recalled. "I went across the road to where I'd left my saxophone with a friend off of Tottenham Court Road, got on the train, went to Liverpool Street, got on the train to Harwich, got on the night boat and went to play with Brötzmann, I think in Essen."[75] In September 1968, in Essen (just fifteen miles from Wuppertal), Brötzmann performed at Internationale Essener Songtage (International Essen Song Days) on the same bill as German rock groups including Amon Düül and Guru Guru, and American underground heroes such as the Fugs and the Mothers of Invention. Widely seen as a crucial event in the birth of the German rock scene, the festival also included folk, poetry, chanson and protest song, as well as talks and seminars, including one by German ethnologist Hannjost Lixfeld on the subject of "the song as a mirror of the social and political situation."[76]

"In the States, it's quite often that, after a concert, young people come and ask me about *Machine Gun* and the time of its creation," Brötzmann observed in 1995. "I think they don't only come from the jazz scene, but from rock and electronic music."[77]

Drummer Steve Noble sheds more light on *Machine Gun*'s cross-genre impact: "We were backstage at a gig we were doing in LA in a rock club, and the guy that runs it is just falling over himself to try and help us and he's so thrilled that Brötzmann's there. It's full of rock musicians because they've all heard *Machine Gun*."[78]

Certainly, more than half a century on, *Machine Gun* remains Brötzmann's most famous recording, and one that continues to inspire younger generations of musicians. Its traces can be heard in the work of underground free-jazz ensembles such as the Finnish quintet Mohel, with its line-up of three horns and two drummers, as evidenced on their incendiary 2008 album *Babylon Bypass*. And it's a constant touchstone for more-established musicians such as Swedish tenor saxophonist Mats Gustafsson. In an email, Gustafsson described, with characteristically breathless enthusiasm, his first encounter with the album:

> "Being a teen and playing punk rock in [his home town of] Umeå... and trying to figure out King Crimson and Mahavishnu Orchestra on distorted electric piano... and already collecting some vinyls of free jazz... I find myself standing in the local record shop "Burmans Musik" in Umeå and listening to a vinyl with a really cool cover. It ALL came over me... fuckin everything. The energy from the punk, the experimental shit from Crimson... the sound of (???)... it HIT me like a sledge hammer by Tor! Brötzmann's *Machine Gun* of course... It changed my DNA, I guess."[79]

Steve Noble is just one of many who are convinced of the lasting significance of the daring and provocative work Brötzmann et al. crafted in the 1960s. "It's like they really did have a kind of revolution," he told me. "They smashed down that brick wall. I come along a generation later and I haven't had to break a wall down. I'm just walking along in the rubble. There's so much information from all these incredibly dynamic players of that generation. If nobody did anything new, it would still be a lot of information that you could really grab a hold of." [80]

Schwarzwaldfahrt

"In the midst of capitalism, playing against capitalism"

Brötzmann's organisational flair wasn't just limited to assembling large and successful musical ensembles. Fuelled by his instinctive distrust of establishment structures, and not a little youthful snottiness, he went on to make extraordinary things happen at the end of the 1960s. Significantly, one extremely important development grew directly out of a prickly yet principled reaction to the perceived capitalist commodification of jazz.

Since 1964, critic and producer Joachim-Ernst Berendt had run the Berliner Jazztage (Berlin Jazz Days) festival, a well-funded annual event which had gained a reputation for catering to mainstream tastes and booking primarily big names from America. In 1968, the line-up included Dizzy Gillespie, Art Blakey and Muddy Waters. To Berendt's credit, he was not unaware of the more experimental energies at play in jazz, and Don Cherry was also on the bill that year. Moreover, as an act of recognition of the burgeoning German free-jazz community, Berendt also invited Brötzmann to bring his ensemble to Berlin Jazz Days, on the condition that all the musicians perform in dark business suits. When Brötzmann was unable (or unwilling) to guarantee that his ensemble would meet the required dress code, the invitation to play was retracted.

Brötzmann was offered a conciliatory place in the Don Cherry Big Band, which also included Germans Albert

Mangelsdorff, Joachim Kühn and Karl Berger, but he turned it down. He had other ideas. To help put these into action, he turned to an old acquaintance, Jost Gebers. Born in Berlin in 1940, Gebers was a bass player and frequent visitor to Wuppertal in the mid-60s with whom Brötzmann had had a short-lived quartet also featuring pianist/violinist Donata Höffer and drummer Manfred Kussatz. Though initially serious about making music, Gebers had realised that his talents would be better served elsewhere. As Brötzmann told Markus Müller: "Jost soon noticed that he had much more fun organising, recording and doing all those other things."[1]

Brötzmann enlisted Gebers in helping him organise an alternative event, conceived as both protest against and antidote to what he saw as Berlin Jazz Days' under-representation of the new European free music and its risk-averse, profit-driven commercialism. Billed as an "anti-festival," the Total Music Meeting (TMM) took place in West Berlin at the same time as Jazz Days, running from 7 to 10 November 1968. While Jazz Days occupied the grand Philharmonie concert hall, TMM was located in a small club called Quartier von Quasimodo. Those arriving at the venue were made immediately aware of the festival's political intentions by a cardboard sign just inside the door, made by the poet (and later free-jazz-championing critic) Wilhelm Liefland, which proclaimed: "In the midst of capitalism, playing against capitalism... double entrance price for jazz critics."[2]

Brötzmann had, in fact, already had some experience of this kind of action. Just a few months earlier, at the end of August 1968, he had taken part in a concert in an underground garage in Cologne — together with Alexander von Schlippenbach, Gunter Hampel, Mani Neumeier and Irène Schweizer — staged as a protest against the marginalisation of free jazz at the Jazz am Rhein (Jazz on the Rhine) festival. Held in Cologne's green and spacious Rheinpark on the banks of the Rhine, Jazz am Rhein was inaugurated in 1967 as Germany's first open-air jazz festival. Its second edition, in 1968, included visiting Americans, hard-bop saxophonist Hank Mobley and trumpeter Maynard Ferguson's Big Band, as well as the Joachim Kühn Trio. Brötzmann et al.'s decision to play in a grimy subterranean carpark while the festival took place in the verdant outdoors was about as literal a declaration of their underground credentials as it's possible to imagine.

This petulant display had its own historical precedent. In 1960, Charles Mingus and Max Roach had protested against the perceived racism, commercialism and economic exploitation of the Newport Jazz Festival by staging the Newport Rebels Festival. Described by US jazz historian Scott Saul as "an anti-festival where the musicians seized the means of production,"[3] this musician-run festival foregrounded performances by young innovators including Ornette Coleman and Kenny Dorham. Running concurrently with the main Newport festival, just a few blocks away in the grounds of the Cliff Manor Walk Hotel, it was a calculated attempt to disrupt the mainstream event by enticing a significant tranche of its audience away, and was endorsed by sympathetic older musicians including trumpeter Roy Eldridge and drummer Jo Jones, both of whom performed at the Rebel event.

TMM aimed to make a similar impact by showcasing some of the most progressive young improvisers in Europe. Brötzmann played twice, with his octet and with von Schlippenbach's Globe Unity Orchestra, which also featured Willem Breuker and Manfred Schoof. Gebers performed in the Donata Höffer trio with drummer Manfred Kussatz. Schoof's quintet played, featuring English drummer John Stevens, who also performed with SME alongside vocalists Carolann Nicholls and Maggie Nichols and saxophonist Trevor Watts.

In an email, Watts recalled how the London-based Ensemble ended up on a largely German bill: "John and I had been invited as SME because the guy who started it all [Gebers] played a bit of bass and he came up to the Little Theatre Club with his then actress girlfriend [Höffer], who played a bit of piano, and they did a set. I remember blood running through the piano keys. It was after that gig, which also John and I played at, that he invited that current version of SME to TMM."[4]

Another Englishman, guitarist John McLaughlin (just a few months short of moving to America to play with Tony Williams Lifetime and Miles Davis), played in Gunter Hampel's quintet TIME IS NOW. Hampel's set provided one of the big surprises of the festival when US experimentalists saxophonist Pharoah Sanders and guitarist Sonny Sharrock (both members of the Don Cherry Big Band, which performed at Berlin Jazz Days on 9 November) joined the quintet onstage as guests. Murky recordings of the set available online[5] reveal anarchic group improvisations, with Hampel's ethereal vibes floating over Sharrock's agitated guitar and Roel Koes adding raw electronic whooshes while drummer Laurie Allen and bassist Arjen Gorter flail and churn. While McLaughlin is virtually inaudible among the clatter, Sanders ups the energy, entering the fray and cutting through the sonic gloom with harsh brays and multiphonic honks.

Gebers told Markus Müller:

"It's not like there was a PA or anything. Everyone played acoustically. Sharrock struggled to take it down somewhat with some riffs, so that you could finally hear something from

Sanders, and in the end he stood there and conducted the whole thing, so that Sanders could stand out. That was pretty weird. And all of a sudden I realised what a gulf there was between the two groups — at least at the time. Despite all the freedom or whatever you want to call it, the Americans were still thinking in very small boxes, while the Europeans were much looser, simply saying: *Let's just do it.*"[6]

During the festival, Don Cherry and vibraphonist Roy Ayers also defected from the Philharmonie, making unscheduled (and sadly unrecorded) appearances at TMM. For many of the European musicians present, these encounters were rare and valuable opportunities to check in with the source of African American free jazz. When one considers that Sanders had been playing with John Coltrane right up until the saxophonist's death the previous year, it's easy to appreciate how these collaborations might have been perceived as an endorsement, a handing on of the flame. The same year, similar trans-Atlantic encounters were happening in London. In March, a double trio recorded a session at Olympic Sound Studios (still never officially released) featuring Evan Parker and Trevor Watts on saxophones, Dave Holland and Peter Kowald on basses, and drummers John Stevens and Rashied Ali (another alumnus of Coltrane's final groups, then briefly resident in London). Watts has also mentioned[7] a trio session around the same time with Stevens and bassist Steve Swallow, a prime architect of US free jazz through his pioneering eary-60s recordings with Paul Bley and Jimmy Giuffre.

Although, according to Gebers, "financially, it was a terrible, disaster," TMM in 1968 was, even by his own modest admission, "quite a success."[8] The festival proved such an energising lightning rod for the European free-music community that it became an annual event, running every November, always at the same time as Berlin Jazz Days, for forty years, until its final edition in 2008. Although Brötzmann quickly stepped away from the organisational side of the festival, he remained a vital presence and key contributor, performing at subsequent TMM's with various different ensembles over the years and designing many of the event's posters. Gebers remained at the helm, running TMM until 2000, when he handed his duties over to Helma Schleif. While TMM remained a pivotal rallying point for European improvisers, it also attracted major American artists, including Cecil Taylor, Sunny Murray, Steve Lacy and George Lewis. At the same time, the musical remit of the festival broadened, embracing not just free jazz and free improvisation but also contemporary classical and electronics, as well as placing musicians from different global traditions — such as Iranian and South African artists and Tuvan overtone singer Sainkho Namtchylak — in unfamiliar and challenging improvising contexts.

If TMM's presence as an essential date on the European festival calendar is now much missed, its influence lives on in events like the Blow Out! Festival in Oslo, which celebrated its fourteenth edition in 2023. Founded by a group of musicians (including close Brötzmann collaborator drummer Paal Nilssen-Love) as an alternative to the commercialism of the Oslo Jazz Festival (with which it runs concurrently in August), the event foregrounds improvised music, serving a similar function for Norwegian improvisers to that provided for German artists by the original TMM.

"It was a kind of paradise in London"

After *Machine Gun*, Brötzmann's next recording project took a step away from the former record's maxed-out cacophony, towards a cleaner, clearer sound. Recorded in April 1969, and released later that year, *Nipples* was also Brötzmann's first album on a label other than his own BRÖ imprint, coming out on the fledgling Calig label.

The rushing velocity of the title track, recorded by the sextet of Brötzmann, Bennink, Van Hove, Buschi Niebergall, Evan Parker and Derek Bailey, unfolds with less formal structure than anything on *Machine Gun* while, at the same time, following what feels like a more conventional linear narrative, with Bailey's amplified strings adding a spry tension. The spaciousness of the arrangement allows more instrumental nuances through, with Van Hove displaying an impish, post-Thelonious Monk unpredictability allied with Cecil Taylor's strident physicality. On the flipside, "Tell a Green Man" opens up the sense of space even further, beginning with nearly five minutes of unadorned double bass and tight, rattling toms. When the tenor finally enters, it's a taunting "can't catch me" raspberry — the very spirit of youthful rebellion. For the remaining ten minutes, the quartet of Brötzmann, Bennink, Van Hove and Niebergall roil and roll through queasy peaks and swells. While Brötzmann achieves a kind of dogged transcendence through the blunt interrogation of harsh timbres, the absence of Derek Bailey's taut twangs prevents the piece from achieving the manic urgency of the title track.

In fact, at this time, Bailey was proving himself to be an important figure for Brötzmann, not just in the studio, but as a facilitator of crucial connections, as Brötzmann forged stronger links with the wider UK jazz and improvised music scene. "Derek was setting up so many important things for us little younger guys," Brötzmann recalled.

> "It was a kind of paradise in London in the late '60s. There was never any money involved in the gigs, but you could play. There was a scene in London going on and our other thing was up in Scotland, in Edinburgh. We had some friends at the Art Institute there — they were students but they were able to organise a little bit of money and they were quite active and organised a lot of things. In between, you could do, from time to time, Manchester or Leeds, or both."⁹

In the capital, Brötzmann was getting to know some of the top progressive jazz players, such as saxophonists Alan Skidmore and Mike Osborne and trumpeter Marc Charig. But it was on one of his trips to Scotland that he first became aware of a cohort of expatriate Black South African musicians — trumpeter Mongezi Feza, saxophonist Dudu Pukwana, bassist Johnny Dyani, and drummer Louis Moholo — who, together with tenor saxophonist Nikele Moyake, had previously formed the core nucleus of the extraordinarily influential sextet the Blue Notes. "These Scottish friends of mine in Edinburgh at the Arts School organised a meeting," he recalled. "Evan was there and Dudu and Mongezi and Johnny Dyani — so that was my first contact."¹⁰

Led by white pianist Chris McGregor — the son of a Scottish missionary schoolmaster — the Cape Town–based Blue Notes had been a sensation in their native South Africa: a super-tight, hard-blowing hard-bop unit widely considered the best band in the country by audiences and critics alike. But life under the draconian horror of Apartheid had made their musical activities almost impossible. As an inter-racial group, the sextet was breaking vicious racist laws every time they met. With the notorious Group Areas Act banning racially mixed performances without special permission granted, each gig was an opportunity for the authorities to harass them. Something had to give. So, when they were invited to play at the world-famous Antibes Jazz Festival in Juan-les Pins, France, in July 1964, the group seized the chance to escape and leave it all behind. After the festival, they decided to stay in Europe, following the example of other defecting South African musicians such as trumpeter Hugh Masekela and pianist Dollar Brand, later known as Abdullah Ibrahim. This also mirrored a similar flight from racial repression pursued by many African American jazz musicians, from Dexter Gordon and Don Cherry to Albert Ayler and the Art Ensemble of Chicago, all of whom, during the 1960s, were drawn to the relatively free social milieu available to them in Europe.

At first, The Blue Notes based themselves in Zurich, where Brand had taken up residence, but following a deliriously received appearance at Ronnie Scott's jazz club in April 1965, they relocated to London (with the exception of saxophonist Nikele Moyake, who returned to South Africa due to ill health, to be replaced by white South African Ronnie Beer). In London, they not only wowed the hard-bop crowd with their air-tight arrangements but also served as a catalyst to the more open-minded musicians on the scene by deploying a tactic learned from Christopher Columbus Mra Ngcukana, an older South African trumpeter and mentor to the Blue Notes, active in Cape Town from the late '40s. "Mra was the Albert Ayler before we even knew or heard Albert Ayler, because he was so-called avant-garde or free-jazz," Dyani told journalist Aryan Kaganof in a 1985 interview. "Mra would say, 'Let's do the 'fowl run.' He'd call free-jazz 'fowl run' where everybody starts screaming."[11] In performance, the Blue Notes would slip in and out of ecstatic bursts of "fowl run," suggesting whole new worlds for artists keen to break free from the strictures of hard bop.

By the time Brötzmann met them, a lack of gigs and divergent interests meant that the Blue Notes had more or less ceased to exist as a working group, but the individual members had become firmly embedded as effervescent stars in London's free-jazz constellation. In 1968, they reconvened as the Chris McGregor Group to record their long-awaited debut album, *Very Urgent,* which, with its easy mix of muscular swingers, limpid ballads and boisterous free-form squalls, encapsulated everything that had so effortlessly grabbed the attention of their British comrades. In the early '70s, they went on to form the heart of one of the most energetic and free-wheeling big bands of the era, the Brotherhood of Breath, again led by McGregor and also drawing on the talents of UK players such as Skidmore, Osborne and Charig as well as another South African exile, bassist Harry Miller.

"To meet all the Africans was a great experience,"[12] Brötzmann remembered. Moreover, two key figures from this milieu would go on to play an important role in his own career a decade or so later.

At the same time as he was making these invigorating overseas connections, Brötzmann was also busy consolidating the scene at home.

Buoyed up by the success of the inaugural TMM, and recognising the galvanising effect of bringing German improvisers together, Brötzmann and Gebers were involved in organising another event six months later at West Berlin's prestigious Akademie der Künste (Academy of Arts). Billed as "Three Nights of Living Music and Minimal Art," the event was instigated by the academy itself and sought to present contemporary art and music together in the same exhibition, and in the same space: the academy's cavernous Hall 2. Gebers was brought in to help curate the musical content, and during Easter 1969 — from April 4 to 6 — the exhibition presented performances by the Alexander von Schlippenbach Nonet (featuring Brötzmann, Bennink, Schoof, Niebergall and others) and the Donata Höffer Group, as well as German trombonist Ed Kröger's Quartet. Fearing that the left-field jazz ensembles might not attract enough of an audience to fill the hall, Gebers also roped in a more conventionally crowd-pleasing ringer: the Alexis Korner Blues Group, led by the eponymous multi-instrumentalist and leading light of the British blues boom. It was, by all accounts, a raucous and somewhat fraught affair. With performances taking place among the art, the attendant hairy freaks began enthusiastically banging valuable sculptures with their beer bottles in time to the music. Academy staff had to step in, and harsh words were exchanged. Gebers was certain an invitation to return to the academy would not be forthcoming.

Brötzmann and Gebers realised they were going to have to make a special effort to secure more opportunities for the radical music they were promoting, so, in September 1969, they founded Free Music Production (FMP), a non-profit organisation originally conceived as what Gebers has called a "kind of management, to negotiate with clubs and organisers."[13] When this approach yielded little success, the pair realised they would need to take matters into their own hands and FMP crystallised as an organisation with, according to an official statement, "the intention of creating, independent from the commercial music industry, a better working condition for todays [sic] creative jazz musicians and composers, and to give the audiences a more suitable possibility for an [sic] general view of the new jazz music."[14]

In many ways, this new organisation's aims overlapped with those of the New Jazz Artists' Guild, which Brötzmann had helped to found in 1966, but he and Gebers went one crucial step further with FMP by also launching a record label of the same name. If the FMP imprint built on the modest success of Brötzmann's BRÖ label, it also very explicitly shared BRÖ's conceptual debt to Charles Mingus and Max Roach's Debut label and its ambition to both maintain artistic self-determination and control the means of production. By the same token, FMP was clearly influenced by the Dutch ICP label and its rebellious impetus to document the anarchic music of the ICP collective, unencumbered by the need to make aesthetic concessions to the music industry.

FMP's first release was a huge statement in every way. Unleashed in 1969, Manfred Schoof's *European Echoes* presented a single thirty-minute composition (split into two halves for the original LP), recorded for radio in Bremen in June of that year. Occupying similar ground to von Schlippenbach's Globe Unity Orchestra, it featured a towering, sixteen-piece ensemble comprising the whole of Brötzmann's *Machine Gun* octet plus an additional eight musicians. It also proposed the most comprehensively pan-European convocation thus far, recruiting not just German, Dutch, Belgian and English players but also pianist Irène Schweizer and drummer Pierre Favre from Switzerland, Italian trumpeter Enrico Rava and Hugh Steinmetz, a Danish trumpeter who worked closely with John Tchicai.

As the album's title made clear, it was conceived as a European response to some of the defining free-jazz statements emanating from the US, and particularly those recorded by larger groups, such as John Coltrane's *Ascension* and Albert Ayler's foundational 1965 masterpiece *New York Eye And Ear Control* featuring Don Cherry and others. Here, however, multiples of instruments — three trumpets, three saxophones, three pianos, three double bases and two drummers — lend the sound an orchestral, old-world opulence and an unprecedented ferocity.

The piece begins with booming drums and Han Bennink's giant Chinese cymbals summoning a ritualistic crash before dashing headlong into an urgent, cacophonous roar with great brassy gales and gusts, ululating saxes, blustering trombones and Derek Bailey's electric guitar cutting through like a rusty knife. Towards the end of the first half, the massed ensemble drops away for a series of smaller but no less urgent groupings: von Schlippenbach, Van Hove and Schweizer's pianos pinwheeling like a Conlon Nancarrow nightmare; Bennink and Favre's drums rattling the very atoms; and Kowald, Niebergall and Arjen Gorter's double basses pinging and slapping like juggernaut fanbelts. After a brief, stabbing fanfare, the ensemble regroups, returning to relentless forward motion and unrelenting group frenzy. An undoubted high-water mark in European free music, it remains one of the most uncompromising and unbridled examples of pure energy-sound-action ever committed to wax.

FMP's next triumph saw them making an unexpected return to the scene of a previous debacle: the Academy of Arts in West Berlin. Following the slightly fractious denouement of

"Three Nights of Living Music and Minimal Art," Gebers was pleasantly surprised when the Academy asked him to stage an expanded free-jazz event in the same location. The resulting Workshop Freie Musik (Workshop Free Music) was a five-day musical symposium, held between 26 and 30 March 1970, in which improvisers held public rehearsals and performances across two large stages in the academy's exhibition hall. In attendance were Brötzmann's group, von Schlippenbach's octet, the Evan Parker-Derek Bailey Quartet, Pierre Favre's quintet and a quartet led by American pianist Burton Greene, who had relocated to Paris in 1969. A leaflet publicising the event described it thus:

WORKSHOP
in the exhibitionrooms [sic] of the Akademie der Künste

free music
intended as a demonstration of the possibilities
of free improvised music
musicians and groups working on a varied musical conception
Public rehearsals followed by a pause for discussions
Informal improvisation in the exhibitionrooms[15]

The event was a resounding success and a vindication of FMP's aim to give free jazz greater exposure. Geber's observed: "Now it became apparent that our initial instinct to bring this music out of the concert hall and club, and into public space, had been right. The constraints for musicians and the audience could be significantly reduced in this way."[16]

In fact, so well received was the event that Workshop Freie Musik became an annual event running alongside the Total Music Meeting as a crucial date in the European improv calendar. In 1998 it celebrated its "30th(-1)" anniversary (counting the 1969 "Three Nights of Living Music and Minimal Art" as its inception) with a final event, before a lack of financial backing hastened its demise. However, during the three decades the workshop existed it, like TMM, not only provided a showcase and social fulcrum for European (and South African) improvisers, it also attracted US free-jazz heavyweights, including pianist Bobby Few, drummer Muhammad Ali, saxophonist Anthony Braxton, guitarist Sonny Sharrock and others. Its influence was enormous, providing the blueprint and inspiration for other crucial events, such as Derek Bailey's Company Weeks festival, which, from 1977 to 1994, invited improvisers and experimentalists from diverse backgrounds and locations to come together in a workshop setting and forge new, often unexpected, collaborations. Company Weeks' atmosphere of playful seriousness owed a great deal to FMP's pioneering Workshop Freie Musik.

"It was really like a heavy political scene"

After spending the last years of the 1960s successfully leading large groups, Brötzmann executed a radical change of direction at the turn of the 1970s, initiating a decade-long — and extremely fertile — period during which he concentrated almost exclusively on the intense and unruly intimacies afforded by small groups.

After briefly playing in a trio with Willem Breuker and Han Bennink, he assembled a short-lived quartet featuring Bennink and Fred Van Hove, with Buschi Niebergall on bass and bass trombone. But in 1970, he settled on the unit that was to be his primary working group for the next five years, a mercurial and unpredictable sax-drums-piano trio with Bennink and Van Hove. "In order to make it easier to work, we lowered the amount of musicians," deadpanned Bennink. "Very practical."[17] Indeed, where larger ensembles like the *Machine Gun* octet used bludgeoning power and overwhelming volume to steamroll the listener like a heavyweight armoured vehicle, the new trio — essentially the now liberated core nucleus of the bigger groups — displayed the nippy manoeuvrability of a motorcycle hit squad.

"I thought it was a very special trio at the time," Bennink reflected.

> "We had fantastic times, but also heavy times… We had really weird gigs sometimes. I remember a kind of Woodstock festival in between Denmark and Germany, Fred was driving a white ambulance he had from his grandfather, with hundreds and hundreds [of] litres of oil in it. Finally we got there, it was shitty weather, it was so windy that I couldn't hit my cymbals. They didn't like us at all, somehow the Peter Brötzmann group with *Machine Gun* at that time belonged to the communists or whatever. Then Brötzmann went for the money but six people were killed by the Hell's Angels."[18]

A heavy dose of this anarchic energy can be found on *Balls,* the trio's 1970 debut album and the second release on the fledgling FMP label. With its confrontational punk-puerile title and macho cover photo showing Bennink, shirtless and svelte, looming over a skulking Brötzmann and Van Hove, it positively bristles with snarling chutzpah. (Read that title as both aggressive flip-off and swaggering brag: It takes balls to make music like this. Have you got the balls to listen to it?) When the trio rushes into full-bore, high-energy group improvisation — Bennink's drums booming cavernously, Van Hove scattering notes as though emptying a bucket of nuts and bolts on the keys, and Brötzmann digging into intense, tightly wound altissimo shrieking — it proposes a super-charged extension of the free-jazz continuum. Yet it also captures the trio pushing further out than ever from any residual patterns inherited from US jazz. As well as percussion, Bennink plays a long-necked gachi horn and conch shell, sparring with Brötzmann's tenor with sputtering moans and semi-vocalised growls and grunts. There's a mischievous joy in Van Hove and Bennink's relationship, as they gleefully exploit their instant telepathy for raw, spontaneous surprise: on "Garten," in the full thrust of a splintered barrage, Bennink throws on the brakes, crunching into a dead stop, which Van Hove immediately fills with ridiculous mutant stride; on the title track, Bennink's tuned percussion warbles like a gamelan orchestra of steel pans, setting off mellifluous ripples of prepared piano. For much of the time, Brötzmann's happy to sit back and let them play, while simultaneously maintaining a gruff presence: his isolated, stabbing honk one minute into the title track is like a surly clearing of the throat, a vaguely threatening reminder of who's in charge.

There weren't many other improvisers on the scene capable of keeping up with this kind of quixotic fire power, but the trio found a somewhat unlikely comrade in the form of trombonist and elder statesman of German jazz Albert Mangelsdorff. Initially brought in to fill out the trio on a few occasions when Bennink couldn't make a gig, he went on to perform regularly as a fourth member of the group. Brötzmann told Gerard Rouy: "I learnt later that he got a lot of hard times from his so-called friends from the other scene because he wanted to play with that Brötzmann or that Van Hove… He was a very,

very important person for us... some people actually started to listen to what we were doing when we started playing with Albert."[19] This vital quartet was documented on three albums — *Elements, Couscouss De La Mauresque* and *The End* — recorded live at a concert at Berlin's Quartier Latin club in 1971 and released that year as the third, fourth and fifth releases on FMP, in a three-LP box set.

The success FMP was having in releasing a rapid and steady stream of uncompromising albums proved influential to communities of improvisers outside Germany. In Britain, Derek Bailey, Tony Oxley and Evan Parker established Incus Records in 1970 as an imprint dedicated to releasing UK free jazz and improvised music. Though Incus's official history maintains that the idea originated with Oxley.[20] Parker has claimed that he was inspired to found the label after observing FMP's operations, telling Mike Heffley: "I brought the idea for Incus back from sort of watching Brötzmann."[21] The first release on Incus, 1970s *The Topography Of The Lungs* by Parker, Bailey and Bennink (later reissued on CD by Parker's psi label and credited to Parker alone) wields a violent, snarling, barbed-wire energy not unlike that encountered on *Balls* — not least because of the fierce unpredictability Bennink brings to both dates.

The album's debt to the ferocity of the German sound is acknowledged in the track title "For Peter B. & Peter K." Moreover, a typed insert included with original copies made clear the ideological and practical aims Incus shared with FMP:

"The bulk of the revenue from any Incus recording will go directly to the musicians...
Once the basic cost of each record is recovered,

thus providing the finance for the next,
the vast bulk of all income will be paid in royalties to the artists.
Incus has no intention of making profits in the conventional sense."[22]

By 1972, FMP had released ten LPs, including reissues of the two albums Brötzmann had released on his BRÖ label, *For Adolphe Sax* and *Machine Gun*. Sensing rightly that FMP was better placed to achieve the objectives it had set out for, Brötzmann wound BRÖ down and permanently ceased its activities. At the same time, as Markus Müller has proposed, FMP entered a distinct second phase that brought the label and collective even closer to realising Brötzmann's collaborative aims while enabling him to spread some of the burden and responsibilities of organisation. On 1 October 1972, Gebers, Brötzmann, Kowald, von Schlippenbach and drummer Detlef Schönenberg signed a partnership agreement that officially positioned FMP as a "cooperative of jazz musicians,"[23] as opposed to the benevolent two-handed dictatorship it had been under Gerbers' and Brötzmann's stewardship. The signatories were now committed to joint decision-making in the areas clearly spelled out in the partnership agreement:

"Producing, selling and distributing records
Promoting those records
Planning and organizing concerts, workshops, tours
Public relations"[24]

In this way, FMP was now fully aligned with the example set by pioneering American collectives such as Chicago's

AACM, who, as George Lewis has observed, were determined to "survive and even thrive while (a) pursuing their art and (b) controlling the means of its production."[25] As much as Brötzmann resisted the organised political left, with FMP he was instrumental in establishing a visionary organisation with unassailable Marxist ideals.

"We played for a long time in the trio with Fred," Bennink told me. "We were very popular in Germany. We played for the Communist Party, we played for students. It was really like a heavy political scene there — not so much for me, but they took the music like that."[26]

While the trio's ostensibly leaderless adventures in collaborative spontaneous composition were no doubt enough to convince some listeners of its socialist inclinations, Brötzmann, Van Hove and Bennink nailed their red flag more firmly to the mast in 1973 with the release of FMP's first 7" single, a crazed interpretation of "Einheitsfrontlied" or "Song of the United Front." Composed in 1934 by Hanns Eisler, with lyrics by Marxist dramatist Bertolt Brecht, the song was a reaction to the Nazi Party's power grab the previous year and its banning of both the Social Democratic Party and the Communist Party in Germany. Over Eisler's stiff march, Brecht's rousing lyrics exhorted members of these two feuding parties to shelve their longstanding differences and present a united leftist front against fascism. The song had become a popular anthem of the German labour movement, and in the trio's hands it morphs into an eight-minute free-jazz excursion, split over two sides of vinyl: beginning with a resolute march, it wanders into a concentrated piano and percussion duet until, on the B-side, Brötzmann appears, adding guttural honks and brays on bass saxophone before leading the final dash into an ecstatic resolution.

It was, in fact, not the first time the tune had been presented in a free-jazz context. In 1970, an arrangement by Carla Bley had appeared on the self-titled debut album by bassist Charlie Haden's Liberation Music Orchestra — a politically engaged thirteen-piece ensemble featuring Bley, Don Cherry, Roswell Rudd and other luminaries of the New York New Thing. Recorded in April 1969 at the height of the Vietnam War, *Liberation Music Orchestra* is one of the most powerful left-wing anti-war statements of the period. At its heart, taking up most of side one, is a medley beginning with "Song of the United Front," reimagined by Bley as a ragged waltz, which segues into three Spanish folk tunes that had been adopted as songs of anti-fascist resistance during the Spanish Civil War. With a mood of nostalgic melancholy established, the suite tips into volatile free jazz, with Michael Mantler's trumpet shooting skywards like artillery rounds while scratchy gramophone recordings of the folk tunes' original arrangements are briefly super-imposed like translucent battlefield ghosts. It's highly likely that Brötzmann was aware of this glorious statement of defiance by his erstwhile American mentors, and the trio's version stands as a worthy addition to the slim canon of anti-fascist out-jazz anthems.

Even so, for all their socialist inclinations, the trio revelled in an impetuous iconoclasm that, in some ways, brought them closer to an anarchistic spirit, and much of this capricious charge emanated from Bennink. Their self-titled second LP, recorded in a studio in Bremen in the same session as "Einheitsfrontlied" and released in 1973, is a relatively focused blast, containing ten short, concentrated pieces; yet, throughout, Bennink is audibly straining at the limits of what can traditionally be expected from a percussionist, expanding his arsenal of instruments to include a Lao mouth organ called a khene, as well as "rhythm-box / selfmade clarinet / gachi / oe-oe / voice / tins / home-made junk."[27]

In live performance, the trio — driven by Bennink's restless energy — generated a volatile blur of high-octane free jazz, vaudeville slapstick and physical theatre. All of this can be seen in full-colour detail in a magnificent twenty-four-minute performance filmed for the German NDR TV channel in February 1974.[28] It starts with Bennink — bearded and wearing a folded kerchief as a headband — shaking a large wooden contraption as Van Hove, with floppy hair and a goatee, agitates the strings inside the piano. Brötzmann — bristly and walrus-moustached — enters with pained bleats and the trio takes off into boiling fire music, Bennink swinging like crazy with his head cranked over his right shoulder, facing away from the drums in contorted ecstasy. A sudden stop and Van Hove takes a solo, pinwheeling through cartoon music, silent movie melodrama, kinetic karate chops and even a manic race through the old music hall song "Ta-ra ra Boom-de-ay." Bennink emerges from behind the kit, swinging around his head a long, green hosepipe with a funnel attached, blowing into a trumpet mouthpiece in the other end and sending out lonesome parps and peals. A ripple of laughter and some amused applause runs through the seated audience, rising to hilarity as Bennink takes the funnel and cuddles it to his skull, using his own head as a mute. Through all of this, Brötzmann is reserved, serious, focused. For a brief, four-minute encore, Brötzmann introduces the theme of "Einheitsfrontlied," sending Bennink, back at the drums, into a clipped marching rhythm, which soon explodes into a super-charged energy flash, with a fizzing hi-hat double swish. Finally, as Brötzmann returns to the theme, Bennink rises from the kit and heads to the back of the hall, running up and down, rattling a drum stick against the wall's chunky corrugations like a boy at a railing. As Brötzmann arrives at the tune's conclusion, Bennink opens a hidden door and smartly disappears through it, vanishing from view without a backwards glance. The show is over.

Bennink's extravagant showboating adds an amusing and sometimes thrilling extra dimension to the trio's performance: a crazy comedy of right-brain spontaneity almost certainly informed and enlivened by his habitual and enthusiastic use of marijuana. Yet, according to Bennink, his antics have always been in the service of the music. "If I stand up next to a chair," he mused, "people think it's a theatrical act. I know that Brötzmann was getting at some moments fucking annoyed about what I did… But I swear I never ever do it when the musical situation is not there and, second, I never will do it to get the piss out of somebody else and putting a crown on my head for myself."[29]

In fact, it's not hard to see Bennink's provocations as extending from his background in Dada. "It was there," he agreed, confirming the serious influence of Dada in even his most outrageous diversions.

"It was like, you play drums but suddenly you go to the toilet and you will be just back in thirty-two measures. In the thirty-two measures you can also make a drum break, but for me that break was going to the toilet and being back exactly after thirty-two — things like that. Moving from the drum kit and playing in the hall was not only a theatrical act — first of all it was a musical act because you get off the stage, by that thing you change the entire sound. You leave somebody else there standing and blowing, but yourself, you play drums in the back of the hall and people don't know where they have to look. I'm always doing it for that. Never being, like people say, clown-esque. If they say clown-esque it makes me unhappy."[30]

To get a clearer picture of just how much Bennink's actions informed the trio's aesthetic, it's instructive to contrast the gig described above with a concert given just eight months later, in October 1974. This time featuring the Hobby Quartet — a lesser-known Brötzmann group featuring von Schlippenbach, Kowald and drummer Paul Lovens — it took place on the wide stage of Warsaw's grand Sala Kongresowa (Congress Hall) at the seventeenth International Festival of Jazz Music (known as the "Jazz Jamboree"), and was recorded in black and white by Telewizja Polska, the Polish state television organisation.[31] Throughout, the group can be seen formulating much of the language of free improvisation that is still used by practitioners today, veering from cacophonous free jazz with stratospheric sax, churning drums and dramatically roiling piano to a more spacious and pointillist approach. It's in these quieter moments that Lovens shines, rattling around the kit, clacking pie tins, wood blocks and sheets of scrap metal perched on his snare, and eliciting harmonic shrieks with a drum stick rubbed on a battered old cymbal. Yet, for all its stylistic daring and simmering energy, without Bennink's performance-art histrionics, the twenty-seven-minute set comes across as far more conventional, perhaps even somewhat static.

In the final couple of minutes of the Polish concert, Brötzmann leads the charge into another brief and fiery encore of "Einheitsfrontlied," confirming the somewhat ridiculous yet indisputable reality of Brötzmann, the glowering refusenik, happily playing his single in multiple crowd-pleasing moments throughout '73 and '74. Of course, performing this leftist workers' anthem in a Soviet satellite state at the height of the Cold War is loaded with ambiguous resonances. Just before the encore, to rapturous applause, Brötzmann gathers a bouquet that has been flung onto the stage and tosses the flowers individually into the audience before giving a perhaps slightly sheepish raised-fist salute. Is it a gesture of socialist solidarity? Of recognition of the Polish people's frustrations with life in the Eastern Bloc? Somehow both at the same time?

"It was total freedom in music, and it was the time for it"

Just four weeks later, on 4 November 1974, Brötzmann, Van Hove and Bennink played another gig behind the Iron Curtain, but this time much closer to home, in East Berlin. Though billed as Brötzmann's first official appearance in East Germany, it was, in reality, just one more happening in an East-West German jazz scene that had come to regard the Berlin Wall as a far more permeable boundary than the authorities envisaged.

Though barely tolerated by the Communist authorities of the German Democratic Republic (GDR), who, somewhat predictably, regarded jazz as a troublesome manifestation of decadent, US-imperialist art, a thriving East German free-jazz scene had flourished since the mid-60s, albeit less visibly and considerably less well documented than its western counterpart. If the building of the Berlin Wall in 1961 had ensured that the rest of the world was effectively kept in the dark about musical developments in the GDR, western audiences had, nevertheless, been given a hint of the depth of talent there by the arrival and success of the East German Kühn brothers. Clarinettist and saxophonist Rolf Kühn (born

1929) had moved to the United States in 1956 and played in the swing orchestras of clarinettist Benny Goodman and trombonist Tommy Dorsey (the first German to do so) before settling in West Germany in 1962. His younger brother, pianist Joachim Kühn (born 1944), defected to the West in 1966 and quickly became a star player with pronounced progressive tendencies.

Moreover, Joachim successfully converted Rolf, who, almost a generation older, had come up in a much more conservative milieu, to more outré stylings. Their 1967 album, *Impressions of New York*, was released on the forward-thinking Impulse! label — home to John Coltrane and other US free-jazz luminaries including Archie Shepp and Albert Ayler — and saw them co-leading a quartet also featuring Coltrane's bassist Jimmy Garrison and Italian drummer Aldo Romano, who had previously played in Don Cherry's Paris-based Complete Communion Band in the mid-60s. Ranging from darkly swinging vamps, pushed along by Garrison and Romano in a deep post-bop pocket, to more turbulent outbursts, it captures both Rolf and Joachim deftly negotiating free-form playing, and comfortably sits alongside other landmark recordings of the new jazz released by Impulse! in the mid-to-late '60s.

Before fleeing the GDR with help from brother Rolf, settling first in Hamburg in 1966 and later in Paris in 1968, Joachim Kühn had enjoyed a fruitful collaborative relationship with saxophonist Ernst-Ludwig Petrowsky — a leading figure in an East German community of players who were enthusiastically embracing free jazz. This serious-minded clique also included pianist Ulrich Gumpert, drummer Günter "Baby" Sommer (who adopted his diminutive sobriquet as a tribute to the early New Orleans jazz drummer Baby Dodds), trombonist Konrad "Conny" Bauer, and multi-instrumentalist Manfred Schulze.

While Kühn enjoyed the exposure and freedoms afforded by life in the west, these musicians and others who remained in the GDR operated in a much more repressed ecosystem with far fewer opportunities to perform and little chance of recording.

Certainly, the two scenes on each side of the Berlin Wall were aware of each other's activities. FMP records were clandestinely circulated among aficionados in the east, while those in the west had been able to tune into concerts by the likes of Gumpert and Petrowsky broadcast on the East German Radio DDR. Yet, the strict political and cultural segregation of the Cold War had made actual contact next to impossible. But that changed in 1972 when West German Chancellor Willy Brandt's administration initiated a tentative thawing of relations: for the first time, West Germans were able to apply for a day permit that allowed them to visit East Berlin as long as they were back on the other side of the Wall by midnight. At the same time, East German authorities, recognising that jazz had become an entrenched part of the culture, began to relax their disdainful attitude to the music. It was in this slightly more hopeful atmosphere that the ever-resourceful Gebers initiated a plan to bring East and West German musicians together.

This came to fruition in November 1972 with a historic meeting. Between the 1st and 5th of that month, the fifth edition of FMP's Total Music Meeting had taken place in West Berlin. On the 6th, Gebers oversaw a visit to East Germany by a crew of musicians who had just played at the festival: the Schlippenbach Trio plus Brötzmann, the Peter Kowald Quintet and the duo of drummer Detlef Schönenberg and trombonist Günter Christman. They arrived at Grosse Melodie, a bar where, since 1971, trumpeter Klaus Lenz had been running regular Monday-night gigs and jam sessions, providing a crucial hotspot for East German musicians. Here, Brötzmann et al. met and played with Petrowsky, Gumpert, Sommer and others. Gebers' unfailing organisational instincts had brought the two tribes together for the very first time, helping to forge connections that would bloom and flourish in the coming years.

Gebers was also keen to record the East Germans, and the following year, FMP released *Just For Fun*, by the Ernst-Ludwig Petrowsky Quartet featuring Conny Bauer on trombone, Klaus Koch on bass and Wolfgang Winkler on drums. FMP's first documentation of free jazz from the GDR — and one of the first widely available recordings of East German musicians — is a furiously tense study in free-form expression, with Sommer clattering a pneumatic snare and Bauer's 'bone moaning and growling with pent-up aggression. With the floodgates opened, FMP went on to release several more well-received albums from the GDR, including *The Old Song* by the Petrowsky/Sommer Duo plus saxophonist Manfred Hering (1974), and *Auf der Elbe schwimmt ein rosa Krokodil* by the quartet of Petrowsky, Bauer, Gumpert and Sommer (1975).

This exciting period of increased contact and fruitful traffic between musicians from the two halves of Berlin provided the context for Brötzmann, Bennink and Van Hove's first official visit in November. The gig was part of a daringly progressive concert series called "Jazz In Der Kammer" (Jazz In The Chamber), which took place in the Kammerspiele, a performance space adjacent to the historic Deutsches Theatre, just a few minutes' walk from the border crossing at the Friedrichstrasse railway station. It was a resonant location, tacitly drawing attention to the ridiculous restrictions imposed on Berliners by Cold War machinations. As Bert

Noglik observes: "This was the bottleneck entry point for visitors from the West; for East Germans it was the end of the line, the last station they could travel to."[32]

Arriving on 4 November, the night after performing at that year's TMM, the trio gave a performance (released on CD in 2022 as *Jazz In Der Kammer Nr.71: Deutsches Theatre / Berlin / GDR / 04/11/1974*) that neatly encapsulates the exploratory power of their live shows at this point. While American free jazz is still an influence — detectable in Brötzmann's wailing gusts, Bennink's savage bursts of power-swing and Van Hove's percussive post-Cecil Taylor kineticism — it's also clear how much of a break with that tradition they'd effected by this point. *Suis generis* moods appear out of nowhere, the piano spraying notes over rattling tin-can percussion and a buzzing mutter from the sax, or Bennink slotting into a clipped military march over woozy stride piano. Bennink is credited as playing drums, but he's also audible indulging in extra-curricular antics: shouting, bellowing into something resembling an alpine horn and playing what could be a clarinet.

Throughout, there's a palpable sense that the trio are free to follow their imaginations anywhere the moment suggests and are keenly aware of just how precious that freedom is. As Brötzmann observes: "It was total freedom in music, and it was the time for it."[33]

The trio of Brötzmann, Bennink and Van Hove released one more studio album in 1975, the aptly titled *Tschüs* (an informal goodbye, perhaps best rendered in English as "Cheerio" or "See you"). Brötzmann's cover design features a black-and-white photo showing what looks like a carriage of some sort on a snowy, mountainous road, pulling away as a black-clad figure resembling the grim reaper waves farewell. Thumbnail photos from the same reel on the album's back cover reveal this to be a van, pulled over perhaps for a comfort break on one of the trio's many cross-country jaunts, but Brötzmann's selected cover shot is tantalisingly ambiguous, imbued with a gloomy sense of valediction. Crudely collaged above this is a cut-out image of a Zeppelin-style airship, almost entirely black, looming menacingly. Is it about to drop a bomb? Perhaps unleash the figurative bombshell that this is to be the trio's last recording?

Yet, despite this sombre visual summary, the music contained in the album's eleven concise pieces is largely joyous and playful. Opening track "Two Birds in a Feather — To Bobby Few" (dedicated to the American free-jazz pianist who had played with Albert Ayler among others) sketches a kind of mutant cocktail lounge with Brötzmann issuing a mellow blues moan and Van Hove tinkling out distracted and increasingly fragmented ripples while Bennink eschews the drums entirely, rattling about somewhere in the distance before freaking out on clarinet. On "Ein Bischen Jazzbesen" (translated as "A Bit of Jazz Brush"), Bennink returns to the kit, rolling out rapid brushwork while Van Hove deals swift whirls and eddies. The closest the album comes to recognisable free jazz, however, is on Van Hove's "Petit Blues Fourrè — Pour G.R. De Lille," which races forward on Bennink's sustained snare roll as Van Hove sprays vigorous splashes.

Across the date, Bennink is on typically restless form, credited with playing "drums, cymbals, schwirrholz [buzzing wood], akkordeon [accordion], clarinets, floor, walls, megaphon [megaphone], etc."[34] On "Lotteduflotte," he can be heard distantly thumping the floor — almost suggesting a solo dance performance — while Brötzmann issues fruity sax parps. "Zigan, Zigan" (the album's only live cut, recorded at West Berlin's Quartier Latin club the night before the studio session) has Bennink again at a distance (so often distant, as though physically excusing himself from the intimacy of the traditional trio format), bashing out metallic clangs that increase in volume and proximity as Van Hove wheels in with a cartoonish prance. "Bierhaus Wendel" begins with Bennink and Van Hove both on accordion, peppering a wheezy drone with impetuous jabs while Brötzmann moons low on bass sax before Bennink interjects with far-off artillery booms and finally settles into martial pomp on the snare drum. "2 B-Klarinetten" has Bennink and Brötzmann skirling manically on clarinets, with Van Hove delivering just one final, somewhat tentative piano chord, as though offering up his last judgement on the trio's increasingly quixotic experiments.

To seal the valedictory mood, the album's closing title track is a brief, tongue-in-cheek bash at a sentimental ditty written by the East German team of renowned film-music composer Walter Kubiczek and lyricist Dieter Lietz for the soundtrack to an early-70s, Spanish Civil War–set TV spy yarn called *Das Licht Der Schwarzen Kerze*. While Bennink taps out a metronomic hi-hat and chatters tunelessly on a clarinet, and Van Hove plays lightly around the melody, Brötzmann gruffly but gamely sings the schmaltzy vocals like an affectionate drunk taking his leave of a friendly tavern. As goodbyes go, it's delightfully silly and self-effacing, signalling the end of one of the most tirelessly questing and notoriously fearsome improvising units operating anywhere in the world — ending not with a roar, but shuffling off into the night with a shrug and wave.

"As far as I remember, when we recorded *Tschüs,* it wasn't clear that that was the end of the trio," Brötzmann told Gerard Rouy. "We made the decision round my kitchen table in my old place that it should be the last recording after we came back from Berlin or from another tour."[35] By 1976, Van Hove had left the trio, effectively ending its run of incendiary performances and trailblazing recordings. When I asked Bennink to explain Van Hove's departure, he was typically blithe, demonstrating perhaps a little feigned forgetfulness. "We kicked him out I assume," he quipped. "We preferred to go on as a duo and getting along together very well."[36] Brötzmann, however, was more forthright: "The reason was that Fred Van Hove had enough of Mr Bennink's ego trips. And he felt, as a piano player mostly playing shitty uprights in the clubs, there was a time when he said, 'That's it for me.'"[37] In conversation with Rouy, Brötzmann added: "Fred wanted to go in another direction, he was just tired fighting against Mr Bennink all the time. He wanted to have his own more personal freedom, not always dependent on a drummer who killed his solos and things like that."[38] Whatever the reasons, Van Hove's exit ended an extraordinarily fecund decade as a close collaborator with Brötzmann. He went on to work in a number of quicksilver duos — most notably with trombonists Albert Mangelsdorff and Vinko Globokar and saxophonists Lol Coxhill and Steve Lacy — and remained a key figure in European free improvisation until his death, aged eighty-four, in 2022.

Around the same time the trio imploded, Brötzmann bade another important farewell. By 1976, he had come to tire of the difficulties of collective decision-making involved in running the FMP label as a working cooperative. For Brötzmann, the label had always primarily been a vehicle for documenting his own work and that of others in his immediate circle engaged in the serious labour of pushing the music forward. But Gebers was becoming increasingly dissatisfied with what he saw as internal constraints on the label's output. He told Clifford Allen: "Our early projects were always the same people. For me, because I wasn't playing, it didn't seem like an accurate representation of who was making all this music. I wanted to release recordings of different and younger people too."[39] By the same token, Brötzmann felt that under Gebers' influence the label was beginning to operate in a direction that he couldn't fully engage with. He told Markus Müller: "Jost had a much larger range of music in mind than I did… I was only interested in the relatively narrow field, observing what was going on around me and what was happening in the States. I couldn't have cared less about the rest, to be honest."[40] Though Brötzmann was circumspect enough not to name names, it's possible he was referring to additions to the FMP stable such as younger pianist Urs Voerkel (born 1949), whose 1976 FMP solo album, *s'Gschänk*, was at a far remove from Brötzmann's furious trajectory: writing in *Melody Maker*, critic Steve Lake identified Voerkel's ornate style as exhibiting a clear debt to early jazz pianists "Jelly Roll [Morton], [Professor] Longhair, Fats [Waller], Pinetop Smith… shot through with obvious classical technique."[41]

In the face of such irreconcilable differences, at the beginning of 1976, FMP ceased to function as "a cooperative of jazz musicians" and entered its third and final stage, with Gebers taking full responsibility for its continued activities. Though Brötzmann continued to release albums on the label, he happily relinquished any claim to authority over its direction. Under Geber's stewardship, FMP continued to be a major force, releasing hundreds of albums and staging major events. Most notable was a series of fifteen concerts performed in Berlin by Cecil Taylor between 17 June and 17 July 1988 in various different formations calling on a pantheon of leading European improvisers. The performances were documented the following year with the release on FMP of *Cecil Taylor in Berlin '88*, a monumental box-set of eleven CDs, which remains a key text in the history of free improvisation. By the time the FMP label finally folded in 2010, it had built an unassailable reputation as a cornerstone of forward-thinking, creative and experimental music. Gebers died in September 2023, a much-revered architect of European improvisation.

"We used what we had and what we found"

As Bennink observed, following the dissolution of the trio with Van Hove, he and Brötzmann regrouped, quickly adjusting their aesthetic to "go on as a duo." For Brötzmann, the decision to continue playing with Bennink had been a difficult one, finally swayed by considerations of musical practicality. He told Gerard Rouy: "My friendship to Fred was even a bit closer than to Han at that time. I was really in the shit to decide what to do, I decided for Bennink because he was the drummer. I mean, I can live without piano players but playing without drummers works for a night but not for ever."[42]

Certainly, Brötzmann recognised that working with Bennink allowed him to explore possibilities and freedoms only hinted at in his previous output: "In the duo work with Han, music-wise, there was much more happening than in *Machine Gun*. *Machine Gun* is a very conservative, organised piece in a way."[43] Bennink, too, was aware that his more wayward musical whims were inspiring Brötzmann to reach new levels of experimentation. He told me: "I started playing wind and brass and violin and trying out the voice of the different instruments. Peter liked that."[44] For sure, in the second half of the 1970s, Brötzmann and Bennink's simultaneously close yet wide-open musical partnership pushed them into strange, uncharted territories, both artistically and geographically

The name of their first duo recording, 1977s *Ein Halber Hund Kann Nicht Pinkeln* (translated as "Half a Dog Can't Piss"), suggests a symbiotic relationship, a reluctant dependency fuelled by an inspired and infuriating clash of personalities that became ever more apparent in the stripped-back sparring of the duo setting: Brötzmann the stentorian figure of intense seriousness, Bennink the hyperactive joker. Across the album's ten live tracks (recorded at the Quartier Latin and at the 1977 edition of the Workshop Freie Musik), it's Bennink's mercurial energy and curiosity that drive the improvisations, revealing him as an intuitive and endlessly inventive genius of instant improvisation as he flits from clattering, punk-Appalachian banjo to scattered piano hammering, from puttering parps on a military horn to a raw sawing of the viola that sits somewhere between the unschooled expressive freedom of Ornette Coleman's violin playing and Henry Flynt's avant-hillbilly fiddle jams. At the same time, he maintains a constant interrogation of what it means to be a percussionist, rattling castanets, tapping drumsticks on walls and floors, and still returning to the kit for exuberant energy pulses accompanied by whoops of excitement and encouragement that drive Brötzmann's tenor into a fervid, devotional register. Exposed in the sparse vulnerability of the duet, Brötzmann can be heard thinking with his breath, making neural connections through the pipes and valves of his horns. Here, over-blowing ceases to be simply a route to volume and intensity, and becomes a means to generate new textures: in an instant, the bass clarinet can flick from chocolaty smooth to sandpaper rough, with a trace of humming, semi-vocalised song. This primacy of timbre over melody marks a decisive throwing off of any lingering debt to jazz and an entry not merely into a new European sensibility but into a defiantly non-idiomatic and joyously unfettered zone that operates as a prescient blueprint for the late-twentieth/early-twenty-first-century free folk and underground DIY improv exemplified by US collectives such as the No-Neck Blues Band and Jackie-O Motherfucker, and British ensembles like Volcano the Bear and Vibracathedral Orchestra.

Schwarzwaldfahrt (or *Black Forest Trip*) — Brötzmann and Bennink's second and final recording as a duo, also released in 1977 — takes them even further away from their immediate reality. The music it contains was recorded over a few days in the spring of 1977, when the pair set off in a Citroen van for the Black Forest in southwest Germany, packing a portable Nagra tape recorder (borrowed from radio producer and journalist Joachim-Ernst Berendt) and the minimum of musical equipment. Based in a hotel in the town of Donaueschingen, the two would set out each morning into a remote, unpopulated region of the forest to record spontaneous, open-air interactions with each other and the austere natural environment surrounding them. "It was a fantastic week," Brötzmann told David Keenan. "It was the edge of from winter to spring: still snow, and cold and rainy and ugly, and a bottle of schnapps and some sandwiches from the hotel, yeah. So we drove around and wherever we saw something which could be used, we stepped out and put the machine on, and that was it."[45] Bennink, too, remembered the excursion with fondness. "It was just the two of us in that immense Black Forest," he told me. "We placed the microphone in the middle of the dripping forest and then started to wander around hitting and throwing stones. Then later, in the evenings, listening to the results from the day. It was a wonderful time. I consider that the best album we made."[46]

Having deliberately left his drums at home, Bennink creates elemental effects from the dull thud of logs, swishing a branch through the air, rubbing sticks together and splashing icy water. At the same time, the freezing temperatures warp the sound of Brötzmann's horns, lending them a wonky, dreamtime tone. As Brötzmann states in the liner notes: "We used what we had and what we found, and with all of that, we made some music, which is in a way the real meaning of improvising. To work with what you have."[47] The result is a Neolithic ur-music that sounds like a direct antecedent of the ritualistic primitivism of the No-Neck Blues Band. Through all of it, the forest itself is a pulsating presence. Birds twitter. Wind buffets the microphone. A motorcycle or chainsaw hums in the distance. An aircraft rumbles high overhead. Let loose in this environment, Brötzmann and Bennink explore their surroundings with a child-like sense of wonder and inquisitive mischief — gurgling horns in running water like infants blowing down straws, or wandering among the trees, playing hide and seek with honking duck calls.

Here, the act of becoming lost in the woods is a way of entering a kind of shamanic consciousness, of accessing the forest as a central archetype of the German mythical psyche: the realm of primal imagination, fairy-tale and weird magic. To play there is to step outside of time and exist in an exquisite cosmic present. It's the same forest where Hansel and Gretel — in a heightened state brought on by the dread fear of being lost and alone — encounter and overcome the eldritch, unspeakable evil of the cannibal witch; the same forest that surrounds the doomed town of Winden in the German science-fiction mystery TV series *Dark*, in which a cave in the woods just outside town becomes a portal to alternate realities that threaten existence itself. In the 1980 novel, *How German Is It (Wie Deutsch ist es)*, in which Austrian American author Walter Abish explores aspects of the collective psychic condition of post-war Germany, a character delivers a speech that seems to echo Brötzmann and Bennink's woodland adventures in spontaneity: "The forest continues to beckon to us. For in the forest are located our innermost dreams and desires… We wander off by ourselves, packs on our backs, haphazardously selecting one path, then another not knowing where the forest is leading us, but willing to let our instincts and chance dictate our journey."[48]

There's a sense of intense intimacy that emanates from *Schwarzwaldfahrt*, indicating an extraordinarily strong aesthetic and personal bond between the two artists that went beyond just making music together. "We had a relationship that no musicians have together," Bennink reflected. "Very intense. We were both in art. Peter was doing, most of the time, the covers for FMP and I made them for ICP. We were both into long walks in the woods and bird-watching. I got on with his kids very well, we played table tennis."[49]

Yet, despite these genuine connections, for Brötzmann the key to the duo's musical success was an element of discord.

"The duo format is a very special thing because you come close, you get to the point, you can do fantastic things but you can fight a lot. It's a fight on stage. You have to beat them and you have to first make space with the elbows for yourself — and then you can think about 'OK, let's see.' But the fight is a very, very important thing. I always liked boxing and the duo format is, of course, a kind of boxing fight. With Bennink, it's never easy. You always have to fight that guy."[50]

Certainly, on the bandstand they seemed an almost comically mismatched pair, displaying what Evan Parker has called "a kind of Laurel and Hardy aspect."[51] While Brötzmann projected an air of stern, even solemn, intensity, Bennink would habitually try to upstage him with physical pranks and unpredictable antics away from the drums. "It was sometimes really too much," Brötzmann chuckled. "I think I was one of the very few who understood what he's up to. That's why I never could really get angry."[52] Indeed, for Bennink, his constant attempts to distract or even annoy his unflappable foil were deliberate and conceptually sound methods of undermining the performance from within, part of a determinedly subversive challenge to traditional notions of artistic performance. "That was what we learned from the Fluxus period," Bennink stated. "That was part of the game and we never had a fight about it backstage."[53]

Even so, Brötzmann eventually began to tire of the tensions inherent in their relationship.

"I was always the guy playing for the people," he said, "but Bennink always says, 'They can kiss my arse.' It was getting more and more in this direction — and music for me means the complete opposite. I want to work with. I want to get something out of the other person and build up something together. With Bennink, it was more pain than fun at the end. Whenever he would call or somebody would call and say, 'Play some gigs with Bennink,' I would say, 'Yeah, one or maybe even two — but that's enough!'"[54]

It's worth considering the extent to which the pair's pronounced differences in temperament were exacerbated by their preferred intoxicants. While Brötzmann was, by this stage, already a heavy drinker, Bennink was a committed and enthusiastic smoker of marijuana. "In the early times, it was not so easy to get the stuff in Germany," Brötzmann recalled.

"Then he was without grass and then he was unbearable. Oh man, you could have pushed him in the toilet! At that time, he wasn't drinking — just drinking milk and smoking day and night. One beautiful summer afternoon in the south of Germany in some wine garden, I got him to drink the first glass of wine. But, in the early days it was just smoking. The first thing in the morning before brushing the teeth he was smoking a joint!"

Despite its ubiquity among musicians in the 1960s and '70s, grass remained a distraction that Brötzmann largely resisted. "I tried it," he told me, "but I got so lazy, I couldn't work."[55] What's more, as far as Brötzmann was concerned, Bennink's prolonged smoking habit almost certainly amplified underlying tensions between them: "Sometimes people say that marijuana-taking over so long a period influences the brain in this very egomaniacal sense — which might be true with him. I think sometimes he doesn't realise that there is another thing than just himself."[56]

Unsurprisingly, by the end of 1977, Brötzmann and Bennink had dissolved their musical partnership. Brötzmann told Gerard Rouy in 2009: "The duo with Bennink went on for about a couple of years, we really had had enough of each other, we'd been playing together for 15 years, which in the world of music is an eternity. So that was cool and even now we're still good friends."[57] In fact, in the years after that intense period, Brötzmann and Bennink occasionally reprised their double act on stage. In late 2006, they performed at the All Tomorrow's Parties festival in southern England on a bill curated by Thurston Moore which also included Sonic Youth, Iggy Pop and the Stooges and many others. Writing for the magazine *Plan B*, I described the performance as follows:

"These titans of European free jazz have spent nearly forty years perfecting their 'good cop, bad cop' routine. Brötzmann is bullish, bristly, collars of his leather coat turned up, never once looking at the punters, doggedly pursuing his own private imperatives, pouring torrents of angry breath through his saxophone. He's got important work to do and doesn't want to be distracted — which is exactly what Bennink's trying to do. Flailing, long-limbed and nimble behind the kit, he's everywhere at once, questioning each of Brötzmann's gruff pronouncements from a mocking angle, knowing the crowd is on his side, giving them surprises in return."[58]

"The good thing with Bennink," said Brötzmann, "even if we see each other and play once every two years, we know that we have a great respect for each other. When we get together for a night or two, it's working. If he is jumping around making his jokes I know for forty years or longer, then I don't have to do anything. I just play my horn. That's all I can do."[59] In the end, much of the respect Brötzmann maintained for his perennial partner hinged simply on the latter's unbounded musicality. "Bennink is one of the best five drummers in the world," he told me in 2013. "And he always was, in whatever style he was playing. He knows that. That's what he lives on."[60]

In his deep rapport with Bennink, we see the first of many strong collaborative partnerships that Brötzmann formed with drummers over the years. From Hamid Drake to Paal Nilssen-Love and Steve Noble, Brötzmann was repeatedly drawn to percussionists with enough stamina and imagination to match his furious energy. "I was always interested in drummers," he said. "The drum was, for me, the synonym for jazz music."[61]

The Nearer the Bone, the Sweeter the Meat

"I could just play. I didn't have to think"

After the fraught theatrics and off-road sonic adventurism of the Bennink years, Brötzmann's next important collaboration marked a return to a conventional trio format and the chance to luxuriate in a more straightforward free-jazz sound.

Just as the duo with Bennink was coming to an end, Brötzmann struck up a friendship with bassist Harry Miller, who had recently moved to Amsterdam from London and begun working with Willem Breuker and others. "I played with him in some Dutch constellations," Brötzmann recalled. "It was a really good time for me to meet Harry. He was such a little strong guy, always busy. The way he played bass was so strong and fantastic."[1]

Certainly, Miller came with plenty of experience. Born in Johannesburg in 1941, he started out playing in R&B groups, including a stint with fellow South African Manfred Mann. In 1961, he relocated to the UK and worked in bands on transatlantic ocean liners, giving him the opportunity to catch the likes of John Coltrane and Thelonious Monk in the clubs of New York. By 1964, he was settled in London, where he quickly became an in-demand player on the capital's jazz scene, playing with some of the most advanced composer-bandleaders of the day, including pianists Mike Westbrook and Keith Tippett and saxophonist John Surman.

He was also — alongside John Taylor on piano, Kenny Wheeler on flugelhorn and Tony Oxley on drums — part of the quintet led by tenor saxophonist Alan Skidmore that caused a sensation by scooping the press award for best group at the 1969 Montreux Jazz Festival and went on to record the epochal 1970 album *Once Upon a Time*. This high-water mark in British jazz was a hugely assured and adventurous date, which pushed the sophisticated mid-60s Blue Note aesthetic of Wayne Shorter and Andrew Hill closer to free jazz. "It's influenced by be-bop and free playing," Skidmore told me. "'Inside-out' we used to call it. It was time and then free, but we would do it without any signals or anything like that. It was magical."[2]

At the same time, Miller was operating in the weird hinterland where avant-garde jazz met progressive rock. He played on King Crimson's 1971 album *Islands*, alongside auxiliary member Keith Tippett, and in the same year contributed to *Septober Energy*, the sole recording by Tippett's monstrous Centipede project — a sprawling, ambitious and stupendously impractical fifty-plus-piece ensemble that included pretty much the entire UK jazz cohort plus open-minded ambassadors of progressive rock and jazz-rock such as Robert Wyatt and Elton Dean of Soft Machine, Ian Carr and Roy Babbington of Nucleus, and Ian McDonald and Boz Burrell of King Crimson, with Crimson's Robert Fripp on production duties.

On top of all this, the mercurial Miller found time to co-found his own label, Ogun Records. Established in 1973 with his wife Hazel and sound engineer/artist Keith Beal, the label was devoted to documenting the work of vanguard UK jazz and improv artists such as Tippett and Trevor Watts, as well the expatriate South African jazz community in groups such as Chris McGregor's Brotherhood of Breath and Miller's own sextet, Isipingo. As can be heard on Isipingo's 1977 debut, *Family Affair*, this Anglo-South African ensemble featuring Mike Osborne on alto sax, Mark Charig on trumpet and Malcolm Griffiths on trombone, as well as Tippett on piano and Louis Moholo on drums, combined head-spinning free turbulence with Miller's deep, soulful, almost Mingus-like compositions.

By the end of the '70s, Miller and Moholo had developed an extremely tight musical bond, forged while providing the rhythm section not just in Isipingo and the Brotherhood of Breath but, most notably, in the high-octane trio led by Mike Osborne since 1969. The trio's debut album, *Border Crossing*, released in 1974 on Ogun, provides a thrilling glimpse of the extraordinary group-mind this configuration had created. It was recorded live at the Peanuts Club on London's Liverpool Street — the same candle-lit, left-wing, pro-CND, folk-jazz-poetry den where Trevor Watts and Paul Rutherford had first formulated their free-jazz approach in 1965, prior to the birth of SME, and where Osborne's trio had performed so regularly that they'd assumed the role of de facto house band. From the first moment, the album crackles with a barely controlled energy, the trio hunkering into a careening, free-bop power-swing tackled at breakneck pace. Through endless, expansive choruses, Osborne's alto unleashes a torrential cascade of rapid-fire notes incorporating both the vinegar-sour attack of Jackie McLean and the unconstrained free associations of Ornette Coleman, while Miller provides an agile and muscular pizzicato throughout, relentlessly driving ahead while always responding to Osborne's synapse-swift melodic flurries with split-second timing. The album's second side is a single suite, which, as Osborne states in the sleeve notes, "is typical of the way the Trio can be heard at a club or a concert, moving continuously from one number to another, changing mood and direction as we feel the music dictates. This is successful because of the degree of empathy between the members of the trio, which has come from working so closely over the years."[3] Here especially, Moholo is a tightly wound, bullish presence, with a thunderous right foot kicking out savage salvos of bass drum punctuation at lightning speed.

A player of exceptional power and imagination, Moholo (born 1940) had thrilled audiences and fellow musicians alike since first arriving in London with the Blue Notes in 1965. Greatly in demand, he holds the improbable distinction of having turned down the chance to work with both John Lennon and Frank Zappa. In March 1969, he participated in Natural Music, a chaotic gig at Cambridge University organised by student, poet and percussionist Anthony Barnett. Billed as an "International Avant Garde Concert Workshop,"[4] it featured performances by John Tchicai, Willem Breuker, John Stevens, Trevor Watts and Chris McGregor. Also present were Yoko Ono and an unannounced Lennon, who together performed a duet of shrieking vocal improvisation and raw electric guitar feedback. Afterwards, an affable Lennon expressed an interest in employing Moholo. Then, in October the same year, Moholo attended the Amougies Festival in Belgium, a sprawling five-day event co-organised by the French free-jazz record label BYG, which showcased some of the biggest names in underground rock, such as Pink Floyd, Soft Machine and Captain Beefheart, alongside heavy-hitters in avant-garde jazz including Don Cherry, Pharoah Sanders, Sunny Murray and the Art Ensemble of Chicago, with Zappa acting as master of ceremonies. Here, Moholo took part in an impromptu jam session with the mind-boggling line-up of Zappa, Archie Shepp, trombonist Grachan Moncur III, bassists Earl Freeman and Johnny Dyani and legendary be-bop drummer Philly Joe Jones, after which Zappa, too, offered him a job. In both cases, Moholo declined the invitation, largely because it would have meant relocating to the US. In a 2017 interview for the *Wire*, he told Mike Barnes: "I was afraid to go to the States… [because of] the stories that we heard of people coming away from the States on heroin. I was quite wild then, so I would probably have been dead by now."[5]

Even so, like Miller, he did have a brush with the rock scene, though his brief participation in the short-lived Afro-rock band Assagai. Named after a South African throwing spear, the group brought together three South African ex-Blue Notes — Moholo, alto saxophonist Dudu Pukwana and trumpeter Mongezi Feza — and two Nigerians — tenor saxophonist Bizo Mngqikana and guitar/bass player Fred Coker — and released two albums, both in 1971. The self-titled debut leads with the outrageously catchy track "Telephone Girl," with Moholo's infectious funk break sitting lazily behind the beat like a pre-emptive hip-hop banger (in fact, in was later sampled in the tune "That's My Bitch" by Jay-Z and Kanye West on their 2011 album *Watch the Throne*). Elsewhere, on tracks like "Akasa," heavy hand percussion, glowering horns and stinging psych guitar take the sound closer to that of the contemporaneous Ghanaian-British Afro-rock group Osibisa. The follow-up album, *Zimbabwe*, pushed even further in this direction (with a cover designed by Roger Dean, who had also created Osibisa's covers). Opening track "Barazinbar" is a darker brew, with a heavy break and towering horns, while tracks like "Wanga" and

"La La" are more like dreamy prog, with Martha Mdenge's wafting vocals intertwined with Pukwana's lilting flute.

However, it was in the realms of free jazz and improvisation that Moholo was most prolific. As early as 1966, he'd toured South America with bassist Johnny Dyani and noted avant-gardists saxophonist Steve Lacy and Italian trumpeter Enrico Rava, resulting in the live album *The Forest and the Zoo*, released under Lacy's name on the ESP-Disk label. In London, he struck up close relationships with the likes of Evan Parker, John Stevens and Derek Bailey. He also came into the orbit of FMP records, recording 1976's *Messer* for the label in a trio with saxophonist Rüdiger Carl and pianist Iréne Schweizer. Commenting on the effect European free-improv had on him and his South African colleagues, he noted: "This is the kind of music that appealed to us and influenced us more than any other kind, more than the so-called Coltrane music... Anything free made sense to us, anything rebellious. We were in a war with the situation of how things were run on this planet at that point."[6]

In 1978, Moholo and Miller both took part in two extraordinarily powerful projects that still stand as landmarks of progressive jazz. The first was the performance at London's Roundhouse and subsequent recording of *Frames (Music for an Imaginary Film)* by Keith Tippett's Ark. A natural descendant of Tippett's Centipede, this twenty-two-piece avant-jazz orchestra included Peter Kowald on bass and tuba, as well as Trevor Watts and Soft Machine's Elton Dean on alto sax, and vocalists Julie Tippetts and Maggie Nicols. The double album, released on Ogun, captures Tippett's ambitious suite in four side-long parts: a grandiloquent, tumultuous journey through abstract improvisation, furious free turmoil and luxuriant charts, coming across like an update of Charles

Mingus's cinematic classic, 1963's *The Black Saint and the Sinner Lady.*

The second important recording that year, also released on Ogun, was *Spirits Rejoice!* by Louis Moholo Octet. Though sharing a name with a 1965 Albert Ayler album and foundation stone of free jazz, Moholo's first statement as a leader is a far more tuneful, if no less serious, affair. Performed by a mix of South Africans — Moholo, Miller and Dyani — and Europeans — Tippett, Evan Parker, trombonists Nick Evans and Austrian Radu Malfatti — as well as Canadian trumpeter Kenny Wheeler, the album is also a collision of styles. Opening track "Khanya Apho Ukhona (Shine Wherever You Are)" is a boisterously up-tempo gallop with strident horn charts and Moholo riding a wave of wild energy, bass drum smacking like a murderous heavyweight boxer while the snare cracks like bundles of street-corner firecrackers. "You Ain't Gonna Know Me 'Cos You Think You Know Me," by contrast, is a soulfully laid-back ballad, both jaunty and brave, defiant in its simplicity, an unmistakable declaration of freedom and fundamental human independence. Indeed, there's an anthemic quality across the whole album that lends it a poignant political punch: Moholo the exile, looking back to the land of his birth with longing and anger, hope and regret.

Once Brötzmann and Miller began to play together, it wasn't long before Moholo was brought on board, and the trio made their live debut in November 1978, playing on consecutive nights on either side of the Wall in West and East Berlin. "To start playing with Louis and Harry was such a relief for me," Brötzmann recalled. "It was never easy with Bennink. It was a lot of fighting. There was always tension. But with Louis and

Harry I got rid of all that. It was just flowing. I could just play. I didn't have to think. I didn't have this fucking arsehole on my side!"[7]

Away from the bandstand, too, Brötzmann the hellraiser enjoyed an immediate rapport with his new bandmates: "Harry was an enjoyable person — smoking, drinking, girls — whatever you needed. And Louis, if he was not too drunk… OK, beer was working, but if he changed to the hardcore stuff, it was over! Harry always kept an eye on him. He was the guy who really kept him working. Not too much smoke, not too much alcohol. Alcohol was not always good for playing, but I was so happy with that group."[8]

Evidence of this camaraderie surfaced with the trio's first album, *The Nearer the Bone, the Sweeter the Meat*, recorded and released in 1979. Just one look at the album cover shows it's a band that's dedicated to the joy of playing: rather than assembling one of his obliquely stylised designs, Brötzmann opts for a single colour photo of the group in action — Brötzmann hunched into a short clarinet, Miller almost bent double over the bass, head down, his right hand a blur, furiously bowing, and Moholo grimacing in eyes-closed absorption as he attacks ride cymbal and snare. Opening track "Long Time Service" dives straight into the heat with Moholo thrashing out a rattling rat-a-tat of snare and high-tuned toms while Miller delivers lurching arco scrapes. Brötzmann enters with scattered spurts over this constant undertow, building in intensity as Moholo's shouts and moans of ecstatic excitement propel the improvisation forward with terrific momentum. As Brötzmann slips into a droning whirl of stunted melodic units, somehow making his clarinet sound like a set of overblown bagpipes, the music accesses a fevered atmosphere of pure thrills.

But what's most impressive is the trio's ability to ease off the volume and open up a more subtle sound palette without ever letting the velocity or intensity flag. On "Kucken Und Drücken," Moholo drops down into an impossibly rapid patter, like raindrops on an upturned wooden bucket, while Miller investigates muscular plucking and abstract arco shapes that find a natural resonance with Brötzmann's dry braying and long, languid lines. The title track is a study in patience, with Miller's fidgety pizzicato details and Moholo's muted barrage and cymbal shimmer guiding Brötzmann into a leisurely ascent from the lower registers of the bass clarinet, like thick coils of smoke slowly rising, performing close minuets with Miller's arco flourishes along the way.

The contrast with Brötzmann's previous trio with Van Hove and Bennink is stark, marking a turn away from fractured abstraction and an arrival at a more explicitly free-jazz-informed aesthetic. Yet, it's also clear just how differently Miller and Moholo approached these open-ended jams than they had the hurtling free-bop of Mike Osborne's trio, joyously revelling in a blunt, forceful freedom. Together, Brötzmann, Miller and Moholo had discovered an entirely new lexicon.

"You always could find some very special players"

Brötzmann was making other important new discoveries around this time, most notably on his first trip to Japan.

Just as they had in Europe and the US, young jazz musicians in Japan had begun to search for new and more progressive forms in the 1960s. Renowned writer, critic and promoter of the new music Teruto Soejima has traced the first detectable rumblings of this youthful energy to two important developments, both in 1962. First, a collective of thirty musicians banded together to form a mutually supportive organisation called New Century Music Research Lab. With a slightly more esoteric spin on the analogous aims and methods of musician-led groups such as the ICP and the Jazz Composers Guild, this cooperative endeavour was guided by three basic principles:

1) We will pursue the structure and content of the art of the future.
2) Through close collaboration with our audience, we will stimulate listeners, not in any superficial way, but by inviting them to understand our true essence.
3) We will encourage younger artists and give the talented ones a space to grow through activities that will also challenge us to grow qualitatively as human beings, hopefully also creating an environment for critical and theoretical discourse.[9]

Secondly, this group established Friday Jazz Corner, a weekly live event held in the Ginparis chanson club in the Ginza district of Tokyo, which presented a rare opportunity for the young artists to perform and develop original modern jazz compositions.

Again, as in the West, this musical blossoming was adjacent to and interconnected with the wider flowering of avant-garde praxes that birthed the Fluxus movement. Soejima describes wild performances witnessed at Friday Jazz Corner, including an event called "From Sign to Creation" at which musicians were given Rorschach images and instructed to perform them as sheet music. On another occasion, a large sheet of traditional washi paper was erected at the back of the stage through which a naked woman burst at the moment the music on stage reached its peak intensity. Soejima also draws explicit parallels between the provocations of Brötzmann's early mentor Nam June Paik and performances by the artist Uchiyama Heogoto, who would "smash glasses on the floor, tear up newspapers, overturn tables."[10]

In July 1964, Yoichi Miyagawa, a drummer and member of New Century Music Research Lab, opened a new club in Ginza called Gallery 8. Crucially, it was Tokyo's first entirely musician-run club, and it afforded the most adventurous young jazz musicians more freedom than they'd ever known. Miyagawa recalled: "We were young and rebellious... We were listening to jazz night and day, much of it what would be called avant-garde today, and Gallery 8 was absolutely the first live space where we could play what we wanted."[11]

By the beginning of 1965, Gallery 8 had taken over from Ginparis as the key hotspot for the most advanced Japanese jazz, and it was here, on 8 May 1965, that Soejima witnessed what he called "possibly the first truly free jazz performance in Japan,"[12] by a quartet led by drummer Masahiko Togashi and featuring Kazunori Takeda on tenor sax, Yosuke Yamashita on piano and Kuniro Takimoto on bass. The group was short-lived, breaking up after just three months and making no recordings, but its importance as an early forerunner of Japanese free jazz cannot be overstated. As Soejima astutely observed, this epochal first performance took place in the very same month that Bernard Stollman founded the ESP-Disk record label in New York and the AACM was established in Chicago.

December 1965 saw the opening of another crucial venue, the Pit Inn, which shifted the centre of Tokyo's avant-garde jazz activity to the hip, bohemian district of Shinjuku, with its night clubs, coffee bars and campus book shops, and provided even more conditions and opportunities for free jazz to germinate. Within just a few years, the scene began to bear fruit, coalescing around a nascent, tight-knit community of young, mutually encouraging free-jazz musicians and leading to the emergence, in 1969, of four key groups with overlapping memberships: trios led by bassist Motoharu Yoshizawa and pianist Yosuke Yamashita; ESSG, a quartet co-led by Masahiko Togashi and pianist Masahiko Satoh; and New Directions, a trio led by guitarist Masayuki Takayanagi also featuring drummer Toyozumi "Sabu" Yoshisaburo and Yoshizawa playing bass, cello, percussion and reeds, including traditional Japanese pipes.

It was this latter group that, in 1969, recorded the album that's largely regarded as the first true classic of Japanese free jazz: *Independence: Tread On Sure Ground*. Throughout, Takayanagi's electric guitar is a brittle, barbed threat, at times quietly plucked, at others surfing the edge of dangerous feedback, while Yoshizawa and Yoshisaburo add unpredictable shading and gestures. It's certainly not difficult to discern an echo of European improv dates such as Parker, Bailey and Bennink's *The Topography of the Lungs*, released the same year. Writing in the liner notes to a 2007 CD reissue, critic and Japanese music expert Alan Cummings claims: "Its sense of focused concentration is more akin to the European free improvisation of AMM or the Spontaneous Music Ensemble than the violent ecstasies of American fire music."[13]

The core players at the heart of the Japanese free-jazz scene released a rapid burst of albums around this time, all with a similar snarling energy: Togashi Masahiko Quartet's *We Now Create: Music For Strings, Winds And Percussion* (featuring Yoshizawa on bass and cello and Takayanagi on guitar, and with Mototeru Takagi on reeds) and Yosuke Yamashita Trio's

Concert in New Jazz (with Takeo Moriyama on drums and Seiichi Nakamura on saxophones and clarinet) were both released in 1969, both further demonstrating a marked affinity with European free improvisation at the same time as they were clearly striving to find a uniquely Japanese identity (a mission and pre-occupation clearly alluded to in the title of Takayanagi's *Independence: Tread On Sure Ground*). Just as it did for many young German jazz musicians, this meant a deliberate turning away from American jazz. As Soejima noted: "Japanese free jazz musicians were cutting their umbilical ties to American jazz and looking around for inspiration in Japanese culture."[14]

This was by no means the only important parallel to be found between the Japanese and German scenes. In both countries, the rise of more challenging and expanded artforms like free jazz, improvised music and psychedelic rock could be seen as just one element of widespread socio-cultural upheavals felt most keenly by disaffected youth determined to disassociate themselves from the bellicose crimes of the parent generation. Mirroring the actions of the Socialist German Students' Union, Japanese leftist and anti-government student organisations rallied under the banner of the All-Campus Joint Struggle Committees — known as the Zenkyōtō — and, throughout 1968 and 1969, staged strikes, campus occupations and violent clashes with police in protest against state capitalism and American imperialism. With Tokyo's free-jazz brethren firmly established in the Shinjuku district, site of a major university campus and hotbed of radical student activity, the musicians bore close witness to these revolutionary actions. In a further striking correspondence between the German and Japanese milieus, some musicians even courted far-left terrorism. Just as the hippie communes that spawned musical collectives such as Amon Düül were also home to leading protagonists in the German Red Army Faction, so members of the mythical Japanese psychedelic rock group Les Rallizes Dénudés became closely involved with the Japanese Communist League's Red Army Faction, with bassist Moriaki Wakabayashi even taking part in the hijacking of Japan Airlines Flight 351 in 1970. In so many ways, German and Japanese youth were united in a struggle for political and expressive freedoms.

The first inevitable contact between German and Japanese free-jazz musicians took place in February 1971 when a group calling itself the German All-stars — including Albert Mangelsdorf, Wolfgang Dauner, Manfred Schoof, Gerd Dudek and bass clarinettist Michel Pilz — arrived in Tokyo to play a handful of gigs. In downtime between shows, Schoof, Pilz and Dudek enthusiastically hooked up with the local underground and played with the Yamashita Yosuke Trio at the Pit Inn. Soejima has quoted Schoof as claiming: "This is a good space. Nowhere in Europe have I found a space dedicated solely to new jazz."[15]

News of this exciting Tokyo scene soon spread to German organisers, and Japanese improvisers found a particularly welcoming reception at the Moers International New Jazz festival that had run in the small north-western German city of Moers since 1972. At the invitation of festival founder and director Burkhard Hennen, the Yamashita Trio played there between 1974 and 1977, sharing bills with European acts such as Willem Breuker and Globe Unity Orchestra and American artists including Anthony Braxton and Steve Lacy. "The Moers festival was always a good address for Japanese musicians," Brötzmann concurred.[16]

It was at Moers that Brötzmann received his first invitation to play in Japan. He told me that this offer was extended to him in 1979 by influential critic and promoter Akira Aida, who was visiting the festival that year, but, as Aida died of a cerebral haemorrhage in December 1978, it's likely that the timelines became confused with the passing of the years. "Aida was the main figure for the new music in Japan," Brötzmann recalled, "and he already had invited Milford Graves to Japan, Steve Lacy, I think Derek [Bailey]. I played with Bennink at Moers and he came and asked us to come over the next year to Japan for quite a long tour."[17] Despite Brötzmann's professed reluctance to undertake any lengthy engagements with Bennink at this time, he recognised a potentially fruitful opportunity and accepted the offer, arriving in Japan for the first time in 1980: "Our first tour was about four weeks long, for the duo, and that was really fantastic."[18] A record of what that tour sounded like can be heard on an extremely rare album, *Atsugi Concert*, released as a limited-edition LP, in Japan only, in 1980. Recorded live at the Rodo Centre in the small city of Atsugi, near Tokyo, on 8 April that year, it's a riotous blast of avant-garde expression, with Brötzmann playing multiple reeds as well as piano, and Bennink contributing on drums, saxophone, clarinet, piano, xylophone, shells, stones and violin.

Once in Japan, Brötzmann had the chance to reconnect with one young firebrand with whom he was already acquainted: trumpeter Toshinori Kondo: "I knew him before because he had played at the Moers festival, and he had showed up in Wuppertal one day with [American cello player] Tristan Honsinger. So, we decided, when I came to Japan, to do things together."

Kondo (born 1948) had been among the first Japanese improvisers to make a truly international name for himself. In 1978, he'd moved to New York City and immersed himself in the febrile downtown scene, playing with saxophonist John Zorn, bassist Bill Laswell and guitarists Henry Kaiser and Eugene Chadbourne, and he made his recorded debut that year on the trio date *Moose and Salmon* with Kaiser and saxophonist John Oswald. By the turn of the decade, he'd also connected with the British scene, releasing *Artless Sky*, a trio with guitarist John Russell and drummer Roger Turner, in 1980. Restless and uncompromising, Kondo was, in many ways, a natural match for Brötzmann, not least in his perception of improvised music as being ideologically adjacent — but ultimately superior — to the radical politics of the day. Soejima has cited him as claiming:

> "When I was in college, it was the peak of the student movement and the fires of revolution were burning all over the campus. But I'm not the kind who could just join in. I was crazy about the trumpet and thought that with my music I could do something even more revolutionary than what they were talking about. Music can go all the way into people's consciousness, something that's even stronger than social revolution. That's why I got into free jazz."[19]

Brötzmann's first foray to Japan sparked a deep affinity for the country, setting the tradition of at least one visit nearly every year from then on. In 2013, he told me: "I loved the country from the very beginning, and I still do. The people I always liked. Of course, some love stories happened too."[20] Romance aside, these regular trips also enabled him to make other important connections with key musicians at the beginning of the '80s. Again in 2013, he claimed: "I met people I am still working with, like the piano player [Masahiko] Satoh or [Takeo] Moriyama, the old, really famous drummer."[21]

Both Moriyama (born 1945) and Satoh (born 1941) had been originators of the Tokyo free-jazz community, with each active in the key groups that had dominated the scene in 1969 — Moriyama in the Yosuke Yamashita Trio, and Satoh as co-leader of the ESSG quartet. Moreover, Satoh had already made early inroads into the European jazz milieu, bringing him into close contact with German improvisers. In 1971, at the invitation of Joachim Berendt, he performed at the Berlin Jazz Festival in a trio with bassist Yasuo Arakawa and drummer Masahiko Ozu, and around the same time, began cutting a number of international collaborations, including *Pianology* with Wolfgang Dauner and *Duologue* with Hungarian guitarist Atilla Zoller (both 1971), as well as 1972's *Spontaneous,* in a quartet with the American rhythm section of bassist Peter Warren and drummer (and former member of Albert Ayler's later bands) Allen Blairman, plus the ever-adventurous Albert Mangelsdorff. Deeply influenced by traditional, Zen-informed Japanese calligraphy, in which each indelible brush stroke must be actioned with conviction and a complete abnegation of forethought, Satoh developed an improvising style through which he strove to fully inhabit and make new every moment. "It's possible to say let's go along this line or let's go along that. But I got really sick of that," he maintained. "I really wanted to go somewhere where there were no guidelines… I try to play what's appropriate each minute or even each second."[22]

If Brötzmann identified an obvious shared ideal in Satoh's commitment to total spontaneity that made eventual collaboration inevitable, his first trip to Japan also led to an important connection with a much less likely figure. Keiji Haino (born 1952) was a young, long-haired multi-instrumentalist with a penchant for brain-bleeding, overdriven electric guitar; he'd been active in psychedelic and experimental rock since the beginning of the '70s, but really hit his stride with the formation of his improvisational free-rock unit Fushitsusha in 1978, initially with Tamio Shiraishi on synthesizer but thereafter with a revolving cast of co-conspirators. Brötzmann's initial contact with him came about almost by chance: "You have to have a kind of management over there [in Japan], and the management we had was the same who was, at that time, busy with Keiji Haino too… and so we decided, 'OK, let's do something together.'"[23] From the beginning, Brötzmann was deeply impressed by the younger musician: "Keiji Haino is a very special guy."[24]

In fact, Brötzmann remained unequivocal in his praise for the musical personalities and kindred spirits he encountered in Japan:

"You always could find some very special players. They all had something special, and that is always fascinating to me. You always had a lot of Japanese musicians trying to play like Americans but you had these other people too who tried to do something else, something of their own, maybe even connected to their own tradition and history — for example, I think Keiji Haino is very much connected to Japanese music and theatre history — and that is always fascinating me because I like surprises, I like challenges and I have to find my own way to react and do my things."[25]

"Sometimes it needs a kick in the arse"

Back home in Germany, Brötzmann cut a second album with Miller and Moholo, *Opened, But Hardly Touched*, recorded live in Berlin in November 1980 and released on FMP the following year. On this double LP, he employs an expanded arsenal of instruments, playing alto, tenor and baritone saxes, E-flat clarinet and a new addition — a Hungarian woodwind called a tarogato. In an email in 2021, Brötzmann told me how the instrument first came into his life:

"It must have been in the late 70s, a Festival in Debrecen, south of Hungary. After the concert a Hungarian man came up to me and invited me to visit his workshop. Debrecen had an important music school, and he was the man for the woodwind instruments. His name — I remember — was Attila Nagy. Entering I saw immediately on a board a number of clarinet-like instruments, no idea what that was. So I saw my first tarogatos, beautiful instruments, different in size and color, some with ivory inlays, some pieces of great craftsmanship. I was invited to play one or the other and I did, learned that there have been two important makers, Shundai and Stohwasser, a little different in system. After trying most of them I had the one in my hands with the sound I liked most, a Shundai instrument in B-flat. We talked a bit about buying/selling, after a while I gave him all the Forints I had earned this afternoon and a couple of hundreds of German marks. He was happy, I was happy and I still love the horn and it accompanied me through all the decades on all my travels."[26]

The tarogato has rarely been used in jazz, though it can be heard played to mellifluous effect by Charles Lloyd on his 2006 album *Sangam,* with tabla player Zakir Hussain and drummer Eric Harland. While Lloyd slots it comfortably into the New Age world-jazz sheen of *Sangam,* in Brötzmann's hands the tarogato is a far more volatile presence, wielded with a brittle, braying urgency. On *Opened, but Hardly Touched*, it rears up like a snake-charmer, skirls like a bagpipe and keens like a Persian ney.

The album itself covers a vast terrain, with Miller and Moholo stretching the possibilities suggested on the trio's debut album, pulling Brötzmann into unexpected territories by sketching outlines of form that overlay the furious improvisations with intimations of more conventional jazz settings. Opening track "Eine Kleine Nachtmarie" rides Moholo's savage, free-form kick drum attack and off-mic vocal exhortations, with Miller throwing in flashing hints of walking bass, until Brötzmann's frenzied tarogato drops out, opening up a space for the rhythm section to race gleefully into the kind of impossibly fast free-bop they perfected with Mike Osborne. "Trotzdem Un Dennoch" proposes a constantly self-deconstructing, elastic ballad cushioned by low tenor moans from Brötzmann, while Miller and Moholo execute daring hairpin tuns as they flip from slow blues shuffles to swinging hard-bop charges with all the panache and precision that Ron Carter and Tony Williams brought to Miles Davis' mid-60s quintet. On "Special Request for Malibu," Moholo cheekily interrupts Brötzmann's slowly uncoiling bass clarinet with a sudden, brief funk break before leading the trio into a home stretch of super-fast power-swing. At once fiercely uncompromising yet warmly accessible, it captures Brötzmann in obvious good humour, revelling in the easy playfulness of his South African colleagues as they tease him into a more conventionally jazz-inflected sound than he'd ever made before.

While Brötzmann had ostensibly been concentrating on small groups throughout the 1970s and into the 1980s, he had at the same time been taking part in a number of much larger ensembles, all of which extended the notion of the pan-European summit suggested by *Machine Gun*, while reaching out to embrace a wider internationalism.

A couple of notable examples were issued on the ICP label. *Groupcomposing* (recorded in 1970 but not released until 1978) convened a veritable supergroup of European improv pioneers from Germany (Brötzmann), the Netherlands (Misha Mengelberg, Han Bennink and his brother Peter on alto sax and bagpipes) and England (Evan Parker, Paul Rutherford and Derek Bailey) for two lengthy spontaneous compositions, each originally occupying one side of vinyl. Coming just two years after *Machine Gun,* it illustrates how rapidly the notion of group improvisation was evolving. There's still plenty of bluster and brawn, not least from Rutherford's gusty trombone and Brötzmann's molten tenor, so much so that Bailey's guitar is often fighting for oxygen. Yet, when things do simmer down — and particularly when Bennink's more ebullient percussive gambits drop out — there's a surprising amount of space, with ad hoc duos and trios briefly adhering: taut guitar and muttering trombone, plunging piano chords with pinging wood blocks, and so on. The second piece takes things even further from the free-jazz template, with an extended section of peaceful abstraction, full of overlapping tones, brassy lowing and delicate rustles. It's an absorbing document of living music in real-time flux.

For the ICP Tentet's 1977 debut album, *Tetterettet,* a crack team of Dutch improvisers including Mengelberg and both Benninks is bolstered by Brötzmann, John Tchicai, American cellist Tristan Honsinger and a bona fide legend of US free jazz, bassist Alan Silva, who had provided the bottom end for Albert Ayler, Cecil Taylor and Sun Ra. Yet rather than leaning into a fire music aesthetic, the date steers a perverse course towards a kind of European Dada cabaret, guided by Mengelberg's impish compositions. In many ways, it's quintessentially Dutch art-music: playful, mischievous, irreverent and gleefully aware that it's breaking the rules, with tunes mashing together ragged cha-cha-cha, comedy vaudeville marches, wonky waltzes, strolling jazz with silly unison vocal scat, and episodes of straight-faced chamber improv. Michel Waisvisz adds a frisson of unpredictability with his home-made crackle-box — a rudimentary electronic noise maker — while Brötzmann wobbles out a vibrato so wide it suggests how Ayler might have sounded if he'd been thinking of the circus instead of the church.

Mengelberg's "Alexander's Marschbefehl" provides a glorious demonstration of Brötzmann as an embodiment of disrupting force, ripping apart the tune's cartoonish march with a sudden impatient irruption of savage energy, snarling and raging like an attack dog foaming at the mouth, incensed by the silliness of Mengelberg's deceptively dainty composition. "In the end I was invited to play this role in the ICP," Brötzmann chuckled.

"Misha was always so happy when I did something which was not on the paper. When they were playing their nice tunes and nicely organised pieces, Misha always liked when I came in and sometimes very suddenly — and not in the concept of the whole thing — I disturbed the whole band. At least in the early years, he wrote all the pieces and arranged them in his very minimalistic way, but he knew sometimes it needs a kick in the arse — and I was a good guy for that."[27]

Despite their undeniable comic effect, Brötzmann's chaotic disruptions were underpinned by a serious conceptual refusal to engage uncritically with the prevailing discourse, an urge shared by artistic and philosophical movements from Dada and Fluxus to Situationism.

Some of the more ambitious large-scale projects Brötzmann took part in during this period were under the auspices of his old mentor, Don Cherry. In fact, since those early days, Cherry had remained a venerable presence in Brötzmann's professional life, providing memorable encounters, continued encouragement and a few surprises. Brötzmann told me: "An early concert with Van Hove and Bennink, we played some radio concert in Cologne and we heard from the back some trumpet playing, and Don Cherry came onto the stage to play with us. This kind of support was very important to us."[28]

Moreover, Cherry had remained an important catalyst for the wider European improvised music scene. In 1967, he took part in the Free Jazz Meeting, an annual festival and showcase for the new music initiated the previous year by Joachim-Ernst Berendt, held in the southwestern German town of Baden-Baden. Performances at the Free Jazz Meeting were broadcast over the FM radio station SWF (Südwestrundfunk, or Southwest Broadcasting), and a recording from the 1967 edition (released on CD in 2018 as *Free Jazz Meeting Baden Baden '67*) captures Cherry performing a free-form improvisation titled "Relationship" with a European cohort, his cornet trading prancing whinnies with Evan Parker's soprano saxophone while bassists Peter Kowald and Buschi Niebergall saw and lunge, and drummer John Stevens scuttles and stutters on the kit. At the same 1967 edition of the Free Jazz Meeting, Cherry convened a fourteen-piece ensemble comprising most of the musicians in attendance — a performance that is, as yet, unreleased. In the following years, Cherry was a regular fixture at the Free Jazz Meeting, often manifesting characteristically omnivorous and quixotic ideas that drew on his burgeoning interests in non-Western music: in 1970 he led a massive, twenty-five-piece orchestra of mostly European improvisers — including Brötzmann, Manfred Schoof, Joachim Kühn, Derek Bailey and others — through an improvised meditation on scales from Indian classical music.

As well as these ad hoc groupings, Cherry also made use of European improvisers in key performing and recording projects, one notable example of which came about as a direct result of the large group he led at the Free Jazz Meeting in 1967. Enthused by the performance, Berendt spent several months discussing with Cherry the idea of forming a large, international band to perform at the 1968 Berlin Jazz Days — at the exact same time that Brötzmann and Geber's first Total Music Meeting was taking place. In the event, Cherry actually formed and led two different ensembles in Berlin: his eleven-piece Big Band played on 9 November, and a couple of days later, on 11 November, he premiered the Eternal Rhythm Group, a nine-piece ensemble which included all the same members as the Big Band, minus Pharoah Sanders and Turkish trumpeter Maffy Falay. This latter performance was recorded and released on the German MPS label in 1969 as *Eternal Rhythm*, one of Cherry's defining works and an enduring free-jazz masterpiece.

The personnel of the Eternal Rhythm Group was a truly international crew, featuring players from several different countries who Cherry had encountered during his peripatetic wanderings: from Germany, Albert Mangelsdorff on trombone, Joachim Kühn on piano (who had first played with Cherry at the inaugural Free Jazz Meeting in Baden-Baden in 1966) and vibraphonist Karl Berger (who had been a stalwart of Cherry's European groups since their mid-60s residencies in Paris, and had accompanied Cherry to New York in 1966 to play on his Blue Note album *Symphony for Improvisers*); from Sweden, trombonist Eje Thelin and saxophonist Bernt Rosengren; from France, drummer Jacques Thollot; and from Norway, the then unknown bassist Arild Andersen.

Rounding out the company was New Yorker guitarist Sonny Sharrock (born 1940). Turned on by John Coltrane, the young Sharrock had wanted to be a tenor saxophonist, but thwarted by a bad case of asthma, had turned to the guitar instead. When the New Thing broke in New York, Sharrock was drawn to free jazz, making an early appearance on Pharoah Sanders' 1966 album *Tauhid* and becoming what Berendt describes in his liner notes for *Eternal Rhythm* as "perhaps the first guitarist who plays free with the full intensity of the New Jazz."[29] In fact, Sharrock repeatedly claimed to dislike the guitar as an instrument, and according to musician and musicologist Dave Stagner, maintained that he was "a horn player with a really fucked up axe,"[30] forging a jagged, heavily-amplified sound full of dense, horn-like lines punctuated by wild feedback bursts that approximated the ecstatic altissimo shrieks of Sanders, Coltrane and Ayler. As Berendt notes, Sharrock "came to Berlin as a member of the Herbie Mann Group,"[31] and he did, in fact, spend several years playing with Mann, an American flautist who achieved considerable commercial success with an accessible soul-jazz sound and who, like Cherry, was an early pioneer of fusing jazz with global influences. Yet, even in this setting, Sharrock was fiercely experimental and uncompromising. A compilation of his guitar solos during performances with Mann (first isolated and committed to a legendary mix tape by Thurston Moore, now reproduced on YouTube[32]) reveals him utterly destroying the tasteful grooves of tunes like Mann's "Memphis Underground" and Sam and Dave's "Hold On I'm Coming" with crazed glissandi, ferocious divebombs and face-melting howls — all delivered with an almost comical disregard for Mann's funky, feel-good vibes.

Sharrock can be heard delivering a handful of typically taut outbursts throughout *Eternal Rhythm*, with an attack like he's assaulting the strings with a razor-sharp cheese wire. These are nestled within the collage of interlinked themes that comprise the single forty-minute title track, originally split across two sides of vinyl. Berendt explained the piece's origins: "When this band began to play — in the rehearsal hall of the Berlin *Philharmonie*, six days prior to this recording — the music sounded like exciting, fiery chaos. Nothing was organised. But then Don passed out motifs and themes and worked out ideas, and all of a sudden melodies, forms and structures became audible; the music achieved order."[33] Both dreamlike and urgent, *Eternal Rhythm* glides through a dizzying range of moods, touching on Ayler-like fanfares, tumultuous free jazz irruptions, joyous Turkish folk melodies and a slow, crashing blues. It also furthers Cherry's world-jazz agenda, with Don playing ethereal flurries on a bamboo flute and Bengali wood flute simultaneously, and — in its most unusual moments — incorporates the tinkling clatter of Javanese and Balinese gamelan, with Cherry, Berger and Thollot negotiating intricate traditional rhythms on *gender* and *saron* metallophones.

Three years later, in 1971, Cherry convened an even bigger ensemble, the seventeen-piece New Eternal Rhythm Orchestra, for a performance at the Donaueschingen New Music Festival, an esteemed and long-running showcase for contemporary classical music held every October since 1921 in the titular Black Forest town in southwest Germany. Once again, the group he assembled was a truly international entity, featuring: Brötzmann, Willem Breuker and Gerd Dudek on saxophones; Manfred Schoof, Kenny Wheeler and, from Poland, Tomasz Stanko on trumpets; Paul Rutherford and Albert Mangelsdorff on trombones; Gunter Hampel on flute and bass clarinet; Fred Van Hove on piano and organ; Norwegian guitarist Terje Rypdal; Buschi Niebergall and American Peter Warren on basses; plus Han Bennink on "drums, Chinese woodblocks, tabla, thumb piano, percussion, plastic hose, horse jaw, etc."[34] On Cherry's nineteen-minute suite "Humus," the group also included Moki Cherry on tambura and Dutch vocalist Loes Macgillycutty.

The piece's debut performance on 17 October 1971 at Donaueschingen was recorded by Südwestrundfunk and released the same year as one side of the album *Actions*. Much like the suite heard on *Eternal Rhythm*, it's an episodic journey, featuring seven distinct themes selected in the moment by Cherry from fifteen motifs the orchestra had rehearsed in the preceding weeks. Both gripping and charmingly ramshackle in its spontaneity, "Humus" touches on themes and ideas from Africa, Hindustani classical music, a Chinese-influenced section incorporating tonalities inspired by minimalist composer (and Cherry's friend and sometime collaborator) Terry Riley, a bluesy, swing-era vamp that Cherry called "the last of the big bands,"[35] plus Balinese music, revisiting breakthroughs made by the Eternal Rhythm Group at the Berlin recording of *Eternal Rhythm* in 1968. "It all started in Berlin," Cherry told Joachim Berendt in the sleeve notes for *Actions*. "The Balinese Gamelang (sic) percussion we used

there really opened it up. That is why we have called the band
The New Eternal Rhythm Orchestra."[36]

Manfred Schoof told Swedish journalist Magnus Nygren:

"It was really interesting because this kind of big ensemble was
completely improvising and there were no things really written
down, they were just given by Don. We followed and we tried
to realise it. We went with him and then we also did some [of
our] own ideas and he followed us, he was an open man, he was
open for everything that was good for him and the music."[37]

On more than one occasion, Brötzmann can be heard
exercising his freedom, breaking through the group sound to
blaze out scorching solo statements of utterly crazed altissimo
shrieking, once again unleashing the same unruly, disrupting
and energising force he brought to performances with Misha
Mengelberg's ICP formations.

The B-side of *Actions* features a sixteen-minute piece
for the New Eternal Rhythm Orchestra (minus Cherry) by
Polish composer Krzysztof Penderecki. Entitled "Actions
for Free Jazz Orchestra," the composition was inspired by
Penderecki witnessing Alexander von Schlippenbach's Globe
Unity Orchestra at Donaueschingen in 1967 and subsequently
attempting to write his own work for improvisers. As Berendt
states: "'Actions' is the first example of a piece where a classical
composer has renounced the hitherto customary (and always
unsatisfactory) orchestral jazz 'imitations' in favour of allowing
exclusively jazz musicians to play his piece."[38] Much like
Cherry's piece, "Actions for Free Jazz Orchestra" shifts from
theme to theme in an unbroken chain, guided by Penderecki
making his debut as a conductor. Notably less dynamic than
Cherry's "Humus," the piece is very much a compromise.

While some of the performers reportedly felt stifled by the lack of space for improvisation, Penderecki aimed to harness the improvisers' spirit of unpredictability, claiming: "If an orchestral musician who has been playing with an orchestra for thirty years or so is suddenly called upon to improvise, he won't manage it. He would first have to learn something which is taken for granted by jazz musicians. They can improvise freely — it is their second nature."[39]

What remains most significant about "Actions for Free Jazz Orchestra" is the extent to which it represented a neat, full circle: while Globe Unity Orchestra had initially been influenced equally by von Schlippenbach's studies in contemporary classical music and the free-wheeling suites performed by Don Cherry's mid-60s band, here a renowned composer of new music sought to emulate Globe Unity, drawing on the skills of improvisers assembled by Cherry. Moreover, "Actions…" has continued to resonate. In 2018, Swedish saxophonist Mats Gustafsson and his Fire! Orchestra were commissioned by the Sacrum Profanum festival in Kraków, Poland, to perform a new, extended reading of Penderecki's piece. Released as the CD *Actions* in 2020, the new version featured almost identical instrumentation (with a tuba replacing one of the trombones), but ran to forty minutes, using a graphic score to provide the ensemble with more scope for extemporisation, thus bringing it even closer to the Globe Unity Orchestra's original seed of influence.

"I never could tell a good player, 'Man, you have to stop now'"

Brötzmann had remained an integral member of the Globe Unity Orchestra since its inception in 1966. Under the musical direction of Alexander von Schlippenbach, the

Orchestra continued to serve as a white-hot crucible of group improvisation on an epic scale, largely populated by adventurous German and Dutch musicians. However, by the turn of the '70s, it had expanded its borders, bringing in improvisers from the UK and elsewhere, as can be seen in a thrilling thirty-minute performance by a nineteen-piece Orchestra filmed at the Berliner Jazztage festival on 7 November 1970.[40] Derek Bailey makes an early appearance, bespectacled and serious, scratching out jagged chords on a crackling, heavily amplified guitar; trombonists Paul Rutherford and Malcom Griffiths blow up huge gales of trombone alongside Albert Mangelsdorff; and Evan Parker slots into the saxophone section with Brötzmann, Gerd Dudek and others; while Manfred Schoof is joined by fellow trumpeters including Kenny Wheeler and Tomasz Stanko.

The three compositions performed give a clear indication of the ambitious tactics and techniques the Orchestra employed at this time. Von Schlippenbach's "Globe Unity 70" is a study in dynamic contrasts, with loudly churning group improvisations (von Schlippenbach laying a thick plank of wood on the piano's keys and pressing down violently to create impossible chords barely heard over massed horns) giving way to more reflective moments (Han Bennink stepping from behind the kit for an extended turn on a long Tibetan horn, growling out digeridoo-like vocalisations). Navigating these episodes, Orchestra members scrabble around with dog-eared, loose-leaf scores on music stands, a brief close-up revealing a graphic instruction of thick, black, horizontal lines. Schoof's "Ode" transitions from free-form billows to a bluesy, swinging, big band riff strafed by urgent horn blasts. And Brötzmann's "Drunken in The Morning Sunrise" (a cheeky play on the show-tune standard "Softly, as in a Morning Sunrise") provides a showcase for its composer, who takes centre stage for an intense tenor solo, rocking back and forth from the waist, clad in black shirt and a hunter's waistcoat, utterly absorbed as he strains at the horn's highest registers and the Orchestra punctuates a wailing cacophony with sudden staccato crashes.

While its musical lexicon was rapidly developing, Globe Unity Orchestra remained somewhat geographically limited, mostly performing in West Germany at festivals such as Berliner Jazztage, Total Music Meeting and Workshop Freie Musik, and suffered a further loss of momentum when von Schlippenbach briefly left in 1971. But from 1973, the orchestra's fortunes revived as Peter Kowald stepped up to co-run the endeavour alongside a returned and recommitted von Schlippenbach. Drawing on Kowald's infectious energy and utopian inclinations, Globe Unity Orchestra began playing abroad and recording, mainly for FMP, beginning with *Live in Wuppertal*. Credited to Globe Unity 73 in acknowledgement of the ensemble's fresh start, the album highlights how, while rightly revered for providing a blueprint for large-scale, ecstatic free jazz, the orchestra also affectionately — often humorously — interrogated earlier styles of jazz and other, more disparate forms: a fleeting version of Jelly Roll Morton's "Wolverine Blues" is a woozy oompah-Dixieland hybrid, and von Schlippenbach's "Bavarian Calypso" ends up as daft as the name suggests. Elsewhere, as on the intoxicating swirl of "Yarrak," there are echoes of the scale and accumulative power of George Russell's mammoth suite "Electronic Sonata for Souls Loved by Nature" (the debut 1969 recording of which Schoof also played on). Side A ends with a brisk march through "Solidaritätslied" ("Solidarity Song"), a revolutionary working song by Bertolt Brecht and Hanns Eisler and a companion piece to "Einheitsfrontlied," the left-wing anthem recorded by Brötzmann, Van Hove and Bennink the same year. The whole of Side B is taken up by Kowald's "Maniacs," another episodic exploration of highly charged, conducted group improvisation.

During the five years that Kowald co-led Globe Unity, the project grew and evolved, both in terms of personnel and artistic ambition. 1977's *Jahrmarkt / Local Fair* is the perfect example. The A-side features a single piece by the pared back ensemble of Brötzmann, Mangelsdorff, Enrico Rava, Paul Lovens on musical saw and AACM-affiliated alto saxophonist Anthony Braxton. For the B-side, Kowald assembled a daring tape assemblage describing a leisurely, dream-like stroll through a fantastic village fair that condenses and collides disparate musical cultures into one dizzying global kaleidoscope: snatches of Miles Davis's "Milestones" and Charlie Parker's "Anthropology" waft in and out of ear shot; gusts of savage group improvisation billow up like angry storm clouds; members of the FMP family can be heard shredding in duos or alone; we encounter a Greek folk group playing traditional tunes and twenty-five Wuppertal accordion players wheezing away with high seriousness, all shot through with tantalising snippets of blues, ballads, beerhall drinking songs and ending with a punchy, big band R&B vamp. It's quite a day out.

To mark the tenth anniversary of its debut recording, Globe Unity gathered another large assembly to record *Pearls* in early 1977, again finding room for Rava and Braxton. If Braxton's presence can be seen as a logical link to the similar large-scale experiments of the AACM, the organisational debt owed by Globe Unity is more explicitly paid in von Schlippenbach's "Kunstmusik II," with its thorny, concatenated clumps of ensemble improvisation. Moreover, it's here that Globe Unity most convincingly fulfils its orchestral promise, with glancing, metallic scrapes and tense whines constructing vertical shapes that sit closer to Ligeti than anything Ellington ever imagined. It's an intense and exhausting set, after which the final, schmaltzy, big band ballad reading of Monk's "Ruby My Dear" soothes like a cup of cocoa and a kiss goodnight.

Still, Globe Unity's ambitions expanded, bringing theatrical and multi-media elements into performances and seeing them play in locations as far-flung as the Ashoka Hotel, New Delhi, in 1978. Brötzmann, too, brought his own wider artistic sensibilities to bear on this generous canvas. He told me in 2013:

> "There are a couple of compositions — big word! — I did for Globe Unity in those times in which I was trying to follow the kind of Fluxus systematic. I wrote pieces mainly with graphic structures, not influenced by who was playing what, just how certain graphic structures solve certain problems, or come from here to the end. I remember we performed, from time to time, one or the other — I don't think it was a big success in a way, because you have to have the right people for that way of thinking. I never could tell a good player, 'Man, you have to stop now.' I just did always the opposite: 'Go!' So there was a kind of contradiction. But I was — and I still am, in a way — very interested in this contradiction, too, because it's a really interesting way of working. But I don't think it works for the real player."[41]

Despite these experiments with form, Brötzmann ultimately remained more committed to the open-ended possibilities of collective free improvisation suggested by Globe Unity rather than the more orchestrated approach favoured by von

Schlippenbach and guests such as Braxton. There was, then, a tension — the "contradiction" Brötzmann hints at — between those keen to explore structure and what Brötzmann calls "the real player." Tellingly, while Brötzmann contributed to Globe Unity's 1978 album *Improvisations*, he was absent from its 1980 companion piece, *Compositions*. By the beginning of the 1980s, Brötzmann had parted company with Globe Unity. David Keenan, in 2012, reported him recollecting that he "got out as soon as it began to ossify."[42]

Globe Unity continued to perform, making a final appearance in 1987 at the Chicago Jazz Festival (notwithstanding a brief fortieth-anniversary reunion in 2006, in which Brötzmann did not participate). Yet its influence has extended well into the twenty-first century, heard in the work of large ensembles such as of Mats Gustafsson's Fire! Orchestra and Circulasione Totale Orchestra, whose 2009 album *Bandwidth* features three drummers closely connected to Brötzmann: Louis Moholo-Moholo (as he was, by then, known), Hamid Drake and Paal Nilssen-Love. In fact, Nilssen-Love's increasingly extravagant iterations of his Large Unit project have probably come closest to the core aesthetic of Globe Unity. His 2018 album *More Fun Please* — credited to Extra Large Unit — features a monstrously swollen twenty-eight-piece ensemble, through which the notoriously ferocious drummer emerges as a composer of some delicacy. Using a combination of graphic scores, conduction, written prompts and conventional notation, he guides the Unit through a remarkable range of shades, with the principal players free to make significant choices throughout. Beginning with eighteen seconds of silence between his signal to start and the first note played, the album's single thirty-three-minute composition moves through fidgety shuffling with hints of Celtic fiddle and accordion to muscular ripples, erupting midway into tumultuous blasts of Globe Unity proportions, before subsiding into gentle Morton Feldman–esque tones that fade into silence. It might never have existed without the explorations set into motion by von Schlippenbach et al. back in 1966.

During his period working with Miller and Moholo in the early 1980s, Brötzmann initiated another major project featuring an expanded group, which was released in 1983 on FMP as the album *Alarm*. It captures part of a performance given in Hamburg on 12 November 1981, organised by the radio station NDR as part of its long-running "Jazz Workshop" series of live broadcasts. As Brötzmann explained in the album's liner notes: "Michael Naura, chief of the jazz dept there, was setting up a series of on-air concerts in a 200-seat studio."[43] With financial backing from NDR, Brötzmann was able to assemble a dream-team nine-piece international ensemble of associates old and new, including the South African rhythm section, Alexander von Schlippenbach on piano, trombones played by Englishman Alan Tomlinson and East German Hannes Bauer (younger brother of fellow trombonist Conny Bauer) and Japanese trumpeter Toshinori Kondo. Tenor saxophones were played by Brötzmann and Willem Breuker plus a US free-jazz original and conduit to the source, Frank Wright.

Born in 1935, Wright had played with Sunny Murray as early as 1964, had been asked by John Coltrane to take part in the recording of his epochal free-jazz blueprint *Ascension* in 1965 (an invitation humbly declined by Wright, who didn't feel he had the requisite skills) and had released his debut as a leader, *Frank Wright Trio*, on the ESP-Disk label in 1966. Wright relocated to Europe in 1969, settling in Paris, which brought him into direct contact with the younger European players. As Brötzmann recalled: "He was one of the first Black Americans we got to know really well, and we all learned a lot from that."[44] With a huge, roaring, uninhibited tone profoundly influenced by Albert Ayler (with whom he'd been friends during his youth in Cleveland, and who had first persuaded him to switch from bass to saxophone), Wright was a natural fit for Brötzmann's group. "[He] was a wild man, in a good sense," Brötzmann said, "made music and lived his own life."[45]

The work documented on *Alarm* is Brötzmann's monumental composition of the same name, coming in at thirty-seven minutes, split over two sides of the original LP. The piece was conceived as a protest against the terrifying escalation of the Cold War nuclear arms race that went into overdrive as the 1980s dawned. More specifically, as Brötzmann explained in the notes, it was an angry contribution to the debate then raging as to whether the West German Army (and US Armed Forces stationed in Germany) should deploy nuclear weapons. Brötzmann's graphic score — reproduced in detail on the album's cover as a scrawl of red and black waves, spirals and arrows with scribbled instructions — was based on official evacuation plans for when the bomb dropped. As Brötzmann explained: "I used graphic instructions for a reaction to a nuclear emergency, a series of waves and straight tones, repeated in a certain way."[46] Here, too, we can discern a link to Brötzmann's youthful alignment with Fluxus, echoing the scores John Cage devised for his *Etudes Australes*, based on astronomical star charts.

"Alarm" begins with horns in unison mimicking the chilling rise and fall of an air-raid siren — a motif that recurs throughout the piece, interspersed with intense energy-burst explosions; staccato piano and stabbing horns crashing into violent tumult; an intensely pained, hopeless, wailing tenor solo; Moholo's frenzied gallop trying to outrun the siren's warning; trombones whirring and buzzing like flies on a pile of corpses; gales of massed horns raised in horror and lamentation. Towards the end, a brief, hopeful sax melody emerges, only to immediately warp into a ridiculous martial stomp and then dissolve into seething chaos — a fleeting caricature of the absurdity of nuclear posturing. Finally, there is only the desolate siren.

There are, of course, obvious musical similarities to "Machine Gun" — a big band making a huge, turbulent sound with episodes of fierce improvisation hung on the most slender of structural premises — but "Alarm" can also be seen as a thematic continuation of the earlier work. While "Machine Gun" was inextricably linked to anti-Vietnam War sentiments, "Alarm," with its strident call for nuclear disarmament, updates an urgent and necessary resistance of US imperialism. Certainly, for many on the left, this was just as much of a pressing concern in the early 1980s as Vietnam had been in the 1960s. When US president Ronald Reagan visited West Berlin in June 1982 and delivered a speech calling not for peace and unification but for the build-up of American arms in West Germany and further Cold War division, demonstrations demanding disarmament developed into full-blown rioting and street battles with police. Brötzmann's "Alarm" plugs directly into this sense of helpless rage, and can be filed alongside Sun Ra's "Nuclear War" (recorded 1982) as an avant-jazz meditation on the ever-present spectre of nuclear annihilation that hung over the world in the early 1980s.

At the November 1981 gig at which "Alarm" was recorded, the piece was intended as just the opening movement in a wider programme. "We had planned two more pieces, one by Willem Breuker and one by Frank Wright," Brötzmann explained. "My piece took about 40 minutes, the first half of the concert. At the end of the performance, [Michael] Naura came to me — while we were still on the air — and whispered that the house got a bomb threat and had to be evacuated. So I had to bring the piece quickly to an end and the audience was asked to leave the hall. We also had to pack up and leave. Police and special forces showed up with all kinds of equipment, gear, dogs — we know all that much better now than then."[47] The implication, and a persistent rumour, is that the show was stopped by the West German authorities, keen to suppress subversive messages and anti-government gatherings. But, whatever the truth, there's something gloriously apposite about Brötzmann's powerful, incendiary piece being halted by an actual threat of explosive violence.

As it happens, the reality of that evening doesn't quite match up to Brötzmann's recollection. A "content log" reproduced on the reverse of the album reveals a tantalising list of tunes by Breuker, Schlippenbach, Miller and Wright, each with "exact transmission times" noted, hinting very strongly at actual performances having taken place. The only piece that makes it onto the record is Frank Wright's "Jerry Sacem," which kicks in just as "Alarm" ends — a gloriously upbeat, crazily swinging, 1940s-style, big band romp with a walking bass, punchy horns and Wright mugging vocal outbursts of "I say lookee here" like *The Jungle Book*'s King Louie in a zoot suit. After just a few minutes, the tune fades out, but it's enough to provide a glimpse of the range the nine-piece Peter Brötzmann Group were capable of — and which audiences were able to enjoy as Brötzmann subsequently took the ensemble on tour.

Sadly, *Alarm* was the last documented project Brötzmann undertook with Miller and Moholo. Just as the trio's working relationship was blossoming, it was cruelly and permanently curtailed when Miller was involved in a fatal car accident on 16 December, 1983. "I was touring in Japan with Keiji Haino when I got the bad news that Harry had his accident and was in Amsterdam hospital in a coma," Brötzmann told me in 2013. "That stupid car crash. Harry is the guy I really sit here from time to time and still think of."[48]

The accident was a major blow to the Dutch improvising community, claiming the lives of not just Miller but also twenty-seven-year-old trombonist Joep Maessen and forty-six-year-old expatriate Scottish trumpeter Jeff Reynolds. For Brötzmann, it marked the premature end of a creative team that had been bursting with potential. With Miller dead, Brötzmann's working partnership with Moholo ended too: "After Harry died, the connection just wasn't there anymore."[49]

The Noise of Trouble

"I was always interested in getting some guys together and making something new"

It should perhaps come as no surprise that, after Miller's death, Brötzmann's next major project marked a radical turn away from the more explicitly jazz-oriented sounds he'd been exploring with the South Africans. In 1986, together with bassist Bill Laswell, drummer Ronald Shannon Jackson and guitarist Sonny Sharrock, he co-founded the avant-garde supergroup Last Exit, proposing an aggressively amplified and violently confrontational hybrid of slippery funk, extreme noise rock and free jazz improvisation.

It's clear that this departure was also very much a response to the prevailing musical zeitgeist of the 1980s, and particularly the backward-looking, so-called Neo-bop school of jazz practised by a younger generation of American musicians including saxophonist Kenny Garrett, guitarist Kevin Eubanks and trumpeter Wallace Roney, and spearheaded by outspoken trumpeter Wynton Marsalis. Dubbed the Young Lions by the music press, these self-appointed custodians of the music demanded a return to the rhythmic, melodic and harmonic fundamentals of traditional, straight-ahead jazz as played in the 1950s, and regarded the free jazz and fusion of the 1960s and '70s as aberrations that deserved no place in the music's history or lineage. Predictably, Brötzmann's attitude to this was, if not scathing, at least somewhat dismissively bemused. In 1990, he told writer Barry Witherden:

"I think that kind of music is a step backwards. I don't know what it is — the business maybe — but in the end you find it everywhere. Not so much in Germany, but… in the States even guys playing more advanced music go back to the old bebop tunes when they play the clubs. I don't understand the young guys playing these tunes. They're good players, they can play the horns up and down, but music for me should be a way to find out where I am and where I want to be. I have my tradition and I know the jazz tradition too but I was always interested in getting some guys together and making something new for myself and the audience."[1]

For Brötzmann, then, Last Exit was both a "fuck you" and an antidote to retrograde conservatism. Looking back on this era, he told Gerard Rouy: "[Last] Exit was a band that happened in a barren period for improvised music. That gave the whole music scene a real kick, it was the right group at the right moment."[2] Even so, Last Exit's aesthetic didn't arrive out of nowhere. The group's challenging sound was, in fact, picking up on a burgeoning interest in combining jazz with elements of funk, punk and alternative rock that had been bubbling up in the work of a handful of progressive improvisers. Prominent among these was Bill Laswell.

Born 1955 in Salem, Illinois, Laswell came up as a funk and R&B bassist before relocating to New York at the end of the 1970s and diving headfirst into the fertile downtown music scene. Taking up residence at producer Giorgio Gomelsky's Zu House loft space, performance venue and creative hub, he began to play with a gang of inquisitive young musicians including drummer Fred Maher, synth player Michael Beinhorm, guitarist Cliff Cultreri and organist Mark Kramer; going by the name of the Zu Band, they accompanied various members of European prog-jazz-rock bands, including Magma and Henry Cow, whom Gomelsky was active in bringing over to perform in New York.

In 1978, assuming the name New York Gong, Laswell and co. backed Daevid Allen, then on sabbatical from cosmic-prog collective Gong, the reins of which he'd handed over to French percussionist Pierre Morelen — an association that culminated, the following year, in the recording of New York Gong's space-rock-meets-punk album *About Time*. After a brief 1979 tour of the US and France as New York Gong, the group parted company with Allen and, under the name Material, recorded two Eps: 1979's *Temporary Music 1*, featuring Laswell, Maher, Beinhorm and Cultreri, and 1980's *Temporary Music 2*, as the trio of Laswell, Maher and Beinhorm, both of which were compiled as their debut album, *Temporary Music*, in 1981. Plugging into New York's adventurous post-punk No Wave scene, the album fuses spiky guitar hooks and glistening synths with jerky riffs and buoyant funk and disco rhythms powered by Laswell's greasy bass lines.

Around the same time, Laswell and Maher were also involved in another equally outré project, together with British guitarist Fred Frith, formerly of art-rock outfit Henry Cow. Formed in 1968, Henry Cow were a serious-minded collective with strong revolutionary Marxist and Maoist convictions who considered collective improvisation to be a crucial element of their praxis — one that was encouraged by no less an authority than Derek Bailey. Frith recalls: "He came to Henry Cow gigs and radiated enthusiasm while unfailingly and cheerfully complaining that we weren't improvising enough."[3] By the mid-70s, Henry Cow performances frequently jettisoned compositions entirely, engaging fully with free improvisation, and the group's 1976 live double album, *Concerts,* featured a whole disc of freely improvised music. Alongside King Crimson, who also (but to a lesser extent) dabbled in improv, Henry Cow's championing of free music made them unusual outliers among 1970s progressive rock bands. When Henry Cow disbanded in 1978, Frith moved to New York and further pursued the spontaneous mysteries of improvisation while becoming increasingly fascinated by the city's loudly energetic punk scene. In 1980, he, Laswell and Maher formed the power trio Massacre as a vehicle for exploring the intersection of these divergent interests. Gerard Rouy cites Frith as explaining:

> "There was a crucial period in the late 1970s and early 80s when actually there was a lot of interest via punk in making a kind of free improvised rock. My group Massacre was one of the pioneers of that idea, there were many others of course, at that moment there were many people coming together from jazz and from the punk scene and I think this is where this particular relationship evolved from."[4]

Massacre was a brief, brutal burst of energy, with its original line-up recording just one album, 1981's *Killing Time,* before disbanding the same year. Yet the album's mix of complex, angular riffs, coruscating guitar textures and open-ended improvisation — and the trio's notoriously ferocious live performances — provided an important early template for ideas that Laswell would later bring to Last Exit.

Also released in 1981, Laswell, Maher and Beinhorm's second album as Material, *Memory Serves,* was even more probing than their debut collection, consolidating a punk-funk sound with the aid of guest musicians including Frith and a phalanx of players drawn from the ranks of the US avant-jazz scene: violinist Billy Bang, cornetist Olu Dara and AACM associates, alto saxophonist Henry Threadgill and trombonist George Lewis. Crucially, the album also featured, on guitar, Sonny Sharrock.

Since the late '60s, Sharrock's career had taken a strange trajectory. In 1969, he'd released *Black Woman*, an undisputed classic of free jazz featuring the all-star personnel of Dave Burrell on piano, Norris Jones (aka Sirone) on bass and Milford Graves on drums — plus his wife, Linda Sharrock, supplying wordless vocals that ran from ecstatic ululations to anguished shrieks and sobs. In 1970, he found himself among the upper echelons of jazz superstars, recording with Miles Davis in a heavyweight group also including fellow electric guitarist John McLaughlin, bass clarinettist Bennie Maupin, drummer Jack DeJohnette, Chick Corea on electric piano and Dave Holland on bass guitar. Here, Sharrock adds barbed chords and gnarled abstractions, heavily distorted through an echoplex pedal, to the malevolent, driving funk of a tune called "Willie Nelson," which appeared the following year as part of "Yesternow," the sinuous collage that constitutes the second side of Davis's album *Jack Johnson* — though Sharrock and the rest of this line-up (with the exception of McLaughlin) were uncredited on the final release.

In 1970 Sharrock released *Monkey-Pockie-Boo*, an exploratory session recorded for the French BYG label, featuring bassist Beb Guérin and drummer Jacques Thollot, plus Linda reprising her role as a raw source of unfettered vocal expression. The whole of the first side is taken up by the seventeen-minute "27th Day," on which Sharrock lays off the guitar for the first half, contributing just a lonesome slide whistle, before exploding into some of his most unhinged eruptions of volcanic fretwork. While this album and *Black Woman* both fearlessly pushed free jazz into ever more abstract territory, Sharrock's next outing took an entirely different direction. 1975's *Paradise* — credited to both Sonny and Linda Sharrock — was a curious melange of bluesy grooves, smooth soul and hurtling electric fusion, all overlaid with Sonny's rough abrasions and Linda's strident exhortations. Sharrock was deeply dissatisfied with the album, telling Ben Ratliff in 1989 that it was "not a good album. We used a bunch of young cats, it's not their fault that it wasn't a good album, but it's my fault because I couldn't really put the direction together."[5] Frustrated and embarrassed by the debacle, Sharrock largely disappeared from music for the rest of the '70s, working as a chauffeur and caretaker.

But Laswell remained a fan. "Sonny was a natural," he told Anil Prassad. "I knew about him when I was 14. I saw him play at the Newport Jazz Festival when I was 15." So, when assembling the cast of contributors for Material's *Memory Serves,* Laswell effected a daring coup: "I brought Sonny out of retirement,"[6] he stated. Laswell's success in persuading Sharrock to pick up his axe again marked the beginning of a long-overdue career revival for the guitarist, and a fruitful relationship with Laswell, who went on to produce a string of albums for Sharrock, beginning with his 1986 solo guitar album, simply entitled *Guitar*. Polished to a bright sheen by Laswell's pristine and glittering production values, on *Guitar,* Sharrock arrived at a new aesthetic, still utterly committed to spontaneous freedom, and every bit as uncompromising as his defining late-60s statements, but now freely borrowing from the in-the-red excess and raw power of heavy metal.

"I first met Peter Brötzmann in NYC in the early 80s," Laswell recalls, "at one of Derek Bailey's Company concerts, at a small artspace named Roulette."[7] The event was held from 16 to 18 December 1982, and as well as familiar downtown faces such as Fred Frith and saxophonist John Zorn, attendees at the Brooklyn venue included trombonist George Lewis, French bassist Joëlle Leandre and a larger-than-life character from Germany whom Laswell had never met before. "I had heard a lot about him," Laswell recalls. "Mostly that he was a heavy drinker, and a kind of threatening character. As I was preparing to move to the back of the venue, Brötzmann appeared in the doorway, buzz cut, huge moustache, all in black, big leather coat, the Soldier of the Road."[8] In a scene played out a million times the world over, it was a shared love of nightlife that sparked a friendship at that first meeting. "Brötzmann said, 'Is anyone going to the bar?' Nobody else was drinking, so I said, 'Yeah, I'm going,' and we ended up there together because we were the only ones drinking."[9] "Bill and I were the only ones who went for a drink," Brötzmann told me. "I didn't know him, he's ten years younger, but I liked him, and we had a beer."[10] "That would set us on a path for the next few decades which could be described among other things as self-destructive,"[11] Laswell adds ruefully.

It was while the two were first getting to know each other that Laswell dropped a fateful name in conversation. Brötzmann told me: "So I asked, 'What are you doing?' And he mentioned, 'Yeah, man, I'm in my studio at the moment with a guitar player. His name is Sonny Sharrock.'"[12] Brötzmann was instantly reminded of meeting Sharrock back at the very first Total Music Meeting in 1968:

"I remembered a Black guy, quite big, with an Angela Davis Afro showed up and was very kind and listened to everything.

He said: 'I'm Sonny Sharrock and at the moment I'm touring with Herbie Mann and I'm so frustrated!' So, he was happy to be with us, and he was sitting in with one or two of the bands. At the end, we said, 'OK, let's try to do something.' We swapped addresses but forgot to keep in contact."[13]

Hearing Laswell mention Sharrock's name over a decade later set off exciting resonances for Brötzmann: "Immediately, a bell rang in my head. I had never forgotten Sonny sitting in in the 60s. Then we decided to put together some kind of band with Bill, Sonny, myself."[14]

As Brötzmann told it to me, the formation of the band hinged on just one more decision: "Then the question was who could be the drummer. To begin with, Bill was leaning towards Bennink, but after all those years playing with Bennink, I didn't want to do it again. Then he mentioned [Ronald] Shannon Jackson."[15]

Born in Fort Worth, Texas, in 1940, Jackson had arrived in New York in 1966, and quickly established himself in the city's jumping hard-bop scene. But, almost immediately, he also found a place in the New Thing avant-garde. His very first recording date, in February 1966, was contributing high-spirited and intuitive clatter to the handful of first-take performances that make up saxophonist Charles Tyler's ESP-Disk recording *Charles Tyler Ensemble*. The session found Jackson working alongside three members of Albert Ayler's then band — Tyler, bassist Henry Grimes and cellist Joel Freedman — and Ayler himself was present in the studio for the recording. Impressed with Jackson's expressive and unencumbered playing, Ayler asked him to join his band, and for around eight months between 1966 and 1967, Jackson was a member of Ayler's quintet. *Live At Slug's Saloon* (recorded

May 1966 but not released until 1982) captures the group —
featuring Donald Ayler on trumpet, Michel Samson on violin
and Lewis Worrell on bass — delivering some of Ayler's most
apocalyptic sermons, with Jackson summoning thunderous,
polyrhythmic barrages, slipping between molten firestorms
and ecstatic marches with extraordinary ease. For Jackson,
the freedom this new aesthetic encouraged was revelatory. He
later recalled:

> "Albert really opened me up as far as playing. I had never
> experienced totally playing before. Up until then my work
> had been playing background: the 'ching-ching-a-ding' line,
> where you played like this person. You played in a groove
> like [Art] Blakey or Max [Roach] or Philly Joe [Jones], and
> at that time Tony Williams was riding the crest of the jazz
> wave. You played like them or you weren't playing! Albert
> was the type of person who wouldn't say "I want this" or
> "I want that." He'd just say "Play! Fill it up with sound!"
> So from that being ingrained in me, it allowed me to just
> play."[16]

Crippling emotional devastation and spiritual doubt
following John Coltrane's death in 1967 and a subsequent
period of heroin addiction kept Jackson out of music for a few
years, but he returned in 1975 as a key member of Ornette
Coleman's new electric avant-funk group, which would go
on to become known as Prime Time. Jackson appears on the
band's first two albums — 1977's *Dancing In Your Head* and
1978's *Body Meta* — employing stumbling, stuttering beats
to underpin entwined, serpentine group improvisations
for alto saxophone, electric bass and two electric guitars.
Prime Time's elusive and disorientating sound was based on

Coleman's harmolodics system, a somewhat opaque concept that challenged conventional Western notions of harmony, melody and rhythm, upsetting preconceived hierarchies and giving the music a slippery, unmoored, unpredictable feel. As explored by Prime Time, it was a challenging aesthetic, at once both oddly accessible in its bubbling grooves, yet almost mystical in the essential impenetrability of its underlying philosophy.

In the space of just a few months in 1978, Jackson participated in the recording of four typically dense and uncompromising albums by Cecil Taylor — *Cecil Taylor Unit*, *3 Phasis*, *Live In The Black Forest* and *One Too Many Salty Swift and Not Goodbye* — in a short-lived but supremely supple and powerful configuration alongside trumpeter Raphe Malik, alto saxophonist Jimmy Lyons, violinist Ramsey Ameen and bassist Sirone. Here, Jackson fully commits to Taylor's waves of ferocious, elemental intensity, but still finds the conviction and ingenuity to leave scattered hints of fractured rhythms throughout. These recordings with Taylor also granted Jackson the singular achievement of being the only musician — apart from bassist Sirone — to have performed and recorded with the three essential architects of free jazz: Ayler, Coleman and Taylor.

Yet it was arguably his work with Coleman that had the most profound effect on the evolution of Jackson's own music. In 1979, he formed The Decoding Society, an electric outfit that very explicitly picked up and developed Coleman's conception of harmolodic funk. Albums like the 1980 debut *Eye On You* and 1981's *Nasty* (the latter released on the German Moers label) proposed a thrilling mix of wafting, lachrymose themes (often with a hint of Coleman's famous free ballad "Lonely Woman"), cranked sax and guitar solos, and warped grooves rushing headlong on rubbery, microtonal bass vamps and

Jackson's restless, deconstructed rhythms. Despite its firm grounding in avant-garde thought, the Decoding Society's music was also surprisingly danceable, incorporating pop and disco influences, and brought some unlikely commercial success that afforded Jackson more opportunities, such as playing on Laswell's mutant-funk album *Baselines* in 1982.

All of which made Jackson a perfect fit for the band Laswell and Brötzmann were thinking of assembling. Brötzmann told me: "I'd played with Shannon Jackson at a festival in southern Germany when he had his first and very good Decoding Society.[17] To Gerard Rouy he said that Jackson had "Something I haven't found in any of the other fantastic drummers I've played with, he has some kind of voodoo… some kind of blues and all those very rough elements, things I haven't found with anybody else.[18] He told me: "So I said, 'Let's do it with Jackson.' I pleaded for Jackson!"[19]

As Laswell explained it to me, it all finally came together in 1986:

"I was playing with Brötzmann in Japan — we had a band with Fred Frith, and Anton Fier was the drummer — I forget what we called ourselves. Then some offers came in Europe to play, and I remember that Fred wasn't available. I was playing at the time with Sonny and, in another configuration, Shannon Jackson, so I accepted the gigs and contacted Shannon and Sonny and I kept Brötzmann, and I said, 'OK, we'll go to Europe and play these gigs.' That's how it started. When we did the first tour, I don't think we called the band Last Exit. I believe that came later. We all kind of got along and it was unique."[20]

"It was a combination of four very different people coming out of really different cultures and backgrounds," Brötzmann told

Gerard Rouy, "working together, doing their thing, trying to combine it, to get it together. Bill Laswell did a fantastic job because he did what a bass player has to do, keep the band together and be the connection between the four of us."[21]

"My God, Brötzmann, what are you doing?"

From the beginning, Last Exit considered themselves primarily a live project. In 1986, Laswell told Steve Lake: "Last Exit doesn't exist like bands exist but comes together for concerts. So, if there's an opportunity for a concert we'll probably do it, because it only takes the time that it takes. We don't have to worry about promotion or rehearsal or any of that bullshit. If the conditions are agreeable to everyone, we'll play a concert."[22]

"It was a live band," Brötzmann concurred in 2013. "And, for a lot of different reasons, sometimes we played bad concerts. For this band, you needed the right equipment — and most of the time the equipment was not so good. Sometimes the whole shit blew up and we stopped after fifteen minutes and people were angry and we were not too happy about it. Sometimes we all — or at least Laswell and I — were too drunk to play any good shit."[23]

A thirty-seven-minute German TV broadcast of Last Exit performing early in their career at the Deutsches Jazz Festival, Frankfurt, in February 1986[24] reveals just what a volatile force they were on stage. A thunderous rumble of bass and low-end tom-toms kicks it off, after a few moments pierced first by the tenor saxophone's harsh bray and then by a stinging electric guitar riposte. Jackson, behind a huge kit with double kick drums, shakes his head from side to side, grimacing, already wet with sweat. Laswell flails and stumbles around the stage wielding low-slung bass with rock star abandon. Sharrock, in a bomber jacket and with guitar worn high, contorts in ecstatic spasms. Brötzmann rocks back and forth on the balls of his feet, almost dancing, veins bulging on his neck, face red as the devil, blowing so hard his head looks fit to burst. After four minutes the first crescendo peaks. Sharrock's already snapped several guitar strings. A raucous cheer goes up in the room.

Last Exit's live performances immediately had a huge impact on audiences, and especially on younger music fans, whose tastes were less hidebound. Swedish saxophonist Mats Gustafsson told me in an email about his experience of seeing the band play when he was in his early twenties: "First time I heard [Brötzmann] live was with Last Exit... two CLASSIC evenings in Stockholm in mid 80s... sitting in front of Sharrock's amp and watching the whole thing... man, that really made it for me. The brutal rock sound... the flow of the jazz... the energy... and the interaction between, first of all, Sharrock and Peter... fuck... out of this world."[25]

"With [Last] Exit, the audience is very young," Brötzmann told Barry Witherden in 1990, "and they don't know what a saxophone can do, what you are able to get out of it. They come after the concert and ask how you did it."[26] With a sound that embraced the shock tactics of hardcore and extreme metal, it's no surprise that younger fans were quick to identify a punk snarl in the group's attitude. "I was conscious of that," Laswell told me. "This was a very unusual experience. We were in the middle of jazz festivals, which for the most part probably hated us. Half of the audience were enlightened and refreshed, and the rest would run away. It was dividing people from the old jazz side, which wanted nothing to do with us because we had made it clear that it's not jazz, and then this younger audience, which was a little punk oriented."[27]

"I had a lot of funny situations after our first fourteen days of touring," Brötzmann told Steve Lake in 1986.

"All these good old jazz fans were saying to me, 'My God, Brötzmann, what are you doing?... What are you doing with these idiots?' On the other hand, a lot of younger people seem really to like it, and of course I'm much more interested in younger people than in old fucked-up jazz critics. I always want to take something to the edge. And with this quartet I can feel it much more than with my, let's say, usual thing. More even than this avant-garde business with Bennink or whatever. This time people have to really decide if they want it or not. And that's great."[28]

Certainly, this idea of deliberately and provocatively dividing the audience was something that Last Exit seemed to revel in. In 1986, Laswell laconically proclaimed: "This is the most special thing that's happened in this area of music for a long time. People may disagree. Fuck 'em." When I suggested to Brötzmann some thirty-three years later that Last Exit must have confused a lot of fans who had followed his adventures in improvisation, he laughed: "Yes, that's good! Let people be confused!"[29]

What was very clear from the outset, was that the members of Last Exit were bound together by both an easy-going camaraderie and an intense musical chemistry born of mutual respect. Sharrock told Steve Lake: "When you work with cats at this level, there's no fear. You can just play, walk out and play and you're not afraid that somebody's not going to be able to hold their shit up."[30] Brötzmann told me: "The jazz people asked me, 'Are you trying to get famous? To make money?'

But I didn't make any more money with Last Exit. It was just about music — and to work with Sonny Sharrock or Shannon Jackson, man, the greatest guys you could find in those years."[31]

Last Exit released their self-titled debut album in 1986, featuring recordings from a gig in Paris during their first tour in February that year, and presenting to the world an aesthetic that seemed curiously in step with the times. Plugging right into Gordon Gekko's quintessential 1980s ethos of "greed is good," almost everything about the album is overblown, overdone and over the top. Last Exit's lurching, bellowing improvisations feel like the product of a culture that has gorged itself on its own excess and heaved up great gouts of glitzy sickness. There's a cartoonish absurdity to it, an aural equivalent to the gut-churning, animated nausea of *The Ren & Stimpy Show*. In its unforgiving, relentless ugliness, it issues a very real — and very serious — challenge to the listener. This is the world we made, it says. How do you like it?

If *Machine Gun* was the sound of youth in revolt, it's tempting to think of *Last Exit* as a mid-life wobble, and one that helped to seal the two-dimensional cliché of Brötzmann as an avatar of punishing volume and power. His input to most of the jams is largely restricted to ripping his guts out in a savage onslaught of harsh over-blowing, while the immense amplification of the band and the album's saturated production values mean he's often buried amid the tumult, with little opportunity for any textural subtlety. In short, he accesses the same raw energy with Last Exit as he did with *Machine Gun*: the quintessential Brötzmann bark.

"He just plays what he plays," Laswell told me in 2019.

"Whatever key is existing, he might not respect that. Whatever rhythm, certainly he wouldn't even know what it is. He applied what he does to Last Exit and that's what made it different. If we'd played without him, it would have been completely different. That band could have been a trio like Cream or Jimi Hendrix or something. But if you add Brötzmann it's this whole different equation. He just jumped in and did what he does."[32]

Yet, when the others drop out and Brötzmann succeeds in finding a little elbow room, the torrent pours forth from his sax with such absolute unforgiving ferocity that it's hard not to admire the 100 percent commitment he brings to the role. Here, all of his experiments with caustic timbres and sustained upper registers are put to the service of gonzo exhilaration. When it combines with one of Sharrock's withering, queasy squalls, the results are genuinely thrilling.

Unusually for Brötzmann's discography, there's also a highly rhythmic backbone to Last Exit, with Jackson laying down rugged shuffles, lumbering beats and frenetic gallops that encourage Laswell to latch on with thick grooves. "The rhythms are not haphazard," Jackson said in 1986. "It's very structured. You can play improvised music and find certain things, okay. But to play a rhythm, a set rhythm that you can get back to at any time, that's what's happening with the rhythms that are being done… The creation of rhythm itself is the thing that I be dealing with."[33] Yet, despite the obvious rhythmic imperative, for Jackson, Last Exit's music tapped into the same primal freedom and expressive purity that defined free jazz. "I haven't played this way since I was with Albert Ayler,"[34] he claimed, also stating: "Last Exit is the second coming of the Ayler principle. I am totally at liberty and have total freedom to create and evolve things."[35]

Last Exit's second album, also released in 1986, was *The Noise of Trouble: Live In Tokyo*, recorded in October that year over two nights, including one at the famous Pit Inn, birthplace of Japanese free jazz. It is, to say the least, a mixed bag. The opening medley plumbs the depths of flabby self-indulgence, with the lumpen twelve-bar blues plod of "You Got Me Rockin" and "Ma Rainey" drooping under Jackson's dopey vocal mumble. Yet, among the missteps, there's some deft group improvisation at work, revealing a band working at a high level of collective groupthink after a successful European tour, and even confident enough to welcome some guests. "Blind Wille" starts off with Sharrock revisiting the rural theme from his *Black Woman* album, and quickly builds into an all-hands-on-deck stomping choogle-boogie, with Japanese free-jazz reeds player Akira Sakata adding a sprightly, piping clarinet into the melee. "Needless=Balls" begins as a honking saxophone duet for Brötzmann and Sakata, with Sharrock adding subtle swells and chimes.

Most surprising of all is the closing track, "Help Me Mo, I'm Blind," which features a guest appearance by none other than post-bop royalty, pianist Herbie Hancock. Laswell was on good terms with Hancock, having masterminded, co-produced and played on the pianist's ground-breaking 1983 electro-funk album, *Future Shock*. "Herbie happened to be in Japan at that time," Laswell told me, "and I said, 'You should come down to this club where we're playing.' The soundcheck was incredible — which we didn't record. When we actually did the gig, it was pretty calm compared to the soundcheck. Herbie was just there doing what he does. A very unusual experience. But I wish we had recorded the soundcheck."[36]

On the recorded performance, Hancock provides a jaunty, Latin-tinged vamp that builds into a light-footed jazz-rock jam that could easily have slotted into one of the Grateful Dead's extended middle sections to their exploratory improvisation showcase "Playing in the Band." Swamped in the mix, dogged and determined, there's Brötzmann growling away like a grizzled old hound worrying at a ragged bone.

Notwithstanding his early dalliance with an embryonic Tangerine Dream (and Bennink's remark that *Machine Gun* had more in common with Captain Beefheart than it did with John Coltrane), Brötzmann had never shown much interest in rock music. In fact, he was known to be downright dismissive about it. Trevor Watts recalled in an email: "I did a gig in Wuppertal with the AMALGAM group of Keith Rowe (guitar) / Liam Genockey (drums) / Colin McKenzie (bass guitar) and myself. It'd be around 1979 or so and both Peter Brötzmann and Peter Kowald came to listen to the gig. They were saying stuff like 'why do you want to play this rock shit?' and generally wanted to undermine the situation, so it felt to me."[37]

But, under the influence of Laswell's eclecticism, not to mention his impressive contacts, Brötzmann came closer than ever to embracing rock, not just with Last Exit but also with a very short-lived quintet called No Material. This was nominally led by ex-Cream drummer Ginger Baker (whom Laswell had worked with while producing Public Image Ltd's *Album*, on which Baker played), and also featured Brötzmann and Sharrock, guitarist, long-time Laswell associate and former member of Material Nicky Skopelitis, plus bassist Jan Kazda, who played on Baker's *African Force* album. This unlikely crew held together for barely a week in March 1987 and played just three gigs, two of which were recorded, leading to a self-titled album in 1989. As the band's name suggests, the performances were fully improvised, but they remain largely lumpen jams held in place by Baker's plodding beats, no matter how hard Brötzmann and Sharrock strain to take things further out.

Around this time, Laswell was also keen to have Brötzmann play with British heavy metal group Motörhead, whose 1986 album *Orgasmatron* he had produced. "The way Peter plays, and the way Sonny plays, where there's a lot of energy and a lot of sound, that's not so different from what Motörhead do. Merely in terms of energy,"[38] Laswell told Steve Lake. The fact that this collaboration never came to fruition remains one of the most tantalising of missed opportunities in twentieth-century music.

Nevertheless, Last Exit did spawn a couple of interesting side collaborations — and genuine friendships — for Brötzmann. Foremost among these was his relationship with Sharrock. "Sonny was such a good comrade," Brötzmann told me. "He was such a great man. We did a couple of small duo tours too, which was always very nice."[39] Evidence of the duo surfaced in 2014 with the release of *Whatthefuckdoyouwant*, a seventy-minute set, recorded in Luxembourg in March 1987, which summons all the coruscating bravado you'd expect from half of Last Exit. Sharrock's brittle shredding and razored glissandi mesh seamlessly with Brötzmann's highest altissimo squonk, and when the tenor turns to a honking gutbucket bar-walk, the guitar responds with brutal, kranging chords. But, for all the fury, there are moments of vulnerability, too: when Sharrock opens up with an unexpectedly intimate and fragile melody, Brötzmann steps back and supports him with a soft, sustained tone, while the raw emotion of his Ayler-ish laments brings aching dive-bombs of longing from the guitar. One year into Last Exit's existence, these two highly distinctive voices were clearly enjoying a heightened simpatico relationship. "There were two guitar players I really liked," Brötzmann told me. "One was Derek Bailey, the other was Sonny Sharrock."[40]

Not every interpersonal relationship within Last Exit was quite so harmonious. Speaking in 2013, less than a year before Ronald Shannon Jackson's death, Brötzmann reflected:

"I like Shannon. It's a pity that he is such a difficult guy. He doesn't trust anybody anymore. I think I was the only one who had no problems with him. He has some paranoia going on. Money was always an issue. Wherever we came, he had some argument with the promoter first. Either the promoter owes him money from some ten-year-old concert, and he refused to play until he got some money, and shit like that. On the other hand, we spent quite some time together, sitting alone in the bar and having coffee and schnapps, and he was really... he is a sweet guy. But as soon as he is involved in this business scene... he always took Laswell as a kind of competition, money-wise. For Bill, what we made, in these times of his big productions, was pocket money. So, he used to fly first class from Berlin to Munich, and Shannon, who really needed the money, he spent his fee to do the same! This kind of shit. Sonny and I, meanwhile, were sitting in the bandwagon and drove eight hours."[41]

With Laswell, Brötzmann created one duo album, *Low Life*, recorded at the beginning of 1987 and released later the same year. It's a dark, subterranean exploration of low-end vibrations with Brötzmann playing bass sax throughout and Laswell running his bass guitar through various electronic effects creating juddering rhythmic experiments and mechanistic loops. "*Low Life* is one of my favourite records," said Brötzmann in 1990, "and it's a pleasure to work with Laswell. He knows all about stuff — electronic things — that I have no idea about. He's able to organise pieces and work with little things and make quite reasonable stuff out of them."[42] Writing in *The Wire* magazine, Barry Witherden astutely noted:

"Despite the use of exclusively low-register instruments there is a considerable range of timbres thanks to Laswell's imaginative exploitation of technology and Brötzmann's virtuosity in the extreme regions of the bass-sax. Laswell weaves ostinato into tapestries of strange textures and hangs them in deserted corridors where they stir in a low wind and where muffled noises echo along the pipework. The strange mechanism, the glimpsed fragments of ritual, the chugging chords evoking a train journey through a dark countryside."[43]

There is, of course, another connotation lurking in the title of *Low Life*. The album's back cover shows photos of Brötzmann and Laswell, collars up against a cold, overcast winter's day in street-level, parking-lot America, drear and steadfast in hangover purgatory. "We were kind of self-destructive, I guess," Laswell told me. "Staying out late and drinking heavy and prostitutes and everything. Everything you could imagine. We were trying to kill ourselves and we failed. But it was a lot of fun."[44]

"I was a bad influence on Laswell," Brötzmann laughed. "We liked night life. We had, for sure, a good time."[45] He told Gerard Rouy: "I liked that way of life, which had to do with just raving, drinking too much, night life was the most important part of the day."[46] By this time, in his mid-to-late forties, Brötzmann was already well into his third decade of hellraising: "I started early, when I was fifteen, playing in the Dixieland band. All the other guys were older. At home, nobody cared about me so much, I could do what I wanted. So, I was hanging out with the guys and the beer and the girls and whatever. Alcohol, the good thing is it's a very social drug, until it turns into the opposite."[47]

After the release of another live album — *Cassette Recordings '87* — Last Exit entered a recording studio in Brooklyn in 1988 and laid down a session that became their only studio album, *Iron Path*. Under Laswell's visionary watch as producer, it presents a markedly different sound to the furious blitzkrieg of their live performances and albums. "I guess it's more of a production," Laswell admitted. "Most people say the worst record we did was the studio record, and the live records were great. I don't agree with that. To me, the best thing we ever did was the studio record, and the live records are just glimpses of what we did live. But I'm probably the only one with that opinion."[48]

For sure, *Iron Path* initially bemused and disappointed some fans and critics, but it has enjoyed a critical rehabilitation in the intervening years as tastes and frames of reference have caught up with what Laswell was trying to achieve with this dense studio construction. With ten tracks, none longer than five minutes, spread over a dreamily segued thirty-six minutes, the album essentially paints an extremely dark ambient soundworld seeded with flashes of free jazz, mutant metal and other fleeting incongruities. Opening track "Prayer" begins with the fog clearing on a desolate mountain top and a temple bell ringing in the gloom before Jackson whips up a galloping clatter, Brötzmann unfurls a sinuous, oriental cry and Sharrock chimes a curiously bagpipe-like Celtic refrain. The title track is an interlude of scattered, Asiatic plucks and more temple gongs nested in huge billowing clouds. "The Fire Drum" is slow and filthy funk with rubbery squelch-bass and Brötzmann howling into the night. "Detonator" is dark funk-metal imagined as a jam by fusion supergroup Weather Report. "Cut and Run" is crepuscular surf-thrash with Jackson transforming the "Wipeout" drum riff into a rallying rhythm for legions of undead beach bums. In "Eye for an Eye," with bass guitar and bass sax kranging mightily, Brötzmann and Laswell sound, as Steve Lake points out in the liner notes, like "they're standing on the world's roof, like Himalayan monks voicing one huge chord."[49] *Iron Path* wasn't merely ahead of its time; it still stands out as a singularly original and imaginative achievement.

It was around this time that Brötzmann's son, Caspar, emerged as a musician in his own right. Born in 1962, Caspar Brötzmann chose a musical path that avoided the jazz-derived language of his father's milieu, instead devoting himself to heroically amplified electric guitar roaring out of the rock tradition. In his mid-twenties, he founded Caspar Brötzmann Massaker (a name that echoed Fred Frith's abrasive, short-lived trio from a few years earlier) with drummer Jon Bleuth and bass guitarist Eduardo Delgado-Lopez. The trio's first couple of albums — *The Tribe* (1987) and *Black Axis* (1989) — announced an explosive sound that melded relentlessly heavy riffs, Hendrix-style feedback sculpture, tribal rhythms and a dour, Ruhr valley industrial scrape 'n' rumble. Given the brash contexts that the elder Brötzmann was busily exploring at this stage, it was inevitable that father and son would collaborate, and in 1990, they cut the studio duo album *Last Home*. It's a savage, snarling date, with Caspar's howling and puking electric guitar butting horns with Brötzmann senior's equally forceful bass and tenor saxes, clarinet and tarogato. While it's certainly tempting to interpret it as some kind of Oedipal clash, beneath the ear-splitting *sturm und drang* lies an easy intimacy every bit as rewarding as the contemporaneous duo sessions Brötzmann cut with Laswell and Sharrock.

In the early 1990s, Last Exit released two more live albums, both drawn from archival 1980s recordings: *Köln,* released in 1990, was recorded in 1986, and 1993's *Headfirst into the Flames: Live In Europe* featured recordings from 1989. Although the band hadn't toured for some years, this steady drip-feed of releases meant that Last Exit still seemed very much like an ongoing concern. But that changed suddenly and irrevocably when Sonny Sharrock died of a heart attack on 25 May 1994 at the age of just fifty-three, putting a tragically premature end to a career enjoying a vibrant late ascendency.

Since being coaxed back into the limelight by Laswell, alongside his work with Last Exit, Sharrock had released a clutch of well-received albums, including an accessible mix of jazz and rock on 1990's *High Life* and, in 1991, the deep jazz masterpiece *Ask The Ages,* featuring bassist Charnett Moffett, former John Coltrane Quartet drummer Elvin Jones and, on tenor saxophone, another former Coltrane alumnus, Pharoah Sanders (with whom Sharrock had crashed Gunter Hampel's performance at the very first Total Music Meeting way back in 1968).

If this was enough to secure Sharrock's eternal jazz credentials, it's also striking just how deeply he'd infiltrated a wider alternative US culture. In 1993, he'd been commissioned, together with drummer Lance Carter of his *High Life* band, to provide the soundtrack and incidental music for Cartoon Network's surreal, late-night animated TV show *Space Ghost*

Coast to Coast. Sharrock's death came during the show's first season, and he eventually received an offbeat tribute during the third season, in 1996, when an entire episode, simply entitled "Sharrock," was dedicated to playing snippets of his music, bookended by a brief cameo by Thurston Moore of Sonic Youth. Moore can also be seen in a video clip from November 1994, clad in a Sun Ra T-shirt, performing an emotional seven-minute tribute to Sharrock, wrenching jagged feedback squalls from an electric guitar accompanied by a free-flailing drummer.[50] It's a clear, heartfelt and explicit acknowledgement of the extent to which Sharrock — both as a member of Last Exit and as a solo artist — straddled the divide between the avant-gardes of jazz and rock.

While Sharrock's death was a great loss to the underground music community, it was a personal blow to Brötzmann. At the time, they had just completed a couple of short duo tours and were planning a European tour. "I had just seen him in New York," Brötzmann told Mike Barnes. "Then I was home for two weeks, and I got the message that he was dead, and that was very unexpected. He had his diabetes but he took care and he was healthy and in a good mood, but things happen."[51] For Brötzmann, it meant the loss of a genuine musical connection and a real friendship:

"He was able to be the wild guy, really completely crazy and the next second he was the sweetest guy you could imagine. So I was really fascinated by that. We had concerts when one string after the other broke and he didn't care, and at the end he played on the two left over and he still played fantastic. I don't listen to music very much, but I listen to very old blues music quite often and that's what the guy was doing. He was able to tell his stories even with one string."[52]

In a cruel echo of Harry Miller's untimely death, Sharrock's passing spelled the abrupt termination of a fruitful creative partnership — and the end of Last Exit. Yet the intense energy generated by Last Exit opened a portal through which artists have continued to venture.

Last Exit were undoubtedly an influence on saxophonist John Zorn in forming the group Naked City, active between 1988 and 1993, featuring Fred Frith on bass, guitarist Bill Frisell, drummer Joey Baron, vocalist Yamatsuka Eye and Wayne Horvitz on keyboards. As demonstrated on their self-titled debut, released under Zorn's name in 1990, the quintet specialised in juxtaposing wildly disparate genres including hardcore punk, grindcore, surf music, free jazz and cartoon soundtracks, smashed together in dizzyingly brief, brutal bursts of sound. Though clearly more through-composed than Last Exit's improvised eruptions, Zorn's vision owed much to the pioneering fusion envisaged by Laswell at the inception of Last Exit.

Laswell and Zorn were able to further explore this idea together through the trio Painkiller, co-founded in 1991 with Mick Harris, drummer from British grindcore terrorists Napalm Death. Their debut EP, *Guts of a Virgin*, unleashed a nightmarishly harsh hybrid of avant-garde jazz and thrash metal, while later albums went on to incorporate elements of dub and industrial ambient. A later incarnation, formed to participate in Zorn's "Fiftieth Birthday Celebration" concert series in 2003, featured master jazz drummer Hamid Drake channelling the hyperactive creativity Ronald Shannon Jackson had brought to Last Exit, while Laswell gleefully latches on with viscous vamps.

Laswell has continued to interrogate the wild intersection of free jazz and improvised rock well into the twenty-first century. His 2020 trio date *On Common Ground*, with guitarist Mike Sopko and drummer Tyshawn Sorey, veers from thrashing free-form firestorms to the kind of lugubrious funk-rock jams he pioneered with Brötzmann et al. All it's missing is a bellicose saxophone scream.

Brötzmann, too, has remained an influence on younger noiseniks, and was happy to collaborate with artists from the grimy underbelly of rock. 2022's *An Eternal Reminder of Not Today* captures a live performance from the 2018 Moers festival that teams Brötzmann with OXBOW, a San Franciscan quartet who, since 1988, have explored an avant-garde conception of noise-rock drawing on free jazz as much as the blues, channelled through the imposing, muscular presence of frontman Eugene Robinson. From Brötzmann's opening notes, sliding into a brooding, bluesy rumble, he sounds utterly at home, unleashing a growling lyricism that lifts the razored slide guitar and Robinson's pained histrionics into stratospheric regions. It's great to hear Brötzmann clearly enjoying himself — but, even here, he pulls no punches. For every chugging R&B lick there's a pay-off of molten, altissimo squealing likely to keep fans of his most energetic outbursts satisfied.

Never Too Late but Always Too Early

"I always just knew what I wanted to play"

Given the raw excesses of Last Exit, one might be forgiven for asking the question, does Brötzmann even play jazz? Certainly, when I put it to Bill Laswell, he opined that Brötzmann's playing — in Last Exit, at least — had little to do with the received idea of jazz: "It's more to do with a kind of energy and he uses a certain kind of raw power in what he does. It's not from the jazz world so much. It's more to do with this raw energy and power. That's why the punk rock people would relate to him. It has that power, that energy. It's a little bit doesn't care about the virtuosity or the jazz. He's not a jazz musician so much — it's a power sound."[1]

When I suggested to Brötzmann that he had, perhaps, never really been a jazz player, he exploded with laughter: "If you mean that I never could be a good bebop player, you are right!"[2] By his own account, this sense of being an outsider, working at a tangent to the conventional narrative of jazz, was forged in his earliest days, when he was first forming his artistic identity:

"I grew up, from the very beginning, from another angle, which had a lot to do with my connections to the other fields of art. I learned a lot in the very young years from Nam

June Paik, also Joseph Beuys, and then that was the time of Stockhausen's good years in Cologne. And so on. I came from that side. So, I didn't care. I just did what I wanted to do. I never was shy, for example, to work with Last Exit, which was a very strange band."[3]

By the same token, while Brötzmann was always happy to acknowledge his affection for jazz saxophonists from earlier eras, he was insistent that none had influenced his own sound. In 1999, he told John Corbett:

"I'm still very fond of the old stuff. I still listen to that, it's nearly the only music I'm listening to. [Johnny] Dodds, [Sydney] Bechet, later on [Coleman] Hawkins, [Illinois] Jacquet, Lester [Young], Charlie Parker of course. But to talk about the influence in my lifetime, I can mention some friends who helped me quite a lot. In the first line, Don Cherry and Steve Lacy. Musical influences, I don't know. Even when I started to listen to Albert Ayler, he was not that kind of influence. I saw some historical concerts, like the last recording of Oscar Pettiford, Bud Powell, Coleman Hawkins, Kenny Clarke. That, somewhere, is in my head, and you can't get it out. So that might be an influence. Or an open-air Coltrane concert in Belgium in the early Quartet days. That was just crazy, that's what you live from, you take energy from. But I can't say there is a saxophone player who has really influenced my way of playing the horn. Not really."[4]

Yet, even from Brötzmann's earliest days, the music he made was, by and large, considered part of the jazz continuum — a fact that earned him slots at jazz festivals and clubs, and brought him into contact with some of the eternal architects of the music. An anecdote he told me about that open-air concert in Belgium illustrates this point beautifully:

"In '66 or so, there was a festival in Belgium, an outdoor festival, in a village called Comblain-la-Tour — that was one of my first foreign festival gigs. I was playing with Kowald and a Dutch drummer, Pierre Courbois. We were invited to play our set, forty-five minutes, something like that. After ten minutes, they unplugged us. But we didn't care: we played. Then, after the work, I went down to the only bar in the village to get some beer. There was standing there this Black guy in a suit, together with another small French guy with a hooknose. I was sweaty and needed a drink. The Black guy realised I needed something; the waiter didn't react and so the Black guy told the waiter, the bar man, 'Hey, give this young man a beer.' That was John Coltrane and Charles Aznavour. Coltrane played that same night, a beautiful concert, with the quartet."[5]

Brötzmann's recollection of that early set being cut short — much like his breakthrough performance with Kowald and Courbois at the tenth German Jazz Festival in Frankfurt in May 1966 — underlines the difficulties he faced in his early days in being accepted by the wider jazz community. As Bill Shoemaker has pointed out, right from the beginning Brötzmann was viciously vilified by uncomprehending critics: according to Shoemaker, the debut performance of von Schlippenbach's *Globe Unity* in November 1966 resulted in "a Berlin newspaper characterising the performance as 'a pandemonium in which Peter Brötzmann played the role of Satan.'"[6]

Nowhere was this hostility — and Brötzmann's seeming obliviousness to it — made more apparent than in a TV programme entitled *Free Jazz — Pop Jazz: unverständlich oder populär?* ("Free Jazz — Pop Jazz: incomprehensible or popular?") broadcast on the West German WDR channel in May 1967.[7] Here, Radio Bremen's music editor, Siegfried Schmidt-Joos, ostensibly moderates a panel discussion on the relative merits of free jazz — represented in the studio by twenty-six-year-old Brötzmann's trio with Kowald on bass and Aldo Romano on drums (with whom the two had worked as part of Carla Bley's Jazz Realities tour the previous year) — and what Schmidt-Joos calls "understandable jazz," represented by a quartet led by thirty-year-old saxophonist Klaus Doldinger, with Peter Trunk on bass, Ingfried Hofmann on piano and Cees See on drums. The show begins with Doldinger's group (clad in the kind of black-tie suits Brötzmann would refuse to wear at Berliner Jazztage in 1968) playing some lightly swinging cocktail jazz. This is followed by Brötzmann's trio (casually dressed in jackets and sweaters) sliding into an abstract improvisation with keening tenor moans, sawing arco bass and scattered drum clatter. Immediately following the trio's performance, Schmidt-Joos addresses the camera with the assurance, "I would like to give you, ladies and gentlemen, a little respite after this sound of carnage," setting the tone for what becomes less of a debate and more of an interrogation, with Brötzmann in the dock.

The all-male panel features record producer Siegfried Loch (who had worked with Doldinger) plus a cohort of jazz critics and journalists: Dr Ingolf Wachler, Werner Burkhardt, Ulrich Olshausen, Felix Schmidt and Manfred Miller. With the exception of the younger Miller, who shows some guarded sympathy for Brötzmann's aesthetic, the assembled experts are overwhelmingly negative in their appraisal of free jazz. In fact, what begins as a discussion about free jazz quickly turns into a series of personal attacks on Brötzmann himself. Brötzmann is accused of possessing none of the standard instrumental technique required to play mainstream jazz, to which he replies: "I'm self-taught and have never had any lessons and I never learned anything. I just always knew what I wanted to play, or most of the time anyway, and went after it, developing my technique, which is my own personal property. I certainly know the notes that I want to play, that I can play." He's then asked if he has the ability to play "Summertime" or "St Louis Blues," to which, unflappably cool, he shrugs, "If I wanted to, I could play you something. I don't do it. It's just not my thing." Brötzmann's calm dismissal seems to enrage bassist Peter Trunk, who interrupts proceedings, shouting across the studio, "The man can't play, he has no technique, he has nothing at all!" Doldinger is equally annoyed, calling Brötzmann's music "musical chaos," "pig slaughter" and "musical vomit." Further performances by the two ensembles only serve to emphasise the conceptual gulf between them: Doldinger plays clarinet on a pleasant piece in a syncopated 6/8 time, and a slinky boogaloo with Ingfried Hofmann switching to Hammond organ. Brötzmann's other two improvisations are uncompromising burns of sustained energy, with Brötzmann, eyes closed, rocking back and forth, demonstrating utter conviction. He isn't there to pander or entertain. He has serious business to do.

Yet, despite all of this, on a deeper level, Brötzmann always somehow considered his music to be intimately connected to the lifeblood of jazz tradition — and certainly much more so than some of his contemporaries in the burgeoning arena of European free improvisation. Once, I simply asked him if he had always felt he was playing jazz, to which he replied:

"I think so. I had big discussions with the English players —
especially with Derek [Bailey]. There was a time when they
didn't call the music jazz. And when all the English came with
their aesthetics and explanations and more moving in the
way of contemporary music, where you need more words to
describe the music… I don't need that. I'm a player. I like to
play. Music is — really, it sounds very naïve and very simple
— but it's my way of life. That's what I need. Really. If you look
at the history of jazz music, sooner or later you come not to
styles or to decades of swing or bebop, you always come to
persons. The whole history is the history of different persons.
For [Thelonious] Monk it was no problem to play with Pee
Wee Russell, for example. That's what I have learned very early
from my American friends: to be much more open. When I
met Dexter Gordon the first time, and he heard me, it was no
problem for him. And, of course, it never was a problem for
me."[8]

Brötzmann's insistence on his music's connection to the
jazz source casts a doubtful light on aspects of an influential
and much championed idea first proposed by journalist,
author and musicologist Joachim-Ernst Berendt in his 1977
essay entitled "*Der deutsche Jazz und die Emanzipation
(1961–1973)*" ("German Jazz and the Emancipation (1961–
1973")). Berendt's assertion was that, beginning in the mid-
1960s, European — and particularly German — jazz artists
developed new styles that effectively signalled the creation
of what he called "a new European jazz."[9] This process he
referred to as "*die Emanzipation*" — the Emancipation.
Mike Heffley skilfully summarises Berendt's definition of
"*die Emanzipation*" as "an emancipation from and to several
things: from American jazz, from the Western art music

tradition, and from the international music industry; and to non-Western music traditions, to early Western (medieval, folk) traditions, and to a social as well as musical liberation."[10]

Certainly, we've seen how, through the formation of homegrown, artist-run labels such as BRÖ, FMP, ICP and Incus, many European artists were effective in escaping the established music industry, and how their essentially left-leaning, collectivist approach to musical interaction proposed a compelling alternative to conventional social hierarchies. But the alleged musical impulses Berendt outlines, with particular reference to the German scene, require closer analysis.

To be clear, Berendt's identification of the introduction of both Western and non-Western folk traditions holds up. While Gunter Hampel's 1965 album, *Heartplants,* is generally considered the first flowering of "*die Emanzipation*" (with von Schlippenbach's contributions representing the first recorded instance of German free jazz), there were other artists making quietly radical statements before this, and not least the ever-progressive Albert Mangelsdorff. On his 1964 album, *Now Jazz Ramwong,* the title track is a modal composition inspired by a Thai folk dance, while "Es Sungen Drei Engel" reworks a thirteenth-century German battlefield folk song.

But the idea of German artists turning their backs on the Western art music tradition is more problematic, especially among some of the younger, more radical improvisers: we've already seen how von Schlippenbach's *Globe Unity* was an explicit attempt to incorporate elements of contemporary classical music and elevate the music to the status of high art, and how the more abstract free improvisers such as Brötzmann and Kowald were heavily influenced by John Cage's concept of indeterminacy.

Yet, these young renegades also espoused headstrong, year-zero tendencies that slot more neatly into Berendt's ideas about the waning influence of American jazz tradition — pithily characterised by Kowald's insistence that the music was concerned with "Kaputtspielphase" ("blowing to pieces") and, most appositely, "father-killing." This latter is, in itself, a complex idea. Ideologically, it is tied to the May '68 generation's urge to escape the lingering shadow of Germany's Nazi past (including its lionisation of Teutonic folk melodies) and start over with a new social and artistic identity of total, forward-thinking freedom. In musical practice, and most urgently in Kowald and Brötzmann's case, that freedom meant leaving behind the metric and harmonic ideas that govern Western music — including American jazz.

This tacit yet central agreement to cease slavishly copying US jazz musicians led to some bullishly absolutist statements of intent from the new improvisers. Gerard Rouy quotes Han Bennink in a 1971 interview claiming: "I play a European music. Five or six years before, we could hear musicians in Europe that were repeating what the Blacks were saying, that were stealing their music and the result was quite sad. Nowadays, and I'm happy about that, I have nothing to do with Americans anymore. They have a musical background that only belongs to them, I place myself on another level."[11] Yet, at the same time, other improvisers offered a more nuanced interpretation. Rouy cites Evan Parker suggesting: "This European movement was not a separate thing, we all knew about the developments in America in the early 1960s. Brötzmann certainly knew about Albert Ayler, Han and Misha played with Tchicai… To me, it's a natural response to what for us was the developing aspect of modern jazz, so the idea of a separate European identity is more a function of cultural politic than a cultural reality."[12]

The notion of a culturally political — thus cynically manufactured — divide between American and European improvisation has been extensively explored and developed by academic and AACM-affiliated trombonist and composer George Lewis in an extremely insightful essay that goes a long way towards debunking "*die Emanzipation*"'s central tenet of a clean and decisive break with US jazz. In "Improvised Music after 1950: Afrological and Eurological Perspectives," he proposes two strands of "improvisative music"[13] that arose in the US in the second half of the twentieth century: the Afrological (or jazz) tradition, exemplified by Charlie Parker, and the Eurological (or New Music) school, embodied by John Cage. In essence, Lewis argues that the emergence of bebop, spearheaded by Parker and others in New York's jazz clubs in the late 1940s, prompted European and American composers working in the classical milieu in the next decade to consider ways of incorporating improvisation into their own music. This, Lewis asserts, manifested most convincingly in the work of Cage and associates such as David Tudor and Morton Feldman, who turned away from conventional notation and began to experiment with open forms and elements of chance. In effect, bebop, with all its structural radicalism and hurtling innovation, was a challenge to centuries of Western musical tradition. However, rather than acknowledging that dynamic, Lewis argues, "the space of whiteness [surrounding New Music] provided a convenient platform for a racialized denial of the trenchancy of that challenge."[14] At the same time, the prevailing narrative of music criticism has refused to acknowledge African American practitioners, such as the AACM, who have concentrated on folding elements of contemporary classical music into their approach, effectively denying them any presence in the so-called Eurological school.

However, Lewis goes on to highlight that, among the European school of free improvisation, an indebtedness to Afrological musical culture has always been more readily acknowledged. He quotes anthropologist and improviser Georgina Born (formerly of Henry Cow) as clarifying:

"Some of the main elements of experimental music practice — improvisation, live group work, the empirical use of small, commercial electronics in performance — were pioneered in the jazz and rock of the 1950s and 1960s. Moreover, the politics of experimental music are similar to those of the advanced black jazz of the '60s. Its musical collectivism, for example, was prefigured by the Chicago black musicians' cooperative, the Association for the Advancement of Creative Musicians (AACM), which became a role model for later progressive, cooperative music organisations."[15]

Lewis states that the term "improvised music," as used by European improvisers was adopted "not to distinguish it from jazz in the sense of critique but to better reflect the European improvisers' sense of having created a native model of improvisation, however influenced by Afrological forms. [Derek] Bailey, like other European improvisers, makes no attempt to deny the Afrological influence upon his own work."[16]

In his book, *European Echoes: Jazz Experimentalism in Germany 1950–1975*, Harald Kisiedu has gone further than anyone in challenging the narrative of "*die Emanzipation*," painstakingly illustrating how "European improvisers' intercultural engagement with African-American musical knowledge was much more prevalent than standard historical accounts acknowledge."[17] Furthermore, he posits that "*die*

Emanzipation" is an especially oversimplifying notion with reference to Brötzmann's journey as an artist, pointing both to his early involvement with the trans-national Fluxus movement, and to his enthusiastic engagement with Black experimentalism, fuelled, in part, by the feeling of kinship that young, left-wing West Germans like him felt with the American civil rights and black power movements.

"I like playing with musicians who are more into free jazz"

Brötzmann's own unfolding career, and the connections he made as it developed, decisively confirm his close adjacency to the radical Black free-jazz continuum and how his activities sidestepped the somewhat artificial consensus of *"die Emanzipation."* One intriguing document of the circles he and Kowald began to move in is the movie *Rising Tones Cross* by German filmmaker Ebba Jahn. It provides a glimpse of the Sound Unity Festival, held in New York City in the gymnasium of the Cuando Community Centre between 30 May and 3 June 1984. Co-organised by Peter Kowald, who'd been living in the city for five months, together with dancer Patricia Nicholson and her husband, bassist William Parker, it was funded by a grant Kowald had secured from the West German government. A *New York Times* article dated 1 June describes the festivals aim as "to bring together European, Asian and American musicians and dancers who work with jazz and other improvised music,"[18] and it's recognised as the precursor to the now long-running Vision Festival, organised by Nicholson and Parker.

Between wonderfully evocative shots of '80s New York at its most glamorously grimy, the film shows performances by US free-jazz luminaries including saxophonist Charles

Gayle, drummer Rashied Ali, and Don Cherry leading the Sound Unity Festival Orchestra. It concludes with an excerpt of a forceful performance of Brötzmann's "Alarm" by an international eleven-piece Peter Brötzmann Ensemble featuring Brötzmann, Gayle, David S. Ware and Brötzmann's old friend Frank Wright on tenor saxophones, Jemeel Moondoc on alto sax, Roy Campbell Jr on trumpet, Masahiko Kono on trombone, Iréne Schweizer on piano, Kowald and Parker on basses and Ali on drums — intercut with shots of Brötzmann hand-drawing the graphic score. Everyone involved is utterly committed to its execution.

There's also a brief interview with Kowald, in which he neatly outlines the attraction he and Brötzmann both felt to Black free jazz:

"I like playing with musicians who are more into free jazz, who play music that is more free… I see that they're constantly in touch with their Black roots. Even when it's not so audible in the type of material they're playing, there's still simply a link to rhythm and the tone structure and everything that comes from inside is always there. I was amazed to see the Whites often play more interesting stuff. But this starts to get a bit boring because so little of it comes from inside because it's so often conceptual and it can lose its value quite quickly… An important revelation of these last five months here was that the White and the Black scene are two very different scenes, very distinct both in terms of the musical formation themselves and the audience. Audiences are totally different, one group at White concerts another at Black ones. And I was shocked by just how far this thing goes, how this break, this split is really there and determines a lot of what goes on. White musicians have a much larger following despite their completely different music. It's not even jazz at all. The themselves call it new music. It is a newer music although it's almost totally improvised."[19]

By way of illustration, there's a sly cut to a performance by John Zorn blowing sax mouthpieces into a bowl of water, making gurgling duck sounds to a strikingly Caucasian assembly. It's notable, of course, that Kowald and Brötzmann are seen fully immersed in the Black jazz community rather than playing in a downtown gallery space — and just how welcomed they are by the Black New Yorkers. "I've noticed that I really do play totally European," says Kowald, "that I don't have all the jazz licks down — which I already knew — and that what I've developed as my own formulations on bass over the years are fully accepted by the jazz musicians here as my personal language, which isn't necessarily from New Orleans or wherever but more from Germany or from the combinations that I've been able to develop in Germany or Europe by working with other musicians."[20]

A couple of years later, Brötzmann recorded with one of the undisputed progenitors of US free jazz, pianist Cecil Taylor, for the album *Olu Iwa*. Recorded in Berlin at the 1986 edition of Workshop Freie Musik, it features an expanded Cecil Taylor Unit, in which Brötzmann is notable for being the only non-American, playing alongside Taylor, trombonist Earl McIntyre, fellow tenor-man Frank Wright, drummer Steve McCall, bassist William Parker and Thurman Barker on marimba. The piece performed — "B Ee Ba Nganga Ban'a Eee!" — is a typically dense and erratic Taylor construction, over forty-eight minutes long, with Brötzmann more than matching Taylor's superhuman energy by erupting into a volcanic solo in the second half.

At the end of October 1991, FMP's Total Music Meeting invited a number of US free-jazz musicians to Berlin to work with leading European improvisers. In all, nine musicians were involved in this transatlantic summit meeting. The three drummers were, from the UK, Tony Oxley and, from the States, Rashied Ali and Andrew Cyrille, best known for his lengthy tenure with Cecil Taylor. The three bassists were Kowald plus Americans William Parker and Fred Hopkins. And the three saxophonists were Brötzmann, Evan Parker and, from New York, the enigmatic Charles Gayle. Across the festival, the musicians met in a variety of configurations including solos, duos and trios. The festival was recorded by Jost Gebers and provided material for a handful of subsequent album releases, including the incendiary *Touchin' On Trane* by Gayle, Parker and Ali. Another encounter, featuring Brötzmann, Hopkins and Ali, was released, in 1994, as *Songlines*, one of the most explicitly jazz-orientated releases Brötzmann ever put his name to and one which, again, highlights his unconcern for the so-called emancipation of European improvisation.

The album's subtitle — *music is a memory bank for finding one's way about the world* — hints at the fact that, for Brötzmann, the chance to play in an intimate setting with two legends of the US avant-garde represented a return to territory imprinted deep in his own musical DNA. Ali (born 1933) had, of course, been the drummer in John Coltrane's final ensemble and had helped propel him into some of his most challenging territory on albums such as the sax/drums duo *Interstellar Space*, recorded five months before Coltrane's death in 1967. Hopkins (born 1947) was a member of the ACCM and a loft-jazz veteran, best known for his work in the trio Air, with saxophonist Henry Threadgill and drummer Steve McCall. This esteemed company seems to stimulate an unexpected reverence in Brötzmann, leading to one of his most restrained and lyrical recordings.

The opening track, "No Messages," begins with drums in a relaxed waltz time onto which Hopkins nails a deep, silky riff. Brötzmann finds himself shadowing the changes, concentrating more on the notes than his habitual textures, trying to colour inside the lines very precisely delineated by Hopkins. At times, as the saxophone's phrasing slides away from the true north of Hopkins' bass, it's almost as if Brötzmann is experimenting with microtones. On "…It Is Solved by Walking," Brötzmann responds to Ali's relaxed flicks of the wrist with throwaway bar-walking R&B phrases. And on "Man in a Vacuum," Ali's simmering polyrhythmic swing marshals Brötzmann's playing into linear forms — even when he's engaged in high, wailing exultations — channelling him into a mode of ecstatic storytelling reminiscent of Charles Gayle. While, to an extent, giving Brötzmann an opportunity to look backwards at the tradition from which his own art sprang, *Songlines* also allowed him to concentrate on some of his own innovations, particularly his use of the tarogato: in the twenty-five-minute title track, a slow, balladic section inspires Brötzmann to twist the tarogato's Middle Eastern sonority into raw, painfully vulnerable cries. Later, in an up-tempo segment, Ali and Hopkins' buoyant rhythmic interplay clearly foreshadows much of Brötzmann's coming work with bassist William Parker and drummer Hamid Drake.

One of the heaviest free-jazz settings that Brötzmann played in was with Parker and drummer/botanist/healer/ martial artist and all-round underground Renaissance Man Milford Graves. Through his early work with Albert Ayler and as a member of the New York Art Quartet, Graves (born just five months after Brötzmann in 1941) was a true pioneer of the New Thing, doing more than anyone to free the drums from their traditional time-keeping role, opening them up to a radical new consideration of tone and timbre. With a laser-sharp focus on his own idiosyncratic practice, he was a sure fit for Brötzmann's own gritty determination to make things new. As Brian Morton has pointed out: "The late Derek Bailey said there was no such thing as free jazz, though he made gruff exceptions for Peter Brötzmann and Milford Graves."[21]

The trio played together only three times, in 1985, 1988 and 2002, each time in Manhattan, New York City. The 2002 performance, which took place in the front room of the famous East Village music club CBGB — a space known as CB's 313 Gallery — was the only one to be recorded, and was subsequently released in 2022 as *Historic Music Past Tense Future*. The music is ferociously dense and aggressive, with Brötzmann ripping the guts out of an alto sax and Parker fighting to find a gulp of air amid the tumult of a bottom-heavy thunder as Graves negotiates cascade after cascade of submerged rhythmic information on the unique kit he'd refined over the years: no bottom drumheads, bongos added to the top-mounted toms, double kick drums and the snare permanently muffled in the off position. The only known recorded meeting of the two titans, Graves and Brötzmann, it's a crucial late addition to the free-jazz canon. As Brötzmann states in the album's accompanying press release: "It's not easy, it's not a little Sunday ride. It's heavy."[22]

William Parker was also a key presence in Brötzmann's next major project after the dissolution of Last Exit: an intense and innovative group, born from a deep love of the music of Albert Ayler, which became known as the Die Like a Dog Quartet.

PETER BRÖTZMANN

"There is a connection between our kinds of music"

From his earliest days as a player, Brötzmann was compared
to Albert Ayler. And it's true that he was consistently drawn to
musicians who had been in Ayler's orbit. Drummers Ronald
Shannon Jackson and Milford Graves had both been key
members of Ayler's groups in the mid-60s, and Frank Wright
— himself regularly compared to Ayler — was an enthusiastic
acolyte who had been inspired to switch from double bass to
tenor sax after hearing Ayler, and later went on to record with
him in 1966.

Ayler, of course, was one of the great visionary founders
of American free jazz, and the most misunderstood. Born
in Cleveland, Ohio, in 1936 into a highly religious family, he
came up playing saxophone in bebop and R&B styles. After a
couple of years stationed in France with the US Army from
1959, he moved to Sweden in 1962, cutting a pair of tentative
early albums and crossing paths with Cecil Taylor in Denmark,
whose band he joined as an unpaid member in the winter of
1962/3. On his return to the States in 1964 he recorded the
timeless *Spiritual Unity* for ESP-Disk with drummer Sunny
Murray and bassist Gary Peacock, announcing a frighteningly
idiosyncratic tenor style that was light-years ahead of any of
his contemporaries. Employing a huge, earnest tone with a
heartbreakingly wide vibrato alongside harsh, multiphonic
brays and sustained investigations of the uppermost altissimo
register, his voice was utterly his own and a major influence on
none other than John Coltrane as the elder saxophonist began
to commit to the expressive possibilities of free jazz in the
mid-60s. As the decade went on, Ayler's aesthetic coalesced
into a wild, highly personal form that drew just as much on
Christian spirituals and the European and Scandinavian

folk tunes and military marches he'd heard overseas as it did on the collective improvisation of early New Orleans jazz. Increasingly troubled by apocalyptic visions and an urgent yet nebulous spiritual imperative, he'd fallen foul of the critics by the end of the '60s, after experimenting with pop and R&B in effort to better communicate his message of redemption through sound to the love generation. After a period of worsening emotional and psychological instability, his lifeless body was recovered from the East River in New York City in November 1970. He was just thirty-four years old.

It's certainly true that there are many similarities between Brötzmann's and Ayler's sound. Both were influenced early on by Sidney Bechet, and particularly his strong, controlled vibrato. Both imbued their playing with a sense of raw, yearning — almost vulnerable — emotion. Brötzmann said: "You only have to listen to Ayler's first ESP-Disk records, with what kind of love and desperation this man played his own stories — and also what honesty. These are three things which are important to me, which touch me. And therefore, dare I say it, there is a connection between our kinds of music."[23]

If much of Brötzmann's early ferocity was born of pragmatic fury and a burning desire to challenge the tainted socio-cultural consensus of post-Nazi Germany, Ayler's intense outpourings were in service to a transformative spiritual rapture. But here, too, it seems Brötzmann recognised something of a kindred soul, claiming: "From the very beginning, the titles of his tunes have documented his longing for another, better world: Spiritual Unity / Ghosts / Truth Is Marching In / Universal Message / Holy Family / Our Prayer / Spirits Rejoice… he really meant it."[24]

Yet, at other times, perhaps annoyed by the constant comparisons, Brötzmann was much more brusque in his appraisal. He told me: "The only thing we had in common, I think, was, when we started, we couldn't play saxophone. I think he developed his way of playing very beautifully, and I found my way of doing my shit. But it's completely a different world."[25] Indeed, Brötzmann consistently brushed aside suggestions that he was directly influenced by Ayler, making a case for the same kind of simultaneous invention that Ornette Coleman and the British-Jamaican alto saxophonist Joe Harriot displayed on different continents at the turn of the '60s. In conversation with Evan Parker and John Corbett, Brötzmann said: "The ESP Ayler things came very late over to us [in Germany], and I was already working the same way years before.[26] He also claimed: "We both tried to do similar or almost identical things at the same point in time, each independently and without knowing anything about each other — each of us within our own culture.[27]

In fact, there's an intriguing possibility that, in terms of influence, the direction of travel might have been the other way around. "I think that is actually the case," Brötzmann told me.[28] It's known that the two met in 1960 while Ayler was stationed in Orleans, France, with the 76 Adjutant General's Army Band. During this time, Ayler would regularly make trips to Paris and even as far as Stockholm to check out the jazz clubs and sit in with local musicians. When the band toured France and Germany between June and September 1960, Ayler made regular visits to a club called the Cave in Heidelberg, around three hundred kilometres south of Wuppertal. "We were a kind of house band there — me and Kowald and different drummers — we played very often," Brötzmann told me. "There was always a slim Black guy sitting there, but then he disappeared. Then, later, I bought the first record that has his picture on it, from Copenhagen, where he is playing 'Summertime' [1964's *My Name Is Albert Ayler*]. Man, I looked closer and closer — there was the guy!"[29] If, as this story suggests, Ayler may have copped some early ideas from Brötzmann, and given that he then went on to exert a magnetic attraction on John Coltrane at a pivotal moment in the latter's artistic development, is there perhaps a possibility that Brötzmann may have, in some small way, indirectly influenced Trane? Here, Brötzmann demurred with uncharacteristic bashfulness: "That would go a little too far."[30]

By the early 1990s, Ayler had largely fallen out of favour with listeners and critics. It was still more than a decade before the comprehensive, nine-CD box-set *Holy Ghost: Rare & Unissued Recordings (1962–1970)*, released by Revenant in 2004, would kickstart a renewed interest in his work. "The man was forgotten, the subject was passe," Brötzmann said.[31] But, for Brötzmann, the fascination had never dwindled, as he discovered during a late-night conversation with Toshinori Kondo around the time the trumpeter relocated to Amsterdam: "Kondo and I had made a night of it — once again… During our session, we talked about everything under the sun and kept coming back to Ayler. We agreed that he should be brought back to people's attention."[32]

Since their early connection at the beginning of the 1980s during Brötzmann's first trip to Japan, he and Kondo had continued to work together, including on Brötzmann's *Alarm* in 1981. The same year, the two had performed in a trio with Milford Graves. More recently, in February 1992, Kondo had participated in a specially convened hometown Peter Brötzmann Tentet performance (released in 1993 as *The März Combo: Live In Wuppertal*) to celebrate Brötzmann's fiftieth birthday, in a gigantically free-wheeling and scalding ensemble that mixed old improv warhorses such as trombonists Hannes Bauer and Paul Rutherford with artists from the noise-rock spectrum including guitarist Nicky Scopelitis and, Brötzmann's twenty-nine-year-old son, Caspar. "We did a lot of things," Brötzmann recalled. "[Kondo] was, from time to time, a guest in my larger ensembles. Sometimes even a guest in the ICP Orchestra in the years I worked with them. Whenever I came to Japan, we did a couple of small things — duos, trios. You know, trumpet players are very hard to find, especially good trumpet players."[33]

During his time in New York, from the late '70s onwards, Kondo had collaborated with Bill Laswell, which helped propel him in some unusual directions, away from free jazz and towards some of the electronic fusions that Laswell excelled at, including a guest appearance on Herbie Hancock's Laswell-produced 1983 electro album *Future Shock*. After moving back to Japan in the early '80s, Kondo formed the ensemble International Music Activities — or IMA — which, on albums like their 1984 debut, *Taihen*, mixed industrial electro-funk, sultry post-modern jazz, ambient synthesizer textures and turntablism. Crucially, this was also when Kondo started to experiment with running his trumpet through electronic effects, transforming the humble horn into a powerful generator of huge swathes of sound. In 2013 (seven years before Kondo's death), Brötzmann told me; "Kondo was one of the first trying to use electronics, which I am usually not a friend of. We had arguments quite a bit about it but, the way Kondo is doing it, I always had the feeling he knows what he is doing, and is trying to find his own way. And I think he did."[34]

If Brötzmann and Kondo were to constitute the frontline in their proposed Ayler project, they needed a rhythm section.

For bassist, Brötzmann turned to an American player he had, by the early '90s, already been working with for a decade: William Parker.

Born in the Bronx, New York City, in 1952, Parker entered the fertile Manhattan loft scene in 1971. Despite brief studies with bassists Jimmy Garrison, Richard Davis and Wilbur Ware, Parker remained, like Brötzmann, defiantly unschooled and largely self-taught. He received his most formative training playing in groups such as saxophonist Jemeel Moondoc's Muntu, Melodic Art-Tet with saxophonist Charles Bracken, and the Music Ensemble alongside violinist Billy Bang and multi-instrumentalist Daniel Carter. As his talents and reputation grew, Parker quickly found himself in demand among elder statesmen of the avant-garde and served in the working groups of both Don Cherry and Sunny Murray.

During the '80s and into the '90s, Parker was associated with major players on the US free-jazz scene, including a lengthy stint in the Cecil Taylor Unit from 1980 to 1991, and he appeared on some of the era's defining albums. His first notable exposure to public attention came through recording with Taylor on albums such as 1985's *Winged Serpent (Sliding Quadrants)* and 1986's *The Eighth*; with trumpeter Bill Dixon he recorded *Thoughts* in 1987 (sharing bass duties with Peter Kowald) and *Vade Mecum* in 1994; and with Charles Gayle and Rashied Ali he cut *Touchin' On Trane* in 1993. But perhaps his most intense and productive relationship was with saxophonist David S. Ware, in whose quartet he performed and recorded alongside pianist Matthew Shipp and a revolving cast of drummers from the group's inception in 1988. On albums like *Great Bliss Volumes 1 & 2* (both 1991) and *Flight of I* (1992), Parker helped infuse Ware's torrential, huge-hearted compositions with a deep seriousness and reverence that lifted them into genuinely spiritual realms.

Throughout this period, Parker was also increasingly drawn to the European scene and particularly artists associated with the FMP stable. Brötzmann told me he first met Parker in New York "in some tiny club on Avenue A,"[35] but, as Parker's biographer, Cisco Bradley, maintains, their paths first crossed while Parker was playing with the Cecil Taylor Unit in Berlin in 1983, following an invitation from Kowald, whom Parker had met in New York the previous year. Brötzmann and Parker struck up an immediate rapport, playing together in New York the same year, and just two years later, in 1985, Parker played in Berlin at the Workshop Freie Musik, both with the Peter Brötzmann Trio (with Han Bennink on drums) and Brötzmann's Alarm Orchestra (also featuring Kondo on trumpet, Johannes Bauer and Alan Tomlinson on trombone, Larry Stabbins and David S. Ware on saxes, Curtis Clark on piano, Peter Kowald on bass and Louis Moholo on drums). That same year, Brötzmann and Parker convened the first of their triptych of Manhattan trio performances with Milford Graves. Concerning Parker's inclusion in the Ayler project, Brötzmann claimed he "was predestined for the part through his work with Milford Graves alone."[36]

To round out the group, Brötzmann called on the talents of a newer musical acquaintance, drummer Hamid Drake. Born Henry Drake in Monroe, Louisiana, in 1955, he moved with his family to the Chicago suburb of Evanston, Illinois, while still a child. There, he learned drums in school and grew up near the home of saxophonist Fred Anderson, a key early member of the AACM, with whom he performed as Hank Drake while still a teenager. During the '70s, Drake and childhood friend, percussionist Adam Rudolph performed with Gambian kora player Foday Musa Suso in the pan-global Mandingo Griot Society, incorporating African sounds alongside funk and soul rhythms. This led to a longstanding association with the godfather of world jazz, and Brötzmann's early mentor, Don Cherry, who guested on Mandingo Griot Society's self-titled 1978 debut album. Following that collaboration, Drake went on the road with Don and Moki Cherry's Organic Music Society and worked extensively with Don right up to the trumpeter's death in 1995. Throughout the '80s, Drake balanced hometown club dates — playing in reggae bands as often as he was part of Anderson's hard-blowing bop-to-free jazz outfit — with higher-profile dates with jazz luminaries such as Pharoah Sanders.

When Brötzmann first met him, during Brötzmann's first visit to Chicago in 1987, Drake (who had by then converted to Islam and taken the name Hamid) was still a supremely hard-working, jobbing musician. With typically voluble *joie de vivre* and irrepressible energy, Drake told me about that first encounter:

"Peter was supposed to come to Chicago with [East German drummer] Günter 'Baby' Sommer and another musician but they couldn't get the visa thing straight. But Peter was able to get his, so he came. There was a venue in Chicago known as the Southend Musicworks that was curated by this guy named Leo Krumpholz. He would bring a lot of musicians from everywhere that were travelling through the States; he would set up performances for them in Chicago, everybody from Evan Parker to von Schlippenbach, European musicians, Stateside musicians — whoever was coming through the Midwest and playing improvised music. So, Peter calls Leo and asks him is there a drummer in Chicago that he could do this concert with because he's booked to play and the other two guys can't make it. So Leo says, 'Yeah, let me call this drummer, Hamid.' Of course, I had known of Peter but we had never met, and so Leo called me and asked if I could do it and I said, 'Sure, but there's this one problem though — what time is the concert?' And he said it would be eight o'clock; I said, 'You have to get a drum set because after I've played with Peter I have to go down the street to this other venue called Edge of the Looking Glass to work with one of the reggae bands I was working with.' At that time I was playing a lot of reggae. This group had a Ghanaian lead singer and Jamaican and American musicians in the group. For this show, we were supporting [Jamaican dub poet and musician] Mutabaruka. So, Leo said, 'No problem, I'll get a drum set for you.' So, everything was cool, I did the soundcheck at the Looking Glass, and then I went to the Southend Musicworks where Peter was, we met and we played a little bit together, did a soundcheck. Then, time was running so I had to go back to the Edge of the Looking Glass just down the street for a moment, and I told the guys, 'Listen, I'm doing a gig down the street with this German saxophone player and you guys are welcome to come if you'd like.' The whole group showed up, sitting in the front row, Mutabaruka and all of them, with their mouths wide open! Mutabaruka asked me if they could get a recording of that concert, because the drummer wanted to play it for all his drummer friends back in Jamaica. Mutabaruka had a radio show at the time, and he wanted to play the concert over the air. They were just blown away. They said they had never heard anything like it, never heard just drums and saxophones. They loved it. They were able to go past their own musical boundaries and check out what we're doing but maybe see the essence is the same. It was really beautiful. After that concert, I said, 'Hey Peter, I have to go down the street now and play a reggae gig, opening up for these guys who were here at the concert, would you like to come?' he said 'Ja, Ja, I come with you.'"[37]

Brötzmann takes up the story:

"We had the first duo gig together, Hamid and I, and we played for two hours in a row, no break, no nothing, and that was the beginning of the second friendship I have with a drummer, after Bennink. After the gig, he invited me to stay at his place, but he said, 'First I have to go and play with this Jamaican band, it's just around the corner, let's go.' So, I went with Hamid, he played another two hours with these guys, then he said, 'Man, I have another gig, around the corner there's a heavy metal band I have to sit in with.' So, it was four in the morning when we finally entered his home. He said, 'Here's your bed, amuse yourself, I might be gone in the morning because I have a piano trio gig.' That was the first impression of Hamid. He's a great guy."[38]

Cut to a few years later, when the Ayler project with Kondo was coming together, and Brötzmann had no doubts about who should occupy the drum stool: "I knew at once that [Drake] was the drummer I needed for the proposed quartet."[39]

"It was about the basics, the spiritual foundations of Ayler's music"

From the beginning, it was obvious that Brötzmann had a clear vision of what he was trying to achieve with the new quartet. Drake told me: "He was starting off on sort of a… maybe you could call it like a new visionary quest."[40] For Brötzmann, it was simple: "I just wanted to point out how important Ayler was for my way."[41]

The group's first album was recorded live in Berlin in August 1993 and released on FMP the following year as *Die Like a Dog: Fragments of Music, Life and Death of Albert Ayler*. Undeniably, it's a deeply loving tribute to Ayler, which celebrates his music while lamenting the shame and pity of the saxophonist's death, dragged like a drowned dog from the East River. From the outset, Brötzmann calls forth his most soulful, yearning tone: a wide, brittle cry, continually surfing the narrow crest of altissimo ecstasy. The long group improvisations are punctuated by brief quotations from Ayler tunes including "Prophet," "Ghosts" and "Bells," rising up out of the melee like rallying calls to regroup on the battleground of love. Brötzmann explained: "It was never about using the old themes or to revive the old times... There are only fragments of themes, second-long quotes we use. No, it was about the basics, the spiritual foundations of Ayler's music. That's what we were going for, and in our own way."[42] Another musical quote, the repeated return to the elegiac theme of Don Redman's "Saint James Infirmary," suggests a sorrowful weeping of righteous outrage over Ayler's cold body laid out on the mortuary slab.

Brötzmann's tenor and alto reach shuddering heights of intensity, but some of the most gripping playing comes when he switches to tarogato, with long, lachrymose calls twisting into knotted contusions, gnarled like an old man's fingers. Kondo's augmented trumpet displays a wide range, from punchy bulletins echoing Donald Ayler, to the shrill whinnying of Don Cherry and even the tight-lipped accuracy of mid-60s Freddie Hubbard. Still, it's his application of electronics that speaks loudest, as he sends the horn puking and shrieking into dizzying whirlpools of psychedelic distortion. Parker and Drake provide a liquid undertow that bubbles along as freely as a newly liberated spirit, and when Parker drops into one of his loping, primal grooves, there are moments when *Die Like a Dog* forcefully fulfils the Art Ensemble of Chicago's vision of music "ancient to future."

The effervescent chemistry between the four of them demanded further collaboration and the group continued beyond this initial foray, taking the name Die Like a Dog Quartet. Even more so than Last Exit, they were a live proposition and all of the albums they subsequently released were taken from real-time performances in front of audiences. "A lot of it is… a question of money," Brötzmann explained. "We have never been in a studio, three days, three nights, no audience — we simply can't afford it. The possibilities which come up are usually organised by Jost Gebers in Berlin. And we have to grab them."[43]

With the debt to Ayler paid in full on the first album, the quartet jettisoned explicit references to his work, developing their own sound and fully improvised approach, and the five albums released under the name Die Like a Dog Quartet, recorded between 1994 and 1999, reveal an ensemble rapidly evolving.

On *Close Up* (recorded in 1994 but not released until 2011) and the two volumes of *Little Birds Have Fast Hearts* (both recorded in 1997 and released a year apart in 1998 and 1999), Kondo's heavily treated trumpet leaps out like a dangerously deranged animal. Though his approach is often posited as an extension of Miles Davis's use of wah-wah and echoplex pedals on albums such as 1975's *Agharta,* recorded right at the end of his phenomenal run of electric albums and just before his extended hiatus from music, Kondo pushes way beyond these innovations, transforming the horn into a mewling, chattering, shrieking, gurgling beast in throes of agony and ecstasy. Here, too, the extraordinary telepathic connection between Parker and Drake is fully formed as they generate an irresistible rhythmic velocity and power, constantly unlocking fresh vamps with quicksilver flashes of instantaneous invention that send the improvisations in surprising new directions.

That's even more apparent on *From Valley to Valley*, which documents the group's North American debut performance at the Fire in the Valley festival in Amherst, Massachusetts, in 1998. For this set, Kondo is replaced by Roy Campbell Jr on flugelhorn, trumpet and pocket trumpet. Born in 1952, Campbell came up playing hard bop before turning to the avant-garde in the 1970s, and his performance on *From Valley to Valley* shows both influences, mixing strident, Lee Morgan–like athleticism with louche smears and growls. With Campbell's more explicitly blues-based phrases — and without Kondo's searing electronic textures — Parker and Drake are pushed deeper into a jazz pocket of implied grooves.

By the time they cut their last album, Die Like a Dog Quartet were operating like an implacable machine imbued with dazzling organic intelligence. *Aoyama Crows* (named after a high-end Tokyo district) was recorded at the Total Music Meeting in Berlin in November 1999, and released on FMP in 2002, with band members flying in from Sweden, Tokyo and New York to make the date. They hit the stage exhausted and jetlagged, which makes the album's relentlessly hurtling energy all the more remarkable. On tenor sax, tarogato and clarinet, Brötzmann is stern and somewhat melancholy but always unflagging in his commitment. Kondo wrenches the trumpet with astonishing virtuosity, one moment loquacious and wry, the next ascending into electronically assisted stratospherics, sounding like a Moog synth solo. Parker and Drake roll and tumble with locked-in intensity, and in fact, some of the album's deepest moments come when the horns drop-out, allowing bass and drums to steamroll ahead with irresistible forward motion. There's even a moment of pure, unbridled swing, with Drake latching onto Parker's deep, walking line with an old-school ride cymbal ting-a-ling, pushing Die Like a Dog Quartet the closest they'd ever come to straight jazz.

In 2000, speaking of the band circa *Aoyama Crows*, Brötzmann said:

> "It's logical that ideas and thoughts of musicians shift over the years. In Kondo's case away from more jazzy references towards various sound areas, electronics but also towards more harmonic and simple solos. You mustn't forget that Kondo and Hamid still play with Laswell and that for him music is definitely in the direction of groove. This is imported into our quartet. Which is okay because we are always open to these influences… there is so much to discover when you're playing together — the new rhythms Hamid has worked out and what William brings in with his minimalism, it's not finished by any means."[44]

Sadly, however, there were to be no more recordings from this quartet. But on the strength of their slim discography, they remain one of the most genuinely thrilling groups of the 1990s.

Probably the most important and lasting legacy of the Die Like a Dog Quartet — and one of Brötzmann's great gifts to the jazz world — was the bringing together of Parker and Drake. From their very first soundcheck together, it was obvious they'd unlocked a supremely deep musical relationship. Drake told Bill Meyer: "William and I knew of each other, but we had never met or played together before. And a few moments after doing our first piece, we both sensed this connection that we had. It was pretty extraordinary, because it felt like I was playing with someone that I had known forever. He had the same feeling."[45]

Since that initial encounter, they've gone on to become one of the undisputed greatest jazz rhythm sections of all time. In April 2000, they cemented their creative partnership with the recording of two stunning albums — their first recorded collaborations outside of Die Like a Dog — beginning with *Painter's Spring* by the William Parker Trio with Daniel Carter on saxes, clarinet and flute. From the off, Parker and Drake are locked into deep, intuitive communion, surging on a boisterous, preternatural rapport. Whether blasting though bullish free-energy music or hunkering into bliss-out trance grooves, Drake's dense polyrhythms and armoured swing coax tough, sinuous lines from Parker. Carter contributes coiled alto and dreamy flute, but to an extent, it feels like mere decoration: here, the bass and drums are a complete, elemental musical force.

The very next day, Parker and Drake returned to the studio as a duo and cut *Piercing the Veil*. Again, it's crammed with astonishingly tight bass and drum jams: the relentless vamp of "Black Cherry" demonstrates how to make a simple hook endlessly rich; while, on "Chatima," Drake's hi-hat and snare shadow Parker's razored arco howl with thrilling precision. But it's when they turn to an array of non-western instruments that this date really blooms, with a handful of inspired duets for tabla and balafon, hand drum and shakuhachi, frame drum and double-reed horn. It's a first glimpse of the duo's growing fascination with ethnically diverse idioms, and convincingly posits an outernationalist manifesto, connecting musical dots to propose an inclusive vision of humanity.

In the years since, Drake has been a mainstay in various Parker-led ensembles, and the two have also worked extensively in trio settings backing a dizzying array of instrumentalists, from veterans such as Charles Gayle and Evan Parker, to younger players including Amsterdam-based, US tenor saxophonist John Dikeman and Norwegian pianist Anja Lauvdal. And some of their very best trio work was done with Brötzmann.

By the time of the 2001 Montreal trio concert released in its entirety in 2003 as *Never Too Late but Always Too Early*, Parker and Drake had been working with Brötzmann long enough to hone and develop their supporting rhythmic interplay into a living force driven by an astonishing degree of telepathic intimacy. Parker's insistent trance grooves are deepened and propelled by Drake's irresistible polyrhythmic blur of rim clicks, toms and cowbell, fusing elements of African and South American rhythm into hypnotic Fourth World rituals. Parker and Drake's sleek mobility enables them to flick into exuberant, breakneck jazz in a flash. Here, Brötzmann gets about as close as he ever has to the root of American jazz, riding Parker and Drake's deep sense of swing and tradition, which, at one point, even breaks down into a dialogue of Max Roach–style hi-hat and hefty Charles Mingus string slaps. Brötzmann's response is to blast his horn into white-of-the-eyes glossolalia, a timeless pre-Babel song that's the perfect voice for this primeval Pangaeic trip. The whole album is a truly phenomenal explosion of music.

For such an outstanding trio, they remained sorely under-documented, performing live much more than recording. In February 2015, they played a run of three nights at Brötzmann's adopted London base, Café OTO, which was recorded and subsequently released in 2023 as *Song Sentimentale* on the venue's own OTOROKU label. With the CD and LP formats containing completely different music, all recorded over the three nights, it provided ample opportunity for the trio to stake out all the different territories they'd come to occupy together up to that point. I attended the final night of that OTO residency and filed a review for *Jazzwise* magazine, excerpted here:

"Word in the room is that, while the first night was a tentative affair with the trio reconsolidating shared territory, the second saw them slotting back into the kind of joyous, spontaneously generated grooves that characterised *Never Too Late But Always Too Early*. On this third and final night, however, the urge to groove seems largely exhausted. Sure, drummer Hamid Drake occasionally drops into a fat funk break but, for the most part, he ranges freely round the kit. Utterly in control with a dancing physicality and power, Drake is mesmerising to watch in action while, at the double bass, William Parker is an equally huge presence: deeply immersed, an artist who genuinely exudes the air of being engaged in a heartfelt spiritual practice. The connection between the two is so strong you can almost twang it like elastic, with tantalising flashes of tightly coiled vamps emerging briefly from the boiling undertow like fleeting new life forms. Brötzmann, by contrast, remains a little aloof, sending long, rasping tenor lines over the top with an unceasing, uncompromising force that challenges the rhythm section to keep up the pace. The second set offers a respite, with Parker setting up a hypnotic pulse on Moroccan guimbre and Drake nimbly finger-tipping a frame drum and singing a big-throated devotional. Brötzmann responds with high, keening tarogato, causing Parker to join in on an oriental double-reed instrument, filling the room with an intense and uplifting energy that reaches way back past jazz towards the mystical roots of self-expression."[46]

While Brötzmann's work with Parker and Drake was, to some extent, a continuation and development of his sadly curtailed trio with Moholo and Miller, it also stretched in much more adventurous directions, linking free-jazz with a more inclusive, pan-global vision. As Parker put it: "Peter was a conduit for new cosmic music that could float over all the rhythms of the world."[47]

With their shared profound connection to Don Cherry, it's little wonder that this openness was notable in work created by Brötzmann and Drake. On their duo album *The Dried Rat-Dog*, cut in a Chicago recording studio in 1994, there's plenty of bullish sax/drums blow-outs in the vein of *Interstellar Space*, but there are some surprising shades, too: "It's an Angel on the Door" features Drake on galloping tablas, with Brötzmann turning the tarogato into a gnarled snake charmer's pipe; and "Open into the Unknown" has Drake tapping an earthy frame drum with deft fingers while Brötzmann unspools lazy clarinet, the two of them sounding like soporific cousins of Moroccan Sufi-trance troupe the Master Musicians of Jajouka.

On *The "WELS" Concert*, recorded live at the Schlachthof Wels festival in Austria in 1996, Brötzmann and Drake teamed up with Mahmoud Gania, the revered Moroccan Maâlem — or master — of gnawa healing ritual music, who resolutely plucks burbling riffs on the guembri bass lute and sings throaty exhortations while Drake explodes at the drum kit with polyrhythmic abandon and Brötzmann broadcasts cavernous blasts over the top. Gania had already worked with Pharoah Sanders a couple of years earlier, recording the Laswell-produced *The Trance of Seven Colors* in 1994, on which the Maâlem plays traditional gnawa tunes complete with an ebullient call-and-response choir and a clattering battery of iron qraqueb castinets, with Sanders adding melodic embellishments and multiphonic shrieks. But the collaboration with Brötzmann and Drake is a much less traditionally rooted affair, more effectively melding free jazz and gnawa into a uniquely propulsive polyglot hybrid. In fact, it worked so well that Brötzmann and Drake went on to record the equally mesmerising *The Catch of A Ghost* in 2019, revisiting their enlivened jazz/gnawa fusion with Ghania's brother, Maâlem Mokhtar Ghania.

For Drake, a practising Muslim who had previously been involved in the Bahá'í faith and professes a fascination with traditional Vedic Hindu beliefs, the chance to explore the explicitly spiritual elements and purposes of gnawa music seemed a natural development. But it's rare that the gruffly pragmatic Brötzmann ever evinced much interest in matters of the spirit. Yet, perhaps his admitted admiration for Ayler's otherworldly yearning suggests hidden depths. Drake told me:

"We went to Morocco together and he went to a lot of different places with me where I didn't expect him to go. I went to meet this elderly Sufi master whose name was Sheik Abdul Hamid when we were in Rabat, and I asked Peter if he wanted to go with me and he said yeah. We spent a couple of hours with the Sheik, and then the Sheik took us to the place where him and his dervishes would meet, and Peter sat on the floor with me and had cookies and tea."[48]

At bottom, Brötzmann was always driven by a wide-open mind that welcomed cultural exchange, revelled in unusual instrumental combinations and was inquisitive about disparate musical traditions — as demonstrated in high-risk collaborations with artists such as Chinese guzheng player Xu Fengxia and Japanese koto player Michio Yagi. Another intriguing example was facilitated when Uli Armbruster of the German ARM record label persuaded Brötzmann to travel to Sana'a, capital city of Yemen, in 2004 to perform with Yemeni musicians. Brötzmann also brought with him Chicago-based Assyrian American drummer Michael Zerang, who told Bill Meyer:

> "The second day, we were taking this trip up in the mountains while Uli was running around trying to find us musicians to play with, and we saw two musicians that were playing for a wedding party. One was playing something like a zurna, a really loud double-reed thing. He was accompanied by a percussionist that was playing this closed-bottom bowl with a skin tightly stretched across it, and he was slapping it with these long strips of rawhide. Brötzmann was like 'I want them!' That would have been fantastic because these guys were just burning. And then he was informed that no, we can't have street musicians come and play this official gig [at the German cultural house]. So we had these five state musicians."[49]

In the end, Brötzmann and Zerang performed with a quintet of classically trained musicians playing violin, cello, kanun zither, darbuka hand-drum and ney flute. "It was a cultural clash, in a way," Zerang recalled.

> "First of all, a lot of the instruments that these musicians were playing were pretty quiet. And these musicians were not

necessarily improvisers, or even really aware of the concept…
At one point, Peter wanted the cellist to take a solo. We played
the written material, and then it was time for the cellist to play
his solo. And he just played the written part again. And he
played it again. And he played it again, not with any variation.
It was kind of difficult conceptually."[50]

Proof of the encounter can be heard on *Berg-Und Talfahrt
— A Night in Sanaa (Live at "Deutsches Haus")*, released in
2009. It reveals an attempted fusion that never quite comes
together, with the Yemeni musicians floundering in the
improvised passages, and Brötzmann somewhat restrained.
But, flawed as it is, it still stands as testament to Brötzmann's
unflagging internationalism and unquenchable thirst for
new connections. Here, too, it's easy to find final proof of just
how irrelevant the rigid notion of *"die Emanzipation"* was to
his musical journey. From ecstatic Fourth World jams with
Parker and Drake through to wide-open collaborations with
Moroccan and Yemeni folk musicians, not to mention the
ongoing spark he enjoyed with leading Japanese improvisers,
Brötzmann was never merely turning *away* from America
but *towards* the whole world in all its teeming beauty and
complexity.

Short Visit to Nowhere

"He was like a whirlwind that came into town"

If Hamid Drake was the first important connection Brötzmann made in Chicago, he certainly wasn't the last. In the course of his constant globetrotting, Chicago became, during the 1990s, a basecamp to which Brötzmann would regularly return. It was also the birthplace of an audacious project that was to be a major artistic concern for over a decade, striking the Windy City like a thunderclap and sending reverberations far beyond. Chicago-based writer, concert promoter, radio host and gallery owner John Corbett put it succinctly: "He left a great impact on this city. And I think it's safe to say that Chicago for a long time was a very special sanctuary for him."[1]

Chicago had, for decades, been a vital outpost of the jazz avant-garde. It was here that Sun Ra launched his Arkestra in the late 1950s, providing a scintillating lightning rod for local musicians drawn to Ra's outlandish Pharaohs-in-space costumes, complex Afrofuturist mythology and compositions that seemed to take Thelonious Monk's modernist innovations as a starting point before stretching out into strange new worlds of exotic dissonance. It was enough to open up a space of infinite possibilities in the minds of many young Chicago musicians. Just a few years after the Arkestra relocated to New York in 1961, the highly adventurous and ground-breaking Association for the Advancement of Creative Musicians (AACM) was founded, in May 1965, by pianist Muhal Richard Abrams, drummer Steve McCall, pianist Jodie Christian and multi-instrumentalist Phil Cohran, who had briefly played trumpet in the Arkestra. The AACM, in turn, provided a nurturing platform for a whole pantheon of progressive and searching improviser-composers, including Anthony Braxton, George Lewis and Roscoe Mitchell, positioning Chicago as a left-field challenger to New York's jazz sovereignty.

In the 1990s, Chicago was experiencing a heady quickening of energies among its underground music communities. Cheap warehouse spaces and vibrant live music clubs like the Empty Bottle and the HotHouse drew an influx of young musicians from across the States, united in displaying a flagrant disregard for genre etiquette. Groups like Tortoise and Isotope 217 mixed elements of jazz, funk, rock, minimalism and lo-fi DIY. Chicago Underground Collective, featuring cornetist Rob Mazurek, guitarist Jeff Parker and drummer Chad Taylor, were beginning to propose a thrilling avant-garde brew of free jazz and deep grooves with nods to both Bill Dixon and the AACM. Polymaths David Grubbs and Jim O'Rourke were straining towards a stringently experimental art-rock through their collaborative project, Gastr del Sol.

At the same time, building on structures and practices put in place by the AACM, a youthful new jazz scene was aflame with feverish activity. And much of that was thanks to the tireless commitment and energy of saxophonist and organiser Ken Vandermark (born 1964). After arriving in Chicago in 1989, he ran an influential weekly residence at the HotHouse in the early '90s, and threw himself into multiple projects, including assembling a coterie of likeminded players — saxophonist Mars Williams, bassist Kent Kessler, trombonist/guitarist Jeb Bishop and drummer Tim Mulvenna — as The

Vandermark 5, charting a boisterous mix of post-bop, free jazz, free improvisation and post-punk noise rock. There was a lot going on. It was the perfect time for Brötzmann to get involved.

"Right around when Die Like a Dog was formed, Peter started coming to Chicago a lot and he started meeting a lot of other Chicago musicians," Hamid Drake remembers.

> "Chicago was starting to become a second home for him in a way because he was really developing a fanbase here — not only with listeners but of course with musicians and people who wanted to play with him. He was like a whirlwind that came into town and then he formed relationships with some of the other great tenor saxophone players who were here too, like Fred Anderson and Von Freeman and people like that. He would come and stay for long periods of time and, oftentimes, would stay at our place, or he would stay at John Corbett's house."[2]

Corbett was an enthusiastic champion of free jazz and improvisation, and he and Brötzmann quickly became firm friends. And it was Corbett who helped organise the project that cemented Brötzmann's relationship with Chicago. In January 1997, Corbett arranged for Brötzmann to play a weekend of gigs at the Empty Bottle and in Unity Temple (a grand, Frank Lloyd Wright–designed Unitarian Universalist church), with seven local improvisers: Vandermark and Williams on saxes, Bishop on trombone, Kessler on bass, Fred Lomberg-Holm on cello, and Hamid Drake and Michael Zerang on drums. This octet's performances were strong enough to encourage Brötzmann to reconvene the group for a studio session and another live date at the Empty Bottle in September that year, as the Chicago Tentet, with — at Corbett and Vandermark's suggestion — the addition of two extra players.

One of those additional musicians was a veteran of the same vintage as Brötzmann: saxophonist/trumpeter Joe McPhee. The two enjoyed an acquaintance that went way back: "I had the pleasure and honour to share the stage and music side by side with Mr Brötzmann many times since our first meeting in Paris in 1977," McPhee said. "He and Han Bennink had an extraordinary duo. Han played everything, even the walls of the theatre, and Peter's enormous sound was like nothing one could imagine. I was playing solo and I shuddered to think how I would follow that."[3]

Joe McPhee's early history reads like the archetypal twentieth-century post-war jazz life. Born in 1939, he began to learn the trumpet aged eight, with lessons from his father, also a trumpeter. By the late '50s, he was hero-worshipping Miles Davis and digging *Kind of Blue*. In 1962, hearing John Coltrane's blazing sixteen-minute tenor blow-out "Chasin' the Trane" — from *Coltrane "Live" at the Village Vanguard* — opened his mind to the transporting possibilities of extended techniques. Then, in 1963, after seeing Don Cherry playing with Sonny Rollins at Birdland in New York City, he was inspired to begin playing pocket trumpet alongside the regular horn.

His first recorded date as a sideman took place the day after he attended the funeral of John Coltrane at St Peter's Lutheran Church, New York City, on 21 July 1967, at which he witnessed epochal performances by Albert Ayler and Ornette Coleman. The album resulting from that recording session, *Freedom & Unity* by the Clifford Thornton New Art Ensemble, is a keystone of the New Thing, and McPhee emerged as a young trumpeter already in possession of considerable talent. On the two tracks he plays on — "The Wake" and his own composition, "O.C.T." — his impetuous slurs and trills add fierce energy to swift, flying free-bop with a nod to New York Art Quartet.

"When I heard the music of Albert Ayler, that completely took me out, and I wanted to play the saxophone,"[4] he told me. In 1968, after two decades of playing the trumpet, he decided to teach himself tenor, and he's one of just a handful of artists who have mastered both instruments. "Whichever instrument I pick up, at that moment, I'm totally invested in that," he says. "I don't think of the trumpet when I'm playing the saxophone or vice versa. It's not possible, for me anyway."[5]

One of his most explosive saxophone recordings — and his most explicitly political statement — remains *Nation Time*, released in 1971. Its cover alone screams revolt, featuring a black-and-white photo of McPhee dressed in dark clothes, with shades and afro, brandishing his saxophone like a Black Panther's AK47: "Yeah, I turned my tenor into a machine gun,"[6] he said. Musically, it's a revolutionary statement, too. Beginning with the call-and-response invocation "What time is it? Nation time!" — echoing poet Amiri Baraka's incendiary pan-African manifesto — it documents a live performance by a band operating from deep inside an amped-up, propulsive, soul-jazz aesthetic, while simultaneously pushing that form to its limits.

Despite his undeniable connection to the source, McPhee has always been something of an outlier, present at some of the most pivotal moments in late-twentieth-century jazz history while simultaneously sticking to a parallel track all of his own. For one thing, he's largely resisted the lure of New

York City, living most of his life 150 kilometres upstate in Poughkeepsie. In fact, right up till the 1990s, McPhee was better known to European festival audiences than in the clubs and lofts of nearby Manhattan: "For a very long time, I could play in Europe, or I could play sometimes on the West Coast, but almost never in Chicago until Ken Vandermark invited me there in the late '90s."[7]

The other key player to round out the Chicago Tentet was the considerably younger Swedish saxophonist Mats Gustafsson. Born in 1964, he grew up in the city of Umeå, in northern Sweden, where his ears were pulled in interesting directions. "When I was a young teenager, the whole punk scene freakin' exploded in Umeå," he told me. "It was a really great scene at the time, with bands like Anders Ångest and Caligulas Barn and other local heroes."[8]

Gustafsson started out playing flute and first got hold of a saxophone in 1979, at the age of fifteen, inspired by seeing Sonny Rollins play at the Umeå Jazz Festival. He started jamming with local punk outfits and "at the same time, I started figuring out the mechanics of free jazz with my comrade Kjell Nordeson on drums. Sax and drum blow-outs in *Interstellar Space* territory. 'Hellre än bra,' we say in Sweden: 'More important to do it than do it well.' So, the punk/garage thing was more or less running parallel with the jazz/free jazz thing… it was all about ENERGY at that time. For me, it was about the same thing."[9]

But it was his early encounter with Brötzmann's *Machine Gun* in an Umeå record shop that really put a fire in him: "In a way, I'm still in shock after the first listening to *Machine Gun*… I don't know if I ever will recover from that!"[10] With his musical codes rewritten, Gustafsson soon realised it was time to strike out for fresh horizons. Still in his late teens, he left for Stockholm, where he immediately connected with legendary renegade saxophonist Bengt Nordström — an early champion of Albert Ayler who met the American during his visit to Stockholm in 1962 and released Ayler's first recordings as *Something Different!!!!!* on his own Bird Note label the following year. "We met at a jazz club," Gustafsson said, "and we started listening to music together and hanging out in the record stores."[11]

It was also around this time that Gustafsson and Brötzmann first crossed paths. "I remember exactly when I met Mats Gustafsson for the first time," Brötzmann told me. "I was touring with Last Exit and we had two nights in Stockholm, and there were two young blonde guys sitting each night in the front row. After the end of the second night, one of them came and asked me questions about playing saxophone. That was Mats, in his early twenties."[12]

Gustafsson's earliest musical projects in Stockholm included, from 1986, a duo with guitarist Christian Munthe and, from 1988, the trio Gush with pianist Sten Sandell and percussionist Raymond Strid. It was enough to secure an invitation to one of Derek Bailey's Company weekends in London in 1990 and a connection to the source of what he calls "'British-style Improv. Technically, I think that's the most advanced music you can play. To be ready, in every single moment, to change direction of the music all the time. Something is happening and you have to react. You can choose to react in a millisecond or you can choose to react in two seconds — but you have to have the technique. And technique is the key to communicate."[13]

It wasn't until Gustafsson first visited Chicago in 1994, at the invitation of John Corbett, that he even began to think of himself as a jazz musician. It was as if meeting musicians like Vandermark, Drake and others gave him permission to reconsider his art. "That was very clearly a jazz community — and a tradition," he reflects. "John took me to this club and I remember Jeb Bishop was in this band and they played a couple of Archie Shepp, Roswell Rudd pieces, and I thought I was in heaven: people my age doing cover versions, but not just cover versions, it was their music... a tenor sax player and trombone player that are clearly inspired by Archie Shepp and Roswell Rudd, but they sound like something completely different. That was a revelation."[14]

If Chicago played a key role in shaping Gustafsson's identity, it was also something of a two-way street. "He had a profound impact on what was going on here," Vandermark told me.

"He has a lot of enthusiasm. It's pretty infectious. He had so much going on — because when he came here I was thirty, he was around thirty, you're talking about people who have developed a lot of their personal languages, you know? He came with so much stuff, technically and conceptually, to a scene that, at that point, Brötzmann had played here, some of the English guys like Evan [Parker] had been in Chicago, but there really hadn't been a strong influx of European players on a regular basis. Mats was really at the beginning of the wave of that. So, this guy comes from Sweden with all of these different things — different techniques, different ideas, different ways of constructing music — and it was exactly what's always fantastic about an encounter like that: it just throws everything into question in the best way. Even if you continue to do what you did before, it's altered by the knowledge, the first-hand experience of working with someone like that."[15]

The fruits of those two initial large-group sessions in 1997 were released as the three-CD set *The Chicago Octet/Tentet* the following year, forcefully revealing that there's a sense of generosity about Brötzmann's Chicago project directly proportionate to its scale.

The groups are undoubtedly led by Brötzmann and guided by his aesthetic, as made clear on his two long compositions: "Burning Spirit," recorded by the Octet, reprises "Alarm"'s air-raid wail of massed brass, opening up a space from which smaller groupings make forays into free territory; and the Tentet's "Foolish Infinity" folds an insistent, Ayler-ish hook into sustained, burning freefall. But Brötzmann also allows equal room for the constituent members' compositions, with divergent voices jostling for space. Unusually for Brötzmann, that often means pieces that are built on through-composed themes, changes and all. Vandermark's "Other Brothers" is a steel-plated R&B honk with a heavy backbeat, while Zerang's "Aziz" is a gloriously dark, prowling blues vamp.

Brötzmann clearly dug it, and the Chicago Tentet became an ongoing concern, performing regularly and negotiating the herculean logistical challenges of extensive US and European tours. As it went on, it picked up guest members here and there, as seen on *Short Visit to Nowhere*, recorded in 2000, which is credited to Chicago Tentet Plus Two, with the core group joined by William Parker and Roy Campbell. And, as the group evolved, it became a space where, increasingly, its members could try out a wide range of compositional approaches, from the conductions of Lonberg-Holm and Gustafsson, and the vamps of Zerang and Drake, to the notated tunes of Vandermark and Williams and Brötzmann's graphic scores. It made for a uniquely multi-faceted and versatile ensemble, committed to exploring a myriad of approaches while always powered by the huge, rambunctious energy that a large group — and especially a Brötzmann large group — can generate.

"I'm much more aware about every tone I am playing"

Brötzmann was a heavy drinker for decades. Life on the road and the constant company of other musicians made it a way of life. By the '90s, however, it had started to get out of hand: "I just lived for alcohol, I didn't eat very much, I just drank, for breakfast, for dinner, for lunch."[16] As for many alcoholics, it was, for Brötzmann, a form of escapism. He told me: "There was a time when I really worked on that plane, whatever I did, in a kind of unconscious state — what other people reached with a lot of drugs or whatever, just to get away. But, through all my life, even in difficult situations, when it reached a point where it would influence my work — the painting work or the music work — then I started to think about it."[17]

At the end of 1999, Brötzmann was forced to face the reality of just how much his drinking could affect his future as an artist.

"I came back one night from a tour in Poland, and I realised, 'Man, I can't move that finger.' It was very painful, coming in waves. So, I called emergency in the night and there came a very young doctor, and he told me it was gout. Then he saw my saxophone and we sat down at the kitchen table, and he stayed for a couple of hours and explained to me what will happen if I carry on drinking: that I will not be able to play, to move, that everything would swell up and then it goes to the heart. After that, I thought, 'That's it, that's enough.' It was my last chance."[18]

Brötzmann quit drinking there and then. "I felt quite soon that it did me good," he told me in 2013. "And I was never tempted. I have bottles at home of schnapps or wine or whatever, for when a guest comes — no problem. If the band goes drinking, I don't stay to the bitter end. Sometimes I watch the guys and think, 'Did I behave in the same kind of stupid way, or even worse?' I think I wouldn't be here if I hadn't stopped."[19]

Brötzmann had already seen comrades fall by the wayside. His old friend, English trombonist Paul Rutherford, had wrecked his own life and career through alcoholism. "It was so difficult for him. He had no work in England anymore. He was making a little money as a kind of doorman; he was living under conditions that even a musician shouldn't have to. Wuppertal is a very cheap town to live, and I told him, 'Man, I'll organise you a cheap place to live here.' There are musicians around in Cologne, so he would have had at least a minimum of work and some recognition. But he never came."[20] Rutherford later died of cirrhosis, in 2007, at the age of sixty-seven.

Swiss bassist Marino Pliakas told me:

"Werner Ludi, a sax player from Switzerland, was like the Swiss Brötzmann. He was also a crazy, radical sax player, the same age as Peter. They were buddies, they played together, and they were both heavy alcoholics. But, at a certain point, they decided both together to stop. They both decided, 'Come on, let's stop, we want to live on a bit.' Maybe for Ludi it was too late because he died [of a heart attack in June 2000, just a few weeks after touring with Brötzmann]. But Brötzmann caught the very last moment and he survived. From there, he just drank mineral water and a lot of coffee."[21]

Perhaps, inevitably, Brötzmann's newfound sobriety prompted a re-evaluation of his playing. He told me: "What I did earlier, I was doing with the same intensity I'm doing my shit now, but I think it's a little different. Not that I think too much about music while I'm playing, but I'm much more aware about every tone I am playing, about the tone in general."[22] He told Gerard Rouy: "I feel much stronger, I do the things I'm doing more consciously... I think it's been good for me. I think the music or the message I am trying to get across is much clearer than it was in my last years of alcohol."[23]

Sadly, however, Werner Ludi wasn't the only old ally Brötzmann lost around this time. In September 2002, aged just fifty-eight, Peter Kowald died of a heart attack at William Parker's home in New York, shortly after completing a concert in Williamsburg, Brooklyn. It was huge personal blow to Brötzmann. Kowald had been more than just a friend. He was the fearless improviser and conceptualist who'd been there from the very beginning, helping the youthful Brötzmann find his radical art. He was the gregarious traveller and utopian networker who'd initiated lifelong, life-changing connections with the English improvisers and first brought Brötzmann and Bennink together. He was owed everything. In the liner notes to 2002's *Never Too Late but Always Too Early* — an album dedicated to Kowald — Brötzmann wrote: "John Corbett reported me a remark Kowald made saying goodbye after a concert late summer in Lisboa this year: I feel good... but my heart... touching his heart in his unforgettable body language manner. Maybe we failed, we didn't read the message. However — he got respect from men and women all over the world. This is not what you can say about a lot of men."[24]

Brötzmann, however, was still tirelessly forging his own new connections wherever he could. In 2004, he joined forces with two Swiss musicians, drummer Michael Wertmuller and bass guitarist Marino Pliakas.

Wertmuller (born 1966) had a background in both improvisation (receiving tutelage from Misha Mengelberg at the Amsterdam Conservatory in the early '90s) and composition (studying under German composer Dieter Schnebel in Berlin later in the decade). By the mid-to-late-90s he was improvising with Werner Ludi, where Brötzmann first encountered him. "Michael played with my old friend Werner Ludi and I was a guest from time to time," Brötzmann recalled. "When I heard Michael, I immediately saw the energy he was able to put out. You immediately could feel that he could play the drums any way. So that was my man, then. We did duo stuff, we did stuff with William Parker."[25]

Around this time, Wertmuller also played in the experimental rock band, Alboth!, which was how he crossed paths with Pliakas (born 1964) "I was a huge fan of Alboth!," Pliakas recalls. "It was one of my favourite live acts — really cool, crazy, complex and fantastic musicians."[26] Pliakas played in a self-described "Hammond Avantcore trio"[27] called Steamboat Switzerland with organist Dominik Blum and drummer Lucas Niggli, combining jazz with hardcore and noise. By the turn of the millennium, Wertmuller and Pliakas regularly found themselves on the same bill.

"Michael and Brötzmann had played together for many years, and they just thought it could be nice with a bass player," Pliakas recalled. "Michael proposed me because we knew each other, and Brötzmann agreed. We knew each other a little bit — Peter and me — we met here and there in some breakfast rooms in hotels at festivals and stuff, but we were not close, didn't know each other so well."[28]

In the Autumn of 2004, the trio of Brötzmann, Pliakas and Wertmuller set off for a tour of the US, beginning with a show at the Knitting Factory in New York. "I met Peter really for the first time on the airplane on the way to New York,"[29] said Pliakas. "I confessed to Peter that I didn't really like playing with reed players — and he confessed to me that, for him, after Bill Laswell and last Exit, the chapter of electric bass was closed."[30] By then, however, the die had already been cast. "The same night, we played together for the first time."[31] In the event, the trio clicked right away. "We immediately found each other musically and personally," said Pliakas. "I was overwhelmed by Peter's sensitivity, the quality of his sound and his ability to build long arches — always ingeniously moderated by Michael Wertmuller on drums. Peter always had big ears and was an intense listener and interactor. If some of his co-players were not able to keep up or had nothing to oppose him, then he just played his thing, naturally. But, with Michael and myself, it was almost a jazzy approach, depending on one another, listening and cheering each other on, allowing crossfades, stopping together."[32]

Recorded in Cologne in 2006 and released the same year, the trio's debut album — entitled *Full Blast* — does, indeed, reveal a unit operating in tight formation. The name is an apt one, too. Despite Brötzmann's professed reluctance to revisit Last Exit, Pliakas's electric bass lends the music a similar metallic sheen, but there's no sign of the former quartet's lumbering shuffles: Pliakas and Wertmuller lock into a furiously propulsive and fluidly agile barrage that's at once implacable and responsive, ploughing ahead with crazed energy but equally able to turn on a dime with split-second accuracy. Brötzmann, likewise, delivers some of his most gale-force blowing while remaining entirely synced-in, switching effortlessly from enormous, panoramic roars to vulnerable, plaintive cries when the bass and drums settle down into an abstract rumbling thunder. It's among the most focussed dates he ever recorded. "This might have been because of Michael's playing," Pliakas suggested. "It might have been an influence, because he's not the usual free-jazz player or the usual free-improv player, like fragmentary or nihilistic, or whatever. Michael, he's a former jazz and rock player and he's a composer, and he's always very conscious of form and what happens in an instant. This might have taken Peter to different musical areas."[33]

Taking the working name Full Blast, the trio quickly became one of Brötzmann's favourite outfits. Speaking in 2009, he said: "I'm still always surprised by it. Michael gives you the image of a kind of sleepy guy but, when he sits behind the drums, he loosens up so much energy, and Marino is the very well-fitting intellectual hat in the middle. It fits quite well together. We use the trio as a base to invite guests like Mats Gustafsson or Ken Vandermark and they all feel very happy with it."[34]

Full Blast subsequently recorded a clutch of arresting albums, including some with sympathetic collaborators including Mars Williams and Keiji Haino (*Crumbling Brain*, 2010), and Ken Vandermark (*Sketches and Ballads*, 2011). They also went on to become Brötzmann's longest-running regular band, touring extensively until almost the very end of his career. By Pliakas's reckoning, by the time of the Covid pandemic, Full Blast had played two hundred concerts in thirty-four countries.[35]

While not every band Brötzmann formed in the 2000s had the longevity of Full Blast, there was another that matched its intensity. In 2008, he put together a new international quartet that saw him, once again, working with Toshinori Kondo, and also brought into the fold two younger musical acquaintances — Italian bassist Massimo Pupillo and Norwegian drummer Paal Nilssen-Love.

Pupillo (born 1969) played electric bass in the Rome-based trio Zu, formed in 1997 with baritone saxophonist Luca T. Mai and drummer Jacopo Battaglia. While the instrumentation suggested something like a conventional jazz trio, their debut album, *Bromio* (released in 1999 and featuring guest trumpeter Roy Paci), revealed a rhythmically complex, aggressively confrontational sound that borrowed liberally from hardcore punk and math-rock, coming across like a brass-driven variation on European prog, with some of the frantic, cartoonish energy of John Zorn's Naked City. Zu were also serial collaborators and recorded a string of albums with noted improvisers: *The Zu Side of the Chadbourne* (2000) with maverick US guitarist Eugene Chadbourne; *Igneo* (2002) with Ken Vandermark, Jeb Bishop and Fred Lonberg-Holm; *Radiale* (2004) with Vandermark and Hamid Drake; and *How to Raise an Ox* (2006) with Mats Gustafsson. Some kind of collaboration with Brötzmann was inevitable.

As a child, Paal Nilssen-Love (born 1974) learned drums on the kit belonging to his father, who ran a jazz club in Stavanger. "I've known him from when he was very young, as his father introduced me to him,"[36] Brötzmann remembered. By the time he was a teenager, Nilssen-Love was already playing regularly with veteran Norwegian free-jazz reeds-player Frode Gjerstad, and when he was just nineteen, he formed the trio Element with bassist Ingebrigt Håker Flaten and pianist Håvard Wilk, before moving to Oslo in 1996. By the turn of the 2000s, he'd started to build an international reputation, and began working with Mats Gustafsson — a relationship that proved particularly fruitful: in 2000 they formed the trio The Thing with bassist Håker Flaten. Named after a track on Don Cherry's 1969 album *Where Is Brooklyn*, The Thing's self-titled debut presented two group originals plus four interpretations of Don Cherry tunes, all delivered with a testosterone-drenched free-jazz attack, powered by Nilssen-Love's ferociously muscular drumming. After recording another heavy free-jazz date with Joe McPhee (2001's *She Knows...*), The Thing started to incorporate elements of garage rock into their sound, forging a scorching hybrid of punk and free-jazz energies. 2004's *Garage* included savagely exploded cover versions of tunes by New York alt-rock band Yeah Yeah Yeahs and '60s garage-rock heroes The Sonics, alongside a wildly aggressive group reimagining of a Brötzmann tune, "Eine Kleine Marschmusik" — which Brötzmann had originally recorded as a solo piece on his 1976 FMP album *Brötzmann/Solo* — with Gustafsson's guttural tone and rocketing pyrotechnics underscoring his own personal debt to Brötzmann. In 2006, Brötzmann, Gustafsson and Nilssen-Love recorded a live trio blowout at the Molde Jazz Festival in Norway, released the following year as *The Fat Is Gone,* with the two younger powerhouses pushing the elder Brötzmann to almost preposterously superhuman feats of blowing. He sounds like he's loving every minute of it.

In September 2008, Brötzmann, Kondo, Pupillo and Nilssen-Love took the stage at the famous Bimhuis jazz venue in Amsterdam, and performed a raging set, released in 2009 as *Hairy Bones*. For the most part, the album's two thirty-plus-minute improvisations are as boisterous as one might expect: Pupillo's distorted bass guitar thunders (showing that Brötzmann wasn't quite as finished with electric bass as he'd suggested to Pliakas); Nilssen-Love clatters with a steely precision, deconstructing the Dionysian abandon of free jazz into an unfolding of concatenated semaphore stutters; and Kondo shoots out heavily treated squiggles and sonic tracers, entwining, serpent-like, with Brötzmann's forthright cries. The less crowded moments reveal other shades: Pupillo's high-tensile solo bass interlude is followed by Brötzmann in an almost tender mood, weeping over Kondo's queasy, sci-fi washes.

Following a now familiar Brötzmann tradition, the quartet adopted the title of their first album as the band name and, as Hairy Bones, released another album, 2012's *Snakelust (To Kenji Nakagami)*, dedicated to the outsider Japanese novelist. Recorded live at the Jazz em Agosto festival in Lisbon in 2011, it's even more savage than their first, with Pupillo and Nilssen-Love straining at the limits of endurance throughout the single fifty-minute piece. As on the debut, some of its most thrilling moments come when Brötzmann and Nilssen-Love take centre-stage, digging deep into an *Interstellar Space* sax and drums face-off.

In Nilssen-Love — who Brötzmann told me was "really an extraordinary drummer"[37] — he had found yet another percussionist with whom he could develop a close and often volatile sparring partnership. Their 2009 duo album, *Woodcuts* (recorded live in Oslo the year before), contains an imaginative range of settings across six tracks. While there certainly are a handful of belligerent meltdowns, with Nilssen-Love demonstrating a phenomenal, sustained pulse-time snare technique, there are also quieter moments that succeed in breaking the mould, with supple-wristed brushwork encouraging strangled tarogato ululations and a low tom rumble bringing forth a bubbling alto.

In 2024, the Austrian TROST label released a previously unheard duo studio date from 2015 as *Chicken Shit Bingo*, showcasing an even more meditative and exploratory vibe. Across eight compact improvisations — none longer than seven minutes — Brötzmann concentrates on the tarogato, a cache of clarinets, including a recently-acquired contra-alto, and a bass sax, offering some of his most considered and atmospheric playing, with low, slow tones placed just so. Nilssen-Love brings several hitherto-unused Korean gongs to the session, sounding them out in real time and evoking a kind of ghostly gamelan in the process. It's a captivating lesson in restraint and the power of the simple gesture.

"I like the fight. I have liked that all my life"

It shouldn't come as a surprise, then, that Brötzmann found a place for Nilssen-Love in the Chicago Tentet. In its earliest incarnations, the Tentet has been unusual as a group of almost exclusively American musicians led by a European. But as it developed, this changed, too. Recorded in February 2009 and released the following year, the five-CD box set *3 Nights in Oslo* captures the Chicago Tentet in its final form, with German trombonist Johannes Bauer as the +1 guest. By this time, Hamid Drake and Mars Williams had left the group, to be replaced by Nilssen-Love and Swedish tuba player Per Åke Holmlander, bringing the total Scandinavian contingent up to three including Gustafsson.

It's indicative of a healthy symbiosis between the fertile improvising communities in Chicago and Scandinavia, which began with Gustafsson's arrival on the Chicago scene. "He was important because he kept coming back," says Vandermark. "He developed a dynamic with the scene here, which has continued until this day, really. He's always been a part of what's happening in terms of the interaction between Europe and this city, since the mid-90s and his returning over and over again kind of built things up and created a bridge to what was happening in Scandinavia."[38]

But it's also clear that the Chicago Tentet provided a robust consolidation of that bridge — and one entirely in keeping with Brötzmann's key role as an international catalyst. Much as the *Machine Gun* band was a concerted attempt to bring together European improvisers from different countries for a collective endeavour, the Chicago Tentet became, under Brötzmann's guidance, an opportunity to forge strong and lasting intercontinental links that transcended borders and petty parochialism.

3 Nights in Oslo also reveals another major change that radically altered the direction of the Tentet. In 2009, Brötzmann told me: "A couple of years ago, we decided to throw away all the scores and papers and we just decided to improvise with ten — at the moment eleven — people. We all had the feeling we don't need it anymore."[39] Vandermark recalled: "We made the large jump from working hard with compositions to trying something that was totally improvised. Because the band was ten or eleven people, trying to improvise together for the first time without any kind of pre-organised material, the first forays into that weren't 100 percent successful, so we went back to working with pieces again for a short time. Then Peter just said, 'Forget it, we're going to improvise.'"[40]

Brötzmann wasn't just aware of the inherent challenges in this approach — he positively welcomed them: "Of course, it's quite a big risk. To improvise with ten people onstage with nothing — it can go wrong. I like the risk. I like the fight. I have liked that all my life."[41]

Brötzmann's curatorial attitude towards the Tentet comes to the fore across *3 Nights in Oslo*, with three of the five discs devoted to smaller groupings investigating a wide range of moods and approaches: Sonore is the blustering sax trio of Brötzmann, Gustafsson and Vandermark; Survival Unit III is McPhee and Zerang, with Lonberg-Holm adding cello and electronics; Zerang and Nilssen-Love play a sensitive percussion duet; and the Trombone Choir has Bauer and Bishop joined by McPhee and Holmlander for a gale of snuffling gusts. But the first and last discs capture the entire eleven-man behemoth in cacophonous, Walls-of-Jericho group improvisation, generating more raw energy than seems possible from a collection of mainly nineteenth-century acoustic instruments. In these bravura spontaneous orchestrations, the Chicago Tentet pushes beyond "Machine Gun" and "Alarm," past "Globe Unity" and even Coltrane's "Ascension," all of which relied, to a greater or lesser degree, on an organising melodic or structural kernel, finally embracing absolute freedom in the large group setting.

At this point, the Tentet was operating along the lines of what the British jazz critic Charles Fox defined as "participatory democracy."[42] "It's very good to delegate responsibility to the younger guys," Brötzmann told me. "Everybody is asked to put his 100 percent into the whole process of the music."[43] In conversation with Gerard Rouy, he expanded the point: "If you get people involved, if you give them responsibility, if you let them have the freedom to decide for themselves what and how to do things, I think that makes the music really alive."[44]

Moreover, in a very real sense, for Brötzmann, this idea transcended mere musical concerns:

"I've always seen this music as more than just formalistic and aesthetics. As I get older, I see it more and more as a kind of social movement of what is possible… You can see and feel how people can learn to live with this situation and feel comfortable with it and investing their energy in whatever they are able to do; not only in the music, but by helping to organise for the band. One person turns out to be better at making phone calls than the others, everybody does his part for the whole band as a family, as a kind of community… I'm not so naïve to think that we could transfer it to a [wider] community. But if people learn to work this way, they can pass it on to their kids, to other comrades around them. Just to know that these things are possible is already a small step in the right direction, I would say… In politics I always was, let's put it this way, something like a socialist."[45]

Certainly, this idea chimes with Marxist critic Ben Watson's view of the improviser's role:

"With Free Improvisation, the composer genius has been brought down to earth, liberated from the alienation of his desk and redefined as a practical leader and fellow worker, open to questioning by the collective and subject to instant recall. In being open, yet spurred by the most progressive ideas available on the planet, Free Improvisation resembles the workers' council, the most radically democratic institution of the twentieth century: it is *that* heroic and utopian."[46]

Brötzmann may well have balked at this doggedly socialist language. It's certainly true that, as the years went on, he distanced himself from the explicit leftism of his youth, increasingly embracing a less strident but perhaps even more genuinely heartfelt sense of humanist-utopian collectivism — as his hopes for the Tentet make clear. In this respect, I suspect he would have preferred drummer Steve Noble's take:

> "A young journalist asked me, 'Where does politics fit in?' and I said, 'Well, it doesn't really, apart from we are some musicians who walk on stage, who haven't decided what to do, we're all soloists, we're all composers, we're all equals.' That's how I would pronounce my politics. I know some might say that's close to anarchism but it's not about being in a club. It's about respecting individuals."[47]

It should be noted that much of Brötzmann's democratic impulse for the Tentet manifested as a very real reluctance to function in a conventional leadership role: "I don't see myself at all as the kind of band leader who decides what kind of music has to be played," he said. "Sometimes I say yes and no to certain things organisation-wise, but I never tell anyone what they have to play; that time is over."[48]

Ken Vandermark was well placed to analyse the values and the leadership style that Brötzmann brought to the Tentet. He told me:

> "The focus was definitely the musical side of it, but I think that also it represented ideas that he has about social structures. He had strong aesthetics for the band but, at the same time, really struggled with trying to tell people what to do. He just

kind of indicated by action. I think there was a social aspect to why he was working in these large groups his whole career and why he always put the responsibility on an equal plane. He comes from a generation that really came to the fore in the '60s. It was a lot of fighting the status quo at that time. You see it with the English improvisers, too: that the composer was perceived as a dictator, and a motion away from composed materials was also a social construct, not just a musical one. I think that thread of thinking ran through all kinds of things in the arts in that period. And I think that Peter, coming from a different generation from everybody in the band aside from Joe McPhee — they're coming from a perspective about leadership representing some horrible, horrible things. I think that social aspect of political power, he was exploring that on some levels with the Tentet, that he was saying, 'What happens when you don't 'lead' the band by dictating what the band should do?' and really fighting that. He's responding to what he sees as the problems with political discourse. With a larger group, I think that he's trying to find a solution to that kind of power play that he sees as dysfunctional in politics — and he's applying that in a socio-musical context with the Tentet, and perhaps with other bands he's working with."[49]

However well-intentioned, it's also true that Brötzmann's abdication of the leadership role could sometimes make things difficult for the other musicians involved. Vandermark explained:

"He didn't articulate directly what he was looking for. I think he was trying to show what he wanted by how he played, and expected everybody to step up and contribute who they were and what they thought of the music at the time by making musical statements and not discussing the music in terms of aesthetics. When people asked him questions, he would dance around it in lots of different ways. When conversations came up, when the band was at times struggling with what was happening and what wasn't happening, he would very quickly discontinue the conversation if he felt that it was providing guidelines or rules. If it was like, 'Well, we should do this and not this'; he really stepped in and said, 'This is really not what this is about, and I don't want to do this if the band is about these kinds of things.' And that leads to problems from my standpoint, in confusion, when you're not willing to articulate your ideas to a group with eleven people, who are all trying to move in similar directions with music that's completely improvised. There were times when I could have benefitted from a clearer picture of what he was dissatisfied with. Not to tell me what to do, but to give a clearer picture of what not to do, because there were times when I felt like I was doing something clear and he seemed very responsive to it and happy with it, but there were other times, not necessarily playing the same material but working in a similar fashion, and he was very dissatisfied. Then I'm left with the question of 'OK, what is it that's not happening here?' and then he wouldn't tell you. That's a struggle."[50]

Mats Gustafsson put it more succinctly: "Peter is the worst band leader I've known in my life, and no one else has taught me so much."[51] Brötzmann, for his part, shrugged off such issues, offering a very simple analysis of the dynamics underpinning the Tentet: "The main thing is, it's fun. To be together with good people, to be on the road, to meet every night some other people, you have situations, and you have to make the best out of it, and everybody works on it. It's really great fun. That's why I choose to play, to be on the road, to play jazz music."[52]

Like many an idealistic venture before it, however, the Chicago Tentet contained the seeds of its own downfall. In November 2012, Brötzmann released the following announcement:

"14 years… The Chicago Tentet

That's a long time for a 10/11 piece band. Time to say goodbye? Time to stop? For sure time to think about the future!

There are a couple of reasons why I decided to stop it, at least for the moment. The first one is the everlasting critical economic situation, actually with no expectation for better times — we Germans and Americans can't count on support from our cultural departments.

The second, much more important, is the music. Hanging together for such a long time — with just a couple of small changes — automatically brings a lot of routine. In general nothing against, you need it sometimes to survive, but if it gets so far that one can't exist without the other — music is over.

In 2011 with the weekends in London and Wuppertal we have reached the peak of what is possible in improvisation and communication with an immense input from all of us. For my taste it is better to stop on the peak and look around than gliding down in the mediocre fields of 'nothing more to say' bands.

I love to work with larger ensembles and I won't say, 'That's it,' but I need a bit of time to think about some changes, the financial situation is important and in a way the financial situation forms and builds sometimes the music. Who can afford to travel with a quintet nowadays, you see what I mean?

I think the next fall will answer the question about the future of a NEW tentet.

Tokyo, 17th of November 2012
P Brötzmann

WE NEED AGAIN AND AGAIN A MORE ADVENTUROUS SPIRIT

Excuse my language A KICK IN THE ASS and what we call in German VERUNSICHERUNG"

Certainly, the "critical economic situation" had been a pressing concern since the beginning. In 2009, Brötzmann told me: "After nearly every gig, I ask the guys, 'Shall we go on?' because money is so small but as long as everybody says, 'OK, we do it,' then we do it."[53] He had, in truth, never particularly let finances influence his artistic decisions. "Making money is fine," he said, "I've nothing against it, but the first thing, I think, should be the work and what you want to do. I've had my hard times and I was quite often ready to sell the horns."[54] As he points out above, most European and American artists generally receive none of the generous state subsidies that Scandinavian artists are able to take for granted, which led to the Tentet sourcing funds from wherever they could: when Vandermark was awarded a $265,000 MacArthur

Fellowship — known as the "genius grant" — in 1999, the first thing he announced was that he'd be investing in the Tentet's US tour the following year. Even so, in the end, fiscal realities outweighed Brötzmann's utopian dreams. In 2013, he told me: "The last tour, we had ten gigs in fourteen days — even a couple of good-paying gigs — but what was left was not even enough to bring to the bank. I feel a little bit responsible for the guys I'm working with, and I can't do that anymore."[55]

Ultimately, though, Brötzmann's decision to disband the Tentet was more to do with his need for "verunsicherung," or uncertainty. In a distinct echo of his departure from Globe Unity Orchestra, Brötzmann largely decided to call it a day because he felt the music was stagnating. He said:

"I had the feeling, even if we reached really a very high level, some of the guys felt very comfortable with what we have reached. This music lives from surprises, from unsureness, from challenges, and that was going away maybe a little bit. I could have fired a couple of guys, and could have asked somebody else, but I thought that wouldn't have been the solution of the problem. I don't know if there was a solution, because to go on in the same way might not bring a band further, music-wise. So, for me it was the right moment to say, 'OK, until here we have reached a lot, high-level music, and it's better to stop instead of working it down to some average improvising band.' I didn't want that."[56]

"To be honest, I had seen it coming," Vandermark said.

"He had voiced concerns about the way the band was working as a unit. Definitely concerns about it becoming a stock performance — that the Tentet comes out and 'does their show.' He fought, from the beginning of the band to the end, to prevent that from happening. That's a very hard thing to do. You walk on stage and, even if you're a radical artist, and I would put Peter in that category, there's a part of you that wants to communicate — not only to the people you're working with but also to the audience on some level. When you walk out and do a kind of performing that garners a strong response in a positive way from an audience, it's very hard to fight that, to keep the thing fresh, to take chances and to fail. Peter was really 100 percent willing to push the group to failure in order to succeed from a creative standpoint. In that way, he was a fantastic leader, because he completely pushed the band to try to take chances. It wasn't always clear to me how he was expressing those things, but he was always trying to keep us from falling into clichés — and it's very easy to do."[57]

Along the way, Brötzmann had taken steps to prevent the inevitable stagnation by inviting unusual guests to sit in with the Tentet. One celebrated example was John Tchicai's appearance with the band at the Unlimited-festival, in Wels, Austria, in November 2011. Vandermark remembered:

"When John Tchicai played with the band, it's this massive group, it's got its reputation, and John played flute! There's so much sound that comes out of that group and he pulls a flute out. I looked at Peter and saw him just smile, laugh and shake his head. But that's exactly the kind of thing that Peter wants. That's John confronting us. He's saying, 'OK, you can be loud but now let's deal with this.' He's throwing it at us and that's what Peter wants from all the people he collaborates with. He wants to be challenged. It's completely part of his make-up and wanting that challenge from all sorts of people from all sides is an act of generosity. He's a provocateur — and that's where his music and his art come from. A big part of his aesthetic is based on that. To see what happens."[58]

Another of Brötzmann's favourite provocateurs was Japanese wild-man Keiji Haino, who also appeared with the Tentet at Wels in 2011. Recalling that live performance, Brötzmann chuckled:

"The piece with Keiji was very interesting because some of the members in the band couldn't stand it. I mean you should expect these guys know everything but, with Keiji, some of them... OK, we were on stage, Keiji, as usual, was somewhere hard to find, so the band got already nervous because we are very disciplined. I said, 'OK, let's start,' and we started, and Keiji steamed on stage, plugged in his guitar and started to scream. It was really a beautiful chaos. That was the thing I wanted — to get the guys out of their beauty sleep, in a way."[59]

But no amount of disruption could stem what Brötzmann saw as the decline into familiarity. So, still basking in the glow of what he considered the group's pinnacle gigs in Wuppertal and at London's Café OTO in 2011, Brötzmann ended the Chicago Tentet's phenomenal fourteen-year run as one of the most powerful and inventive improvising groups of all time. "Maybe I was a little proud when we could sustain such a high quality for so long, and always pushing each other and challenging each other — but that, I was afraid, was going away. It's no reason to be sad about it. We did it for fourteen years. It was a good time."[60]

I Surrender Dear

"I hate your fucking instrument. Would you like to play?"

At the beginning of the 2010s, Brötzmann had two important trios on the go, both featuring powerful drummers. One of these which he dubbed the Heavyweights[1] — saw him reconnecting with a couple of old Japanese free-jazz comrades, pianist Masahiko Satoh and drummer Takeo Moriyama. Brötzmann had been an admirer of Moriyama's work for a long time:

> "In the very early '70s, there was this trio, Yosuke Yamashita, the piano player, with Akira Sakata on sax and with Takeo Moriyama, the drummer. Our trio, the Van Hove/Bennink trio, and this trio always were fighting about the jobs. Our trio tried a lot of other little things, a lot of other ways, but with the Yamashita trio, it was power play free jazz — very well done. It was really a very good trio. You don't find a drummer like Takeo Moriyama anymore. He has studied some years in the States and his way of playing the drums reminded me always of Joe Jones and Philly Joe Jones: really jazz, singing in the drums. I mean, he tunes it, he knows the skins are not really just skins. He knows what to do with them."[2]

Since those early days with Van Hove — and notwithstanding his '80s collaborations with Cecil Taylor — Brötzmann had hardly ever worked with a pianist. "The piano, it's an instrument made for European traditional music," he explained over the phone from his home in Wuppertal.

"If you work with the piano — whether you want or not — you start to think in harmonics, in melodies. What I hate is all that classical, virtuoso, European piano playing. That's why, when I was very young, I was trying to understand what Cage was doing and I was listening to his prepared piano pieces where no playing is happening. And then I was lucky to meet Nam June Paik who was actually in his very beginning and his education a piano player. And he was creating instruments, for example when I was his assistant here in the Wuppertal exhibition with a lot of prepared pianos. That was quite a good lesson for me — that you can use instruments in any way you want to use them. But these very modernistic piano players just exist out of technique. If you look through my shelves here, most of my vinyl or CDs are piano players — James P. Johnson, Fats Waller. I am a friend of stride piano players like that. I mean, Ellington comes from that. Even Monk comes from that, you can hear it in his playing. All this early piano playing in the jazz history I like very much because these guys, if you look at their hands sometimes on the photographs, they are working class people's hands. They couldn't do the very sensitive bullshit; they had to treat it somehow to get something out of it."[3]

All of which made his choice to play with Satoh in the Heavyweights a curious one. "Satoh, he has a very bright way of intellectual playing but on the other hand, he really can do the heavy shit too, so it's interesting with him," Brötzmann explained. "I think he found for himself a very strong and intelligent way to handle it and really has found his own way of doing things. He gets some strong sounds out of the thing, and I like that very much."[4]

The Heavyweights' sole album, 2012's *Yatagarasu*, is a mammoth session in every way. There's an enormous grandness of scale in Satoh's architecture, in the way he combines the tumultuous, declamatory chords of McCoy Tyner with the leaping geometrics of Cecil Taylor, creating a cavernous environment that amplifies the emotional and dramatic impact of Brötzmann's playing. There's a booming threat in the constant, burning ferocity of Moriyama's boiling snare, attacked with an incandescent insistence that recalls the brawn drummer Marc Edwards brought to Cecil Taylor's *Dark to Themselves*. And there's an elemental implacability in Brötzmann's monumental tenor tone, staring down the craggy, desert-scorched rock face of eternity. *Yatagarasu* sounds like three restless gods of war at play.

The other major trio Brötzmann initiated around this time was, to a degree, the result of happenstance that saw him thrown together with two British players: bassist John Edwards and drummer Steve Noble.

John Edwards (born 1964) began playing bass around 1987, and by the beginning of the '90s had already begun gigging with improvisers on the London scene, including drummer Roger Turner, saxophonist Lol Coxhill and vocalists Maggie Nichols and Phil Minton. By the middle of the decade, he'd established himself as a mainstay of the capital's free-improv community. Steve Noble (born 1960) studied with Nigerian master-drummer Elkan Ogunde before going on to tour with avant-garde jazz-pop group Rip, Rig + Panic alongside Don Cherry's stepdaughter, vocalist Neneh Cherry, and appearing on two of their albums: 1982's *I Am Cold* (with Don Cherry) and 1983's *Attitude*. He, too, gravitated towards free improvisation, and struck up a relationship with Derek Bailey, taking part in Bailey's Company Weeks in 1987, 1989 and 1990. Like Edwards, he was soon ensconced as one of the busiest and most in-demand improvisers on the London circuit.

Both possessed of quicksilver imaginations, laser-sharp attention to detail and unstinting energy, Edwards and Noble naturally began playing together, and by the 2000s had become the most consistently inventive and downright entertaining rhythm section in the UK, playing with a host of musicians and forming the backbone of high-energy trios with saxophonist Alan Wilkinson and guitarist/clarinettist Alex Ward. With Wilkinson, they recorded the full-throated free-jazz date *Obliquity*, in 2006, and with Ward — as the trio N.E.W. — they cut the serrated No-Wave/free-jazz collision of *NEWtoons* in 2008. They also provided the backline for the wildly propulsive avant-garde organ trio Decoy with pianist Alexander Hawkins, recording, in 2009, both the trio's debut, *Spirit*, and the first of a handful of collaborations with Joe McPhee, *OTO*, captured live at the eponymous London venue.

After first opening its doors in 2008, Café OTO had swiftly established itself as the premier purveyor of experimental and improvised music in the capital. Tucked away on an unprepossessing but bustling side street in the then decidedly ungentrified Dalston area in the Northeast of the city, the sparsely decorated former paint factory built its reputation by programming not just local improvisers but also inviting international musicians to perform. Often as not, when visitors came to play, they were teamed with Noble and Edwards, who became a kind of unofficial house rhythm section at OTO.

One of the first major stars to undertake a residency there was Brötzmann, who, in January 2010, settled in for a three-night stay.

Released in 2012 as the inaugural release on Café OTO's in-house record label, OTOROKU, *The Worse the Better* documents the first time Brötzmann, Edwards and Noble played together, on the second night of that 2010 residency. It's as busy as the night-time streets just outside the venue's wide window wall. Edwards and Noble are on extremely hyperactive form, with Noble, in particular, given to tinkering barrages of miniature detail. With Edwards cutting from thick-fingered dabs at the strings to saw-toothed arco, and Brötzmann leaping straight into the alto's highest possible registers, they create the impression of a universe rushing towards what psychedelic mystic Terence McKenna termed "maximum novelty": that bright, flashing moment when all possible information is suddenly made available in one single, overwhelming burst. But rather than reaching that obliterating crescendo, the trio slides away from it, into a slinking deceleration, with Brötzmann hunching into a slow, wounded moan before sitting out for a bass and drum section — a simple development of the basic jazz construct of "trading fours." Incredibly, Brötzmann is, here, still finding new sonic ground. There's a point around halfway in where he launches into a flickering, pixelated signal that seems to contain too much data for the ear to fully comprehend — as if, rather than changing the way he's playing, Brötzmann is rewiring the very act of hearing. Convinced of this trio's near limitless potential, Brötzmann decided to keep it together as a touring unit, which he dubbed the English Trio.

Around this time Brötzmann also began working with Jason Adasiewicz, a young vibraphone player out of Chicago. Born in 1977, Adasiewicz studied jazz drums at DePaul University and only took up vibraphone after he quit his studies. In his early years as a vibraphonist, he was active in Chicago's omnivorous indie-rock scene and was, by his own admission, not especially tuned in to the jazz avant-garde. "I didn't even know who the AACM was," he said, "until I dropped out of school and started working at the Jazz Record Mart."[5] It was while putting in time at this venerable record store — owned by Bob Koestler, founder of long-standing Chicago jazz and blues label, Delmark Records — that Adasiewicz first started to pick up on the jazz leftfield. "I worked there along with a lot of Chicago musicians like [trumpeter] Josh Berman, [saxophonist] Keefe Jackson and [drummer] Frank Rosaly, and I found out about all these artists. Peter was definitely one of them, and that was at the height of him coming to Chicago."[6]

It was 2011 when Adasiewicz first crossed paths with Brötzmann. "Peter was in town, and he came out to a show at a bar called the Hideout where I was playing with a trio that [cornetist] Rob Mazurek had with myself and [Tortoise drummer and percussionist] John Herndon. He was just hanging out in the back, and we get done and he pulls me aside. Some of the first words out of his mouth were, 'I hate your fucking instrument. Would you like to play?' So, that's how we started."[7]

Despite Brötzmann's professed dislike of the vibraphone, it's easy to see why he was keen to work with Adasiewicz. *Going All Fancy* documents their very first performance, recorded at the Vision Festival in New York in June 2011. That year, the festival honoured Brötzmann's seventieth year, inviting him to play in a few different configurations. On the festival's second night, Brötzmann appeared in quartet with Joe McPhee, William Parker and bassist Eric Revis; a quintet

with Ken Vandermark, Mars Williams, Kent Kessler and Paal
Nilssen-Love; and a duo with Adasiewicz. The duo date is a
revelation, with Brötzmann clearly lifted by Adasiewicz's hard-
hitting physicality, but also drawn into more a contemplative
soulfulness by the vibes' ethereal washes. "Within my style,"
said Adasiewicz, "I think he saw the percussiveness and the
intensity, but there was room for him to play a ballad. And
[in me] there was someone that wanted to accompany him
playing a ballad, and not trying to push him into his comfy
intensity that he was so known for. He was a balladeer too. He
was a crooner."[8]

Brötzmann and Adasiewicz cut another duo date, *Mollie's
in the Mood*, recorded live at the Hideout in Chicago in
September 2012 and, like their debut, released in a limited
edition on Brötzmann's partially reactivated BRÖ label. The
following year, in July 2013, Brötzmann, Noble and Edwards
recorded *Soulfood Available* at the Ljubljana Jazz Festival.
Then Brötzmann pulled a surprise move by asking Adasiewicz
to join the trio with Steve Noble and John Edwards, effectively
merging the two working bands. This new quartet made their
debut in August 2013 at the A L'Arme! Festival in Berlin and,
the same month, played at a two-day residency at Cafe OTO.

Mental Shake, released on OTOROKU in 2014, captures the
last set on the second night at OTO, revealing the incredibly
dense yet thoughtful new sounds the quartet were making.
A first glance, the notion of adding vibes to the trio's already
extremely busy and crowded attack seems like a potentially
awkward meeting. Yet it works admirably, thanks in large part
to Adasiewicz's unerring ability to find innovative and creative
ways of engaging with the other musicians. When Noble
rolls out a clatter of chimes and gongs, the vibes lock into a
sharp, metallic pattering. When bass, drums and sax tumble

into boiling turmoil, Adasiewicz floats over the top with an echoing, celestial shimmer, as though glancing up from the furious engine to navigate by the stars. And when the drums drop out, meticulously placed note clusters from Adasiewicz provide a thrilling tension, provoking a plaintive lyricism from Brötzmann's rasping tarogato. It feels like eavesdropping on a new language being born.

At the heart of this quartet's astonishing symbiotic rapport was the deep, rhythmic connection Adasiewicz immediately struck up with Noble — something that Brötzmann had fully anticipated.

"He saw how much Steve and I were going to click," Adasiewicz said. "We both embrace swing. The language still comes from swing, and we're both not afraid to do that, within whatever space we're in. That's also what he loved about Han and what he loved about Hamid. I think that's what he loved about drummers. I'm from a drummer standpoint, too, and, whenever I play with Steve, I always feel like it's just so natural. From the first gig, Steve and I were like, 'Where have you been?'"[9]

Noble, meanwhile, had been deepening his own connection to Brötzmann. *I Am Here Where Are You* is a red-blooded duo date recorded live in Brussels in January 2013. "It was a gig that didn't really pay much," Noble recalled, "and John already had a gig he could do so he went off and did that, and I played a duo with Peter — and that became a regular thing. John is a busy musician so there were times when a duo was quite the right thing to do. I think we did two or three duo tours."[10]

The opening title track of *I Am Here Where Are You* begins with Brötzmann unfurling one of his instantly recognisable yearning fanfares — a move he would increasingly employ to begin a performance — with Noble straight away crashing into a split-second hyperkinetic response of boiling energy. "He'd often start with that fanfare," Noble said.

> "I used to love that because you've had a different day each day — you might be traveling, you might not be traveling, you might have had a shit journey, you might have had a good journey — but it's his way of just going straight in, and then I think there is a lot of interplay, and who knows where it would go? It might keep going upwards till you get above the clouds into the sunshine, or it might just be that after a couple of minutes it's like, 'No, let's take it somewhere else'"[11]

That's very much in evidence on *I Am Here Where Are You*, on which, after the opening barrage, the duo quickly find room for a more spacious, quasi-ritualistic interlude, with Noble setting up rolling tom patterns and Brötzmann wrenching thorny curlicues from the tarogato. But it's also readily apparent just how much Brötzmann enjoyed being goaded into action by Noble, yet another drummer quite adept at matching Brötzmann's intensity with his own heroic athleticism. "We did a trio with [pianist] Keith Tippett," Noble told me.

> "I remember on the first night, I'm in the middle, I've got Peter on my left and Keith on my right. Peter's going for it, and I'm thinking, 'Woah, you've just taken a step up'; and I thought, 'Right, I'm going to try and get up to your level.' So, I do that and I'm pushing him and then he moves up again, and then I move up again, and then he moves up again — so you're always pushing each other."[12]

"It's quite a challenge for me. I was never afraid of that"

Despite Brötzmann's life-long love affair with the drums, in 2015 he began a fruitful collaboration that was entirely drum-free. It was a pairing that would move away from jazz and conventional free improvisation, taking him beyond familiar comfort zones, and would endure right up almost to the end of his life.

Heather Leigh was born in West Virginia in 1976 and raised in Texas. While still a teenager, she started experimenting with DIY music-making. "I bought my own Tascam 4-track recorder in high school and my earliest recordings were me overdubbing acoustic guitar and voice," she said. "When I started playing and recording myself, every aspect was an improvisation."[13] She was at university when she first started playing the pedal steel guitar. An amplified cousin of the Hawaiian lap-steel guitar, played in the horizontal position with foot pedals to change its pitch, the pedal steel guitar has long been a staple of American country music, but Leigh approached it with an intuitive, self-taught curiosity: "Not having proper training on any instrument and not really being drawn to sound from a technical perspective... meant that, even from my earliest days playing music, I wasn't trying to sound like anyone else.[14]

In the 1990s, Leigh began playing with Houston-based underground acid-folk improvising duo Tom and Christina Carter — aka Charalambides — and, at the beginning of the 2000s, formed the duo Scorces with Christina Carter. Their self-titled 2001 debut album is a deeply transporting affair featuring two long-form drone meditations for organ and voices. But it was as a pedal steel player that Leigh would go on to make the biggest impact. After relocating to Scotland and settling in Glasgow in 2004, she was soon deeply immersed in the most subterranean levels of the international DIY underground. In 2005, she recorded the coruscating free-jazz/noise date *Blood Shadow Rampage* as part of Dream/Aktion Unit alongside Thurston Moore on guitar, double bassist Matt Heyner of the No-Neck Blues Band, drummer Chris Corsano and alto sax firebreather Paul Flaherty, and appeared with eccentric Houston-based outsider artist Jandek in a performance subsequently released in 2008 as *Glasgow Sunday 2005*. She also pursued a solo aesthetic, achieving considerable acclaim with her first proper studio date, 2015's *I Abused Animal*, which proposed a hypnotic suite of vulnerable folk-song confessionals with pedal steel accompaniment ranging from woozy slide to roaring overdrive.

In 2015, Leigh was invited to perform at the Glasgow-based Tectonics festival of new and experimental music. She recalled: "They said, 'You can play solo but, if you want to do a collaboration, we're really into the idea of you playing with someone that you've never played with before.' I had in the back of my mind that I'd like to play with Peter. I knew his music and I had seen him play when I was a teenager living in Texas. I had met him in Glasgow when he was playing with Paal Nilssen-Love the year before, but I assumed he wasn't familiar with my music or even the instrument. So, I just emailed him and said, 'Let's do this.'"[15]

"I had, to tell you the truth, no idea what a pedal steel is. I had to look that up!" Brötzmann laughed. "Then I learned that it's used in country and bluegrass music and so on. But, from the first soundcheck I realised that, with Heather, it is quite a different thing and it's quite a challenge for me. I was never afraid of that."[16]

Leigh continued: "I was fully prepared that, when I asked him to play, he would say, 'Fuck off, I don't know who you are, why would I play with you?' But it's a testament to his openness and commitment to the music that he could say, 'I'll do it and if it's a shite concert, who cares? We tried.' And then we played that first concert, and we just knew this is the start of something special."[17]

Indeed, the duo's first album — 2016's *Ears Are Filled with Wonder*, recorded live in Krakow in 2015 — shows both players stretching out into hitherto unexplored territory. Leigh deals in an overtly psychedelic palette: providing a queasy cushion of microtonal arpeggios for Brötzmann's plaintive tarogato; matching the clarinet's wild, altissimo keening with high, Hendrix-like swoops of distortion; and embracing the tenor sax's smoky tone with a haunted, dreamlike swirl. There's a grace and solemnity about it that seems a million miles from fidgety free improvisation. "I really can't stand a busy call-and-response improv style," Leigh said. "it's nice to have some space there and just let things develop. We both give each other a lot of space and neither of us are in a supporting role. It's like that music can't happen without one of us there. It can feel quite compositional, like from the beginning to the end is a whole piece."[18] The album's single, twenty-eight-minute improvisation unfolds thoughtfully as a cavernous lament — an abstract, blues-drenched, late-night corollary to Brötzmann's previous string-and-sax work with Japanese koto player Michiyo Yagi.

At this point, the quartet with Adasiewicz, Edwards and Noble was still an ongoing concern. But, by 2016, Brötzmann had started to display signs of restlessness. After a seventeen-year hiatus, he'd started to drink a little again. Some of those in his close orbit detected something like a fractious vibe. Things came to a head in May that year when the quartet were due to play the last date of a tour at the Art Institute in Chicago, and Brötzmann and Adasiewicz argued backstage before the concert. Adasiewicz told me: "I always told myself — just from hearing stories from other cats, whether they were yelled at onstage or yelled at off the stage — the moment something like that happens, I'm walking away. And that's kind of what happened."[19] Adasiewicz quit the band moments before they hit the stage.

"I feel like part of him kind of lives off that friction sometimes within his bands,"[20] Adasiewicz added. Certainly, in the ongoing antagonism present in Brötzmann's relationship with Bennink, and the frustration felt by members of the Chicago Tentet, the frazzled energy of emotional conflict had often been channelled into heightened performances. And that seems to have been the case in the quartet's gig that night. Speaking of a recording of the show (which, to date, remains unreleased), Adasiewicz said: "Listening back upon it, I think it's one of our best. It's unbelievable. We walked onstage, Peter and I were completely at odds, and Steve and John were just, like, 'I don't know what the fuck's happening.'"[21]

The trio with Edwards and Noble limped on for a few months longer, but something had changed. "Steve said they did a show in Moscow [in November 2016]," Adasiewicz recalled. "It was a double bill — him and Heather did a duo and then the trio played. I think Steve said the trio only played for fifteen minutes."[22] By the beginning of 2017, the trio had run its course. Steve Noble told me: "I thought the trio and the duo stuff I was doing with Peter would last at least another year. It was a surprise and a disappointment."[23]

But with Leigh, Brötzmann found a musical collaboration he wanted to continue exploring. The duo toured extensively, becoming Brötzmann's favoured live configuration and yielding a couple more live albums. Then, in 2017, they recorded their first studio session, released in 2018 as *Sparrow Nights*. Whereas the live dates tended be long, continuous sets, *Sparrow Nights* comprises smaller, more deliberately sculpted pieces, ranging from just two to thirteen minutes. Even so, the intrinsic mood and vocabulary they'd developed remains essentially unchanged. A thick smoke of apocalyptic melancholy lies over these improvisations. "This World Is Love" has Leigh conjuring a dreamy, two-note wash over which Brötzmann moans in aching despair. For "This Time Around," Leigh pushes her axe into the red, with strafing screeches of controlled feedback summoning desperate sax slurs. The aptly named "River of Sorrow" unfurls an otherworldly hum, with the clarinet cawing like a crow against a blood-red sky.

Interviewing Brötzmann and Leigh over coffees among Cafe OTO's afternoon laptop crowd in September 2019, it was obvious to me that the two shared a very warm and intimate affection, which had been deepened by several years in each other's company. "We've been around the world at this point," Leigh said. "It's fantastic. We like travelling together. We have very similar interests outside the music — nature, botanical gardens, museums — so it's very easy to travel and see things. What happens during the day, of course, influences the music that we play in the evening."[24]

It was an easy familiarity that Steve Noble could entirely relate to. "He wants to be on the road all the time," he told me. "A day has twenty-four hours in it. A gig lasts for about one hour. So, there he is with somebody that he enjoys the company of."[25]

Moreover, Brötzmann valued the new sonic challenges the duo presented. "The way I work with Heather is a completely different way of thinking about sounds, about the instrument," he said. "In these years, we have developed a very special way to handle each other so that the whole thing is really getting a kind of unique universe."[26]

"We're always discovering new things with each concert," Leigh agreed.

> "Consistently, when we're touring and we're playing, we leave the night and think, 'Oh wow, we hit some new shit tonight, something else is happening.' And I have learned so much playing with him. It has been really liberating and it is always a challenge. It's never comfortable and easy. I remember very early on, when we played in Krakow — it was a residency and it was Peter, me, Steve Noble, Joe McPhee, William Parker, Per Åke Holmlander, so I was sort of thrown in with all these guys — and I remember I pulled Peter aside and I said, 'I need to tell you something. I don't read music. I don't talk about music in that way. I just play. I play by feel.' And he said to me, 'I don't even know what a note is!' We shook hands and were like, this is a good start! But it's been very interesting playing on a sort of jazz circuit, a lot of festivals and things like that — and it's been quite amazing how, while sometimes people can be sort of confused or taken aback by it, they're also very embracing of the sounds too. It can be such a great feeling when you're walking off the stage and you can feel the audience are sort of 'What just happened?'"[27]

"It's not the time for just sitting at home and playing nice music"

In his final years, Brötzmann was still tirelessly forging new connections, often with much younger musicians. In August

2019, he recorded *B.A.N* with Steve Noble and Brussels-based electric bassist Farida Amadou (born 1989), and the following month at his penultimate Café OTO residency, he and Leigh played with twenty-six-year old French percussionist Camille Emaille, who he'd met the previous year at a festival in Chile. Yet, looking ahead to the state of the music in the twenty-first century, he reserved some misgivings about up-coming generations of improvisers. "They come mostly from a completely different background nowadays," he sighed.

> "It started years ago when certain conservatories and music schools took free improvisation or free jazz as a part of their programme, which is from the very beginning a complete contradiction. And now you have, worldwide, these so-called educated musicians. They learn everywhere the same shit and what they don't learn is what to do with it. They can play, of course, all up and down and everything, they know everything — and it's good to know — but they have no idea what to do with it. It's so very rare that you find, from all these hundreds of musicians, thousands every year going out of conservatories, there is nearly never one you would say, 'Oh!' What they learn to do — beside music, counterpoint, composition and things — is how to sell themselves, which is already the wrong start. They have special classes about marketing now! If it goes on like this then I can't be too optimistic. Young people make a band, and it has to be a production on CD. It has to be successful shit. They don't learn that the person itself doing it is the most important thing, to find out what's going on with yourself. You have to be thrown into cold water and swim — and get better. And then, while doing that, you might develop an idea of where you want to swim to."[28]

For Brötzmann, this criticism wasn't just about the stultifying effects of too much education on a young musician. It was bound up in what he saw as a fundamental disconnection from the essential social — even spiritual — foundations of jazz:

"I think what fascinated me from the very beginning in this music was that it has a lot to do with just a normal life, the difficulties, a lot to do with surviving. People nowadays, I think they don't understand the blues anymore. I think people are missing this kind of experience and this kind of knowledge. I mean, remember, when was Martin Luther King shot? Before that, Black people were still hanging in the trees in the South or disappeared in the swamps. That was still happening, churches were still burning. And that was my entrance into trying to understand this music, in a very naïve way, of course. But I'm still learning. I remember, years ago, I played a concert in Atlanta, and I had a day off. It was a Sunday, and I went in one of the churches, a Black Baptist church. Of course, I was the only white face, and I hid myself a little bit behind a pillar, but I saw a Reverend there on the stage. I didn't understand everything that he was talking about but the way he was doing it, I learned in these short minutes a little bit more about bringing what you have to say over to the people."[29]

If Brötzmann's words, spoken in 2013, seem to signal a lack of faith in younger musicians' commitment to the rage and yearning that historically burnt at the heart of free jazz, he was surely unaware of the rise of a new generation that would later forcefully address important issues that remain every bit as urgent as they were in the 1960s. "Liberation-oriented" free-jazz collective Irreversible Entanglements came together in 2015 after meeting at an event organised by Musicians Against Police

Brutality in response to the NYPD's fatal shooting of twenty-eight-year-old African American man Akai Gurley, and have vociferously spoken out against racism and colonialism across a series of albums beginning with their 2017 self-titled debut. Similarly, trumpeter and vocalist Jaimie Branch made trenchant criticisms of racism and right-wing US politics on tracks like "Prayer for Amerikkka pt. 1 & 2" from 2019's *Fly or Die II: Bird Dogs of Paradise.*

Yet, these outspoken younger artists remain something of an exception. And Brötzmann isn't the only elder statesman to have bemoaned — however mistakenly — a seeming lack of political awareness in contemporary avant-garde musicians. In 2019, Archie Shepp said:

> "I don't think that the musicians since my period have taken up the idea of musical response, I think that the young people today are more pacifistic when it comes to fascism and neo-fascism. Unfortunately, they are content to accept right-wing, conservative ideas, they don't want to engage those politically, they don't want to get involved. I think the ideas of today are more of financial success and to gain popularity. Music, especially Black music, no longer addresses the themes that concern politics."[30]

There was, perhaps inevitably, in Brötzmann's reflections also a certain amount of nostalgia for his roaring youth: "Music in our early days — you can ask Evan, you can ask Bennink about it — it was, beside making music, it was a social adventure in a way. I think that's very, very important. You didn't exchange your thoughts and ideas via the net, you really had the guys together. It was for me always the main important thing about playing this kind of music." Here, he took a puff of his cigar and added with a grin: "Nowadays everybody behaves so nice, nobody's drinking any more, nothing is happening, no playing cards, no poker games."[31]

Right up to the end, Brötzmann was always happy to reconnect with key comrades from those halcyon days. In May 2018, he celebrated the fiftieth anniversary of the recording of *Machine Gun* by convening a trio with von Schlippenbach and Bennink for a gig in Lila Eule, the very same club and former radical left-wing political hub in Bremen where the album had originally been recorded in a single after-hours session. Released in 2019, the album, *Fifty Years After... (Live At The Lila Eule 26.05.18)*, documents that meeting. Half a century on, it would, perhaps, only be natural for the fierce energy that powered *Machine Gun* to have diminished somewhat, and to an extent it had — but not by much. From the opening salvo of Brötzmann's unmistakably throaty tenor bray, it's clear the trio means business. Bennink churns up crashing barrages that seem simultaneously to sit halfway between a skipping swing and a free boil, while von Schlippenbach deals out choppy clusters, eliciting some unforgiving skronk from Brötzmann. Yet, there are some intriguing subtleties at play, too. Playful as ever, Bennink can't help slipping in a slinky shuffle on the brushes here and there, coaxing Monkish phrases from the piano and some bar-walking blues honks from Brötzmann. All in all, these seasoned warhorses sounds like they're having a grand old time.

The CD inner sleeve for *Fifty Years After...* features a touching photo of Brötzmann and von Schlippenbach embracing, with Brötzmann nestling his face into the pianist's shoulder in a display of genuine brotherly affection. But some of the old antagonisms still prevailed. In 2019, Heather Leigh told me: "Last year, we played a festival in Berlin at the old Academy of Arts. The last concert was Schlippenbach, Bennink and Brötzmann, and Peter walked off stage when everyone wanted a bow. He was so angry with Bennink!"[32] Brötzmann chuckled: "It was so terrible. Sometimes I have enough of him."[33]

Much of the revolutionary zeal that powered *Machine Gun* also remained intact in Brötzmann's later years. In 2019 I asked him if, with global fascism on the rise, we need another *Machine Gun*. He deadpanned: "We need a bigger gun."[34] Though tempered by age and experience, his idealism was still aligned to an urgent pragmatism:

> "If you look around the world — and I can't do my work without doing that because I travel all over the place and see the shit happen wherever I go — or you even have to just read the newspapers, it's not the time for just sitting at home and playing nice music. If you look at what we do to this planet then there is no minute to sit there satisfied with everything, with anything. So, it's still the same impetus in a way. The rage still is there but, of course, it's much more controlled. I'm not frustrated, I wouldn't say that, but sometimes I'm desperate. There is no time to be frustrated. You have to work, and I think the human being is defined by what he is working on. I suppose that's a good thing that, with the music, you always are together with a handful of people, and you don't just do the music, you discuss what's important for you and it keeps you alive and it keeps you thinking about things."[35]

In his heart, Brötzmann yearned for a fundamental re-evaluation and restructuring of Western society. He told Gerard Rouy:

"We have to get back to the essentials in a way; we need a bit more humility. I'm not aiming at only musicians but at all this over-blown world we are living in. It needs another kind of consciousness to be creative and it needs solidarity, which is almost non-existent. It's understandable, everybody has to fight to survive somehow in his own little world and forgets to look outside; everybody's in the same shit. Let's get together, let's do things together, I would say that we've got ourselves into quite a rut and it's been going on in waves over the years, but I hope we can get out of it. Without virtues like solidarity, we won't make it."[36]

Crucially, as he saw it, his duty lay in helping to bring about incremental change through the act of performing music. He told me:

"What we can do with the music is to open up ears and sometimes brains [to let people know] that there are other things happening than just the things you get in your ears and brain twenty-four hours a day. Sometimes you have an audience in some small town somewhere and nobody knows more or less about you, and then you have a couple of young girls, after the concert they are coming with tears in their eyes. I think that's what it is about: to reach the single soul and move them somewhere else. That's already quite a bit. We won't make the big revolution. Who does? But you have the feeling you can move things a little bit."[37]

In this respect, he humbly saw himself as one of a long line of messengers, with a cast-iron faith in the consciousness-raising properties of creative music:

"If you follow back the history of jazz music, it's full of crazy guys, naïve guys, bright guys, whatever, but they all had to send a message. You can say that about Fats Waller or James B. Johnson or you have it still in Miles Davis. I can't be on the same level as these guys, but I can try to come a little closer. For me it's important. And, from time to time, I'm glad if some younger musician comes to me and says, 'Hey Brötzmann, I learned this and that from you.' That happens. And, I must admit, I like to hear that, especially from young audiences with no idea about the history of improvised music. But if they have a chance to hear the music, some of them get touched by it and then it starts to open their mind. That's already something. I'm quite a sceptical guy but without any hope I couldn't do the work."[38]

In fact, it's astonishing just how many minds and hearts Brötzmann was able to reach while doggedly pursuing a hugely uncompromising and avowedly uncommercial artistic mission. By his last years, he was a unique figure in the world of free jazz and improvisation who had achieved a level of celebrity that cut across scenes, generations and nationalities. "I am always so surprised," he admitted in 2019. "In the last year, I went more and more over to South America and people greet me on the street or in the airport or wherever. Then I think we have done a little bit."[39]

"There was a really wonderful experience we had when we did a tour of Japan and Australia," Leigh added.

"We were playing a show in Brisbane, and Peter and I had walked and had a coffee, we're on our way back to the gig and we're walking down the street and I see these kids — and when I say kids we're talking fourteen, fifteen, sixteen — youngsters who looked like they were dressed to go to the club or something, fluorescents, knots in the hair, everything — we're walking and I see them whispering to each other, pointing at us, then all of a sudden they flip out, they run up and say, 'Are you Peter Brötzmann?' They're freaking out, virtually crying, they were screaming. I couldn't believe it. They were hugging him. And then we played the concert, and those kids weren't all there, but it was yet more kids that after came rushing to the stage to meet Peter. It was such a beautiful thing."[40]

Perhaps a huge part of his appeal was that, going into the twenty-first century, he had come to embody a kind of freedom. In 2021, he made a brief but reverberant cameo appearance in director Sebastien Meise's movie *Grosse Freiheit* (*Great Freedom*) — also the name of a famous street in Hamburg's red-light district. The film tells the story of Hans, a young man imprisoned in a Nazi concentration camp for his homosexuality who, upon liberation into a peacetime Germany where being gay is still a crime, is transferred directly to prison. After repeated persecution and incarcerations, he is finally released in 1969, just after homosexuality has been decriminalised in West Germany. Bewildered by his new freedom, he stumbles into a gay bar named Grosse Freiheit, orders a shot at the bar and is then drawn to the sound of a saxophone honking and squealing in a back room. Entering the darkened space, he is confronted by Brötzmann's Full Blast trio on stage, laying down a furious free-jazz firestorm to the excited whoops of an entranced audience. Of course, Full Blast's appearance here is somewhat anomalous: in 1969, you'd have been unlikely to see a grizzled eighty-year-old playing free-jazz, and Marino Pliakas's electric bass is out of place. But, in other important ways, Brötzmann's presence is exactly right. Here, he is the emblematic elder emissary of hard-fought freedom in all its manifestations.

"You use what there is and that's what we musicians call improvising"

From his earliest days until the very end, Brötzmann maintained his practice as a visual artist, working in downtime between tours in his home studio, tucked away in a quiet backyard in Wuppertal's Luisen quarter. Some of the works he produced were directly related to his music — graphic scores like the complex schematic on the cover of *Alarm*, or the sets of cards he created, called *Signs and Images,* which could be used to create structured improvisations. There was also his more functional graphic design output: the countless flyers and posters he produced for FMP with an instantly recognisable style utilising the unique, block-lettered typography he developed while still a student at the School of Applied Arts in Wuppertal.

And, of course, there were the album covers, where he drew on all his artistic training to create some unforgettably striking images. *Machine Gun* employs a bold, Situationist Pop-Art style that wouldn't have looked out of place hastily pasted up in a riot-strewn Parisian street in May '68. *Woodcuts* is an explicit recognition of the technique he used to render so many of his designs: a rugged, blunt style actualised using delicate, handmade Japanese tissue paper (a conceptual balance of strength and fragility that finds echoes in his music). *Yatagarasu* — named after a mythical Japanese crow-deity — is a gruesome assemblage of decaying, possibly oil-damaged feathers, strung up in a symbolic act of human folly, underscoring Brötzmann's call for a better, kinder humanity.

Alongside all of this, he also diligently followed his calling in the fine arts — though he was, to begin with, somewhat reticent about it. Hamid Drake told me: "Before his visual art started to become public, if you ever visited Peter at his home, and spent time in his studio, you would see it. Although he did say he was a visual artist, that was something that was known only by just a few people. He didn't really talk about it so much."[41]

That began to change following two high-profile exhibitions of his work in the early 2000s. In 2002, Mats Gustafsson curated Objects and Paintings, a large collection of Brötzmann's early paintings, objects, posters, and graphic works, at Ystads Konstmuseum in Ystad, Sweden. The following year, John Corbett helped arrange the first showing of Brötzmann's art outside of Europe, at the Art Institute of Chicago. The exhibition, entitled *The Inexplicable Flyswatter* (and catalogued in a book of the same name), collated early paintings, collages and lithographs, from around the time of Brötzmann's first solo exhibition in Nijmegen, Netherlands, in 1959, through to 1964, the year after he worked as an assistant at Nam June Paik's *Exposition of Music — Electronic Television* at the Galerie Parnasse in Wuppertal. More than half of Brötzmann's pieces collected here show a fixation on the repeated image of a flyswatter. Corbett writes in a monograph included in the book: "An ideal Dadaistic image, the flyswatter unites elements of humour and violence in a versatile visual schema."[42] A staunch champion of all Brötzmann's art, Corbett went on to present a number of exhibitions of Brötzmann's visual work at his own Corbett VS. Dempsey gallery in Chicago in the following years.

As part of his seventieth birthday celebrations, Brötzmann presented a hometown show at Wuppertal's Gallery Epikur in

2011, as catalogued in *Arbeiten 1959–2010*. The reproductions in this collection begin from the same starting point as *The Inexplicable Flyswatter* but offer a more complete overview of the artist's work, revealing the various techniques and motifs that consumed Brötzmann over the decades. Early collages frequently introduced coarse materials such as sand, tar and wax (a visual corollary to Brötzmann's musical preoccupation with texture), and later developed into elaborate assemblages of feathers and wood and metal "object boxes." He also repeatedly returned to landscapes — in paints, watercolours and woodcuts — with a dual focus on German industrial scenes and the areas around Wuppertal where he took his favourite country rambles. Latterly, he began to introduce remembered scenes and incidences from a life on the road, from sexually bold erotic reminiscences to bittersweet tributes to musical comrades. "The Damage Is Done" (2010) is a large painting dedicated to Joe McPhee, portraying a capsized yacht and a figure just managing to keep his head above water; a metaphorical condition known all too well to musicians who've spent a lifetime on the margins. Throughout the whole collection, Brötzmann constantly returns to images of flight and altitude, from bridges and clouds to stubby Zeppelin airships — the same urge for transcendence that fuelled his most soaring musical statements.

Published in 2021, *Along the Way* is a lavishly illustrated volume documenting pieces made while on the road between 2010 and 2020. Dark, semi-abstract industrial landscapes in watercolour and felt-tipped pen capture the muted greys, greens and browns of his native Ruhr valley. There's a selection of hastily drawn pornographic images in ink, many involving women and dogs, which invite us to become voyeurs of some private, erotic dream zone. Most arresting are Brötzmann's three-dimensional objects and assemblages, including brutal collisions of wood and metal, as well as a series of tiny, self-contained worlds made from used Fuji instant camera cartridges — which he called Instaboxes — begun while he was confined to his home during Covid lockdowns. What all these works have in common is the feeling that they have been created on the fly, using whatever materials were to hand. "Being on the road so much, the time-space between the tours is not long enough for preparing big canvasses and starting oil paintings," Brötzmann explains in a typically terse written introduction. "You use what's on the table — paper, cardboard, an empty cigar box, pens, felts, brushes, ink in a glass or a Chinese ink stone. You use what there is and that's what we musicians call improvising and that's what the works in this book are about (and my life too): IMPROVISATION."[43]

For Brötzmann, the hours he spent in solitude in his studio were a necessary counterbalance to the gregarious life of the touring musician. "It's a thing you do alone," he said.

"You are alone in the studio. That's a completely different thing from music. You are on stage, mostly with a bunch of other guys and you work and that's it! You can't change it. In my studio, I can work on it, I can come back the next morning and say, 'My god, what kind of shit is that?' and so I start again, and again, and again. And you are alone. It's a kind of — especially getting older now — it's a kind of meditation, too, for me. It gives me some quietness and some kind of relaxation. I don't have to prove anything. I don't have to get famous. I'm famous enough! I can do what I like."[44]

With so much of his life spent on the road, always in close proximity to other musicians, his home in Wuppertal became a sanctuary of sorts. In 2019, he told me:

"I live at the same place now for thirty-five years, since I split from my wife. I have two floors — small but nice — with my apartment downstairs and upstairs an apartment for guests. The garden is mine and in the backyard is the studio for painting and playing. The landlord is a nice guy who promised years ago, 'I won't raise your rent in your lifetime.' It's in the middle of town, I can walk for everything I need. Wuppertal is not a beautiful town, but it has a certain rough charm. The landscape around is very fine. Walking, you can be in the woods in twenty minutes and, if you take the car, in twenty minutes you are in forests. That's very important for me."[45]

But when the first Covid restrictions came down in March 2020, Brötzmann, like so many of us, was forced to spend much more time at home than he'd ever anticipated. With travel and live concerts all but impossible, it meant the longest hiatus from touring and performing he'd ever experienced. It can't have been easy. He once told Gerard Rouy: "Music without an audience is just nonsense."[46]

Of course, I wondered how he was coping during this enforced curtailment. At the beginning of 2021, almost a year into the pandemic, I spoke on the phone to Evan Parker, and asked him how he felt the lockdowns and travel bans might be affecting Brötzmann. He told me: "He's the original soldier of the road. He's got his regular schedule — Japan this year, America this year, Europe this year — it's remarkable the way he's kept his life together. Now I guess he's painting more. Going for walks."[47] The next day, I emailed Brötzmann to ask how he was getting on and received this somewhat gloomy reply: "A very strange life nowadays. Since a year I live quite in quarantine, busy with graphics and so on... And an end is not in sight. Hard to stay optimistic."[48] Brötzmann turned eighty in March 2021, and I found myself feeling strangely upset that he would most likely be spending this landmark day alone.

His health was a worry, too. As early as 2013, he told me: "I have serious lung damage from smoking too much, all the black shit like Dutch or German tobacco. Sometimes I can't climb mountains, stairs are difficult. Wuppertal is in a valley, and sometimes, when the air is really locked in and not moving, I feel it."[49] Steve Noble told me: "He's got glassblower's lung. He suffers greatly. But I think the fact that he plays so often, it keeps him steady. Being out on the road, that's what he likes — blowing."[50] Around the beginning of the 2000s, Brötzmann had also begun to develop chronic obstructive pulmonary disease (COPD), which blocks the airflow and makes breathing difficult. It was a wonder he'd been able to play so forcefully for so long.

These difficulties certainly led to a gradual evolution in his playing style. Though always possessed of a tender lyricism that was often overshadowed by his ferocity, in later years this gentleness became even more pronounced. Marino Pliakas told me in 2020: "In the last year, people tell me they were surprised by the fragility of Peter's playing. It's not always screaming. It's fragile, it's intimate, it's almost chamber music."[51]

This was beautifully foregrounded in a studio session Brötzmann cut in 2018, released in 2019 as *I Surrender Dear*, comprising a dozen tracks, all solo tenor performances, most of which interpret some of his favourite tunes culled from the history of jazz and the Great American Songbook. Brötzmann tackles standards like the title track, "Lady Sings the Blues" and Gershwin's "Nice Work If You Can Get It" in a leisurely fashion, employing a mellow, smoky tone that finds him both vulnerable and sentimental. Mixed in with these homages are a few of his own compositions, such as "Dark Blues," essayed as a simple, unhurried refrain. In his liner notes, Brötzmann claims "the only idea for this recording was to show — mostly to myself — the connection between what has been and what there is right NOW."[52] As such, he also allows himself, on one or two occasions, to hint at the extremes for which he was better known: Sonny Rollins' "Sumphin'" is more boisterous, taking off with looping fanfares and grizzled growls, while Misha Mengelberg's tribute to the saxophonist, "Brozziman," unleashes a more familiar howling energy. But it stands as clear proof of just how two-dimensional his reputation as the pugnacious tenor terrorist really was. In fact, for those paying attention, it should have come as no surprise. As far back as 1984, he'd recorded the wide-ranging solo studio date for sax, clarinet and tarogato *14 Love Poems*, which, among its many moods, contained some equally thoughtful and delicate moments.

But now it looked like the pandemic was threatening his ability to play at all. Pliakas said: "The Covid period was a disaster for Peter's health. He had been suffering from COPD for years, but constant touring and playing proved the best therapy and strengthened his lungs. The Covid break brought him down from 100 to zero. This inactivity weakened him dramatically — and in his condition Covid was a constant serious threat."[53]

Mercifully, Brötzmann managed to avoid catching Covid, but during the same period, he developed pneumonia, which brought him dangerously close to the edge.

Yet, Brötzmann's indomitable energy saw him through. In summer 2021, when restrictions began to be lifted, making both international travel and live music more possible, he was among the first artists to begin making tentative arrangements to play again. He had a high-profile gig scheduled for the opening night of the Jazz Em Agosto festival in Lisbon in July with Bennink and von Schlippenbach (which was subsequently cancelled). A month later, at the end of August, a special festival was held in Wuppertal, belatedly celebrating his eightieth birthday. BRÖTZ 80 saw him joined by friends and associates old and new, including Mats Gustafsson, Fred Lonberg-Holm, Hamid Drake, Camille Emaille, Heather Leigh and his son, Caspar, for three days of concerts, including Brötzmann's first live performances since February 2020.

One of these performances, with Leigh and Lonberg-Holm, was released in 2023 as *Naked Nudes*, with alto and tenor sax, pedal steel and cello making for one of his more unusual trios. Leigh conjures gauzy clouds, wobbling tremolo and doom-laden dive-bombs, while Lonberg-Holm lays a sombre foundation of deep, electronically augmented arco and rough scrapes. Within this meter-free ambience, Brötzmann is free to wander, daubing plaintive calls, compact bluesy phrases and more gnarled clusters. It's a lonely sound, the horn somehow lost and peering through a lugubrious murk. BRÖTZ 80 was, by all accounts, a joyous affair. Yet, the music here is decidedly elegiac — mournful, even — as though Brötzmann is taking time to reflect on a long life lived fully and without compromise, and the many sacrifices incurred.

In November 2021, he issued the following statement via Facebook:

"FRIENDS, I THINK IT IS TIME FOR A COUPLE OF WORDS BEFORE RUMOURS TAKE OVER. FIRST OF ALL: I AM STILL ALIVE! MOST OF YOU KNOW THAT SINCE 20 YEARS I AM CARRYING AROUND THIS C.O.P.D. AND COVID-TIMES DIDN'T MAKE IT EASIER. BESIDE THAT I SCRAPED PAST PNEUMONIA WITH ANTIBIOTICS AND THAT REALLY BROUGHT MY BODY DOWN. OK, I SURVIVED AND NOW I AM ON A GOOD WAY TO RECOVER. THOUGH I HAD TO CANCEL ALL MUSIC ACTIVITIES FOR THIS YEAR I AM SURE I WILL BE ON THE ROAD AGAIN IN 2022. FOR THE MOMENT I CAN SAY IT IS NOT THE PLAYING, IT IS THE TRAVEL WITH ALL THE RESTRICTIONS I AM CONCERNED ABOUT. SO I HAVE TO LOOK FOR DECENT AND MORE COMFORTABLE WAYS TO TRAVEL. MIGHT NEED YOUR UNDERSTANDING AND EVEN HELP FOR THAT."[54]

Eight months later, I saw for myself just how tired Brötzmann was, when I was invited to the Kongsberg Jazz Festival in Norway, at which he was scheduled to appear. My flight into Oslo was delayed so I missed my ride. I was instructed to wait around for a couple of hours until Brötzmann arrived and then to share a car with him. During the couple of hours' drive to Kongsberg, we sat in the back and chatted. Brötzmann seemed shattered from the travel, and short of breath, pausing every few minutes to puff on a Ventolin inhaler. He said he'd been unsure about whether to come while there was still a risk of catching Covid. "My doctor said, 'Don't do it,'" he confided. Then, of his recent brush with pneumonia: "I almost died."

Looking ahead to the gigs he was booked to perform during the festival, he candidly expressed some misgivings about the shape he was in and his ability to continue: "If I am onstage and I play some half-arsed shit… then it's goodbye."[55] He told me he was booked to play a duo gig with Hamid Drake the following month, but whether or not he would do it depended on how his performances this weekend went. By the time we arrived at the hotel, he seemed somewhat revived and strode into the lobby, wearing a long, wide-shouldered coat, black jeans and stylish cherry-red cowboy boots, leaning forward into the job ahead.

The next afternoon, he played a solo set in a small gallery space. Before starting, he told the packed room: "Today is a special day. I will do something I don't usually do — talk before I play." When a ripple of laughter had subsided, he explained: "My lungs are fucked up. I thought I would see how it works — *if* it works." After a slight chuckle, he began. It was immediately apparent that his playing had changed, favouring shorter phrases and concise statements. On clarinet, he bathed in a warm, chocolaty tone, pushing up into wobbling ululations and clipped altissimo cries while, on alto sax, he was still able to unleash savage volume and intensity, if only in short bursts. The performance was clearly an effort. Brötzmann paused between pieces to puff on his inhaler and called for an intermission after half an hour. Returning for a second set, he managed around ten minutes before announcing, "I'm afraid that's it for me today. It doesn't work anymore. I'm sorry." On receiving a standing ovation, he told the room, "You're too kind." I think he meant it. The following evening, he played a short, almost valedictory set with Heather Leigh.

When I got home, I emailed him to see how he'd felt about the weekend's performances. "It was worth a try," he replied, "though travel was a pain in the ass but with assistance I made it home. I think I/we made some decent music though it's hard to concentrate when the lungs tell you they don't want that challenge. It had to be and all in all I come to a positive conclusion for the future."[56] The following month he made the duo gig with Drake, at the Summer Bummer festival in Antwerp, and then, in November, he performed at Berlin Jazz Festival in a trio with Drake and Moroccan guembri player Majid Bekkas. In an echo of his 2020 album with Drake and Maâlem Mokhtar Gania, *The Catch of a Ghost,* the set was released in May 2023 as *Catching Ghosts.* Brötzmann plays short, telegraphic statements, one moment straining upwards, the next floating down into tenderness and sensitivity and, throughout, leaving plenty of room for Bekka's vocal exultations. It was to be his last album released during his lifetime.

"Just stopping is out of the question"

No one was more surprised than Jason Adasiewicz when Brötzmann decided to reactivate the quartet with John Edwards and Steve Noble. Since their last performance together in Chicago in 2016, Brötzmann and Adasiewicz had not spoken at all. Then, in November 2022, Brötzmann emailed Adasiewicz out of the blue. "I wasn't expecting an apology or anything," Adasiewicz told me. "And I don't think he was expecting an apology from me either. But it was as close as I could have gotten from him. It was along the lines of 'I know we've had our differences and we ended bad.' And then, this sentence: 'but I haven't stopped thinking about you.' That tore at my heart."[57]

Brötzmann explained that he had a residency coming up at Cafe OTO and was keen for the quartet to play at it. The suggestion was well timed for Adasiewicz, who was then just emerging from an extended sabbatical away from music.

"I was like, 'Yeah man, let's just brush this under the rug and do this'. Looking back on it, if he would have contacted me maybe six months earlier, I probably would have said no, and I don't know how I would be wrestling with myself now with how we know everything played out, and never talking to him again. I can't thank him more, him having the guts to reach back out to me. It really hit me really hard."[58]

At the beginning of February 2023, the quartet played two nights at another of Brötzmann's favourite club venues, Pardon To Tu in Warsaw, and then travelled direct to London for two more nights at Cafe OTO, Brötzmann's final residency there, and his last ever performances. Adasiewicz recalls meeting Brötzmann in the hotel lobby before making the short walk to OTO:

"He was just standing there, swaying back and forth, and you could see he was just completely beat down. We started walking to OTO and, halfway, he put his arm against one of the buildings, completely short of breath. He's eighty-one years old. Most people would be like, 'I'm done, I'm going home.' But no. The sets in Warsaw were blistering but then OTO comes along, and he ups it. Just the fact of being at OTO, I think, charged him up. He goes on to just kill it, gladiator style, just charging ahead."[59]

The OTO shows were, indeed, a tour-de-force that showed Brötzmann was not just undiminished but finding new things to say. For *Jazzwise* magazine, I reported:

"Despite his reduced lung-power, Brötzmann still whips up a raging storm, ripping fierce howls and cries from a clarinet, with Noble's incredibly swift and unrelenting pulse-time thunder goading him into accessing more and more violent vibrations. Where he once showed heroic stamina in keeping this kind of barrage up for long periods, Brötzmann's now dealing in shorter bursts, pouring all his intent into relatively brief but no less intense blasts. When he stops to catch his breath, Adasiewicz leaps in to maintain the energy, revealing just what a physical player he is, plotting abstract geometries with an extremely hard attack. Blown with less force, Brötzmann's tone on tenor sax is shorn of his customary guttural buzz, revealing, in quieter moments, a mellow warmth that illuminates his love for lyrical players like Ben Webster. Noble and Edwards respond by suggesting the outlines of a mesmerising slow blues, encouraging Brötzmann to explore a tender sentimentality, uttering luxuriant phrases that hang in the air like cigar smoke."[60]

"It was like the quartet was reborn," Adasiewicz enthused. "He was so excited. The cab ride to the airport, we were talking about the future, and how we'll get [John] Corbett to get the CD [of the 2016 Chicago show] out, a new recording from the quartet that'll get us some more work." But there were already intimations of trouble ahead. "He used to be so stubborn about carrying his horn," Adasiewicz remembered. "But this time, he was getting help at the airport. He was in a wheelchair, getting wheeled to the gate." Within twenty-four hours of getting home to Wuppertal, Brötzmann was rushed to hospital. To Adasiewicz, it seemed that, on that final night at OTO, Brötzmann had literally given it his all: "He played so fucking hard. With the condition of his body, is that what sent him over?"[61]

On 23 March, Brötzmann issued the following statement via Facebook:

"TIME FOR SOME FACTS:

YES, I HAD A COMPLETE BREAKDOWN COMING HOME FROM WARSAW AND LONDON AND YES, EMERGENCY, RE-ANIMATION, INTENSIVE CARE AND YES, OUT OF HOSPITAL SINCE 10 DAYS AND TRYING TO ORGANISE MY DAILY LIFE AND NO, I HAVE NO IDEA WHAT THE FUTURE WILL LOOK LIKE AND NO, I WON'T BE ABLE TO PLAY IN THE (NEAR) FUTURE, MEANS NO TRAVEL AND NO STAGE. NO GOOD NEWS, MY FRIENDS, BUT IT IS HOW IT IS AND YES, I WILL DO MY BEST TO STAY WITH YOU IN WHAT FORM AND FUNCTION EVER. ALL GOOD AND NOTHING TO COMPLAIN. BEST TO YOU ALL"[62]

In 2013, when I asked Brötzmann if he would always carry on playing, he replied: "I think I have to. I will do it as long as my body functions and as long as my brain doesn't give up."[63] He had finally reached the point where he simply couldn't do it anymore. In the middle of June, Michael Gottfried of ACT records (who had released Brötzmann's final album) spoke with him and told me: "It was hard for him to talk. And he knew he'll never be able to play again. But, at the same time, he was making plans to express himself artistically in different ways. That was real impressive to witness."[64] In one of his very last interviews, published by the German national newspaper *Die Zeit* the same month, Brötzmann reflected: "I can't complain. But you always want a little bit more. And right now it doesn't work. I'm 82 now, I've had an eventful life and I've never taken it easy. If blowing doesn't work anymore, then I have to concentrate on the fine arts again. Just stopping is out of the question."[65]

Peter Brötzmann died peacefully in his sleep, at home in Wuppertal, aged eighty-two, on 22 June 2023.

There were many tributes paid to Brötzmann in the weeks and months that followed. But the one he would have approved of the most took place at his beloved Cafe OTO in February 2024, almost exactly a year to the day after his very last gig there.

3 Days of Music Dedicated to Peter Brötzmann brought together twenty artists who had been associated with the great saxophonist at different stages throughout his nearly sixty years on the road. As ample testament to the generosity and curiosity Brötzmann brought to his collaborations right to the end, the ages of the oldest and youngest participants were separated by more than half a century. It was a truly international affair, too, drawing on the talents of British, European, Scandinavian and American comrades. Over the three days, the musicians appeared in multiple configurations of duos, trios, quartets and quintets — some well-established, others brand new — summoning moods that touched on diverse facets of Brötzmann's life and work.

Some of his very earliest fellow pioneers were there: Sven-Åke Johansson sang and recited Dadaist texts with a poised and diffident piano accompaniment from Alexander von Schlippenbach; Han Bennink and Evan Parker revived the

Laurel and Hardy routine with a duo set that was as much about joking around as making music. The rhythm sections were strong, with John Edwards and Steve Noble playing in a variety of settings, bringing their urgent energy to the fore, while Hamid Drake and William Parker imparted a booming depth to everything they touched, including a careening trio with British pianist Pat Thomas. Chicago buddies were well represented: the eternally youthful Joe McPhee delivering a moving poetic recitation with sensitive counterpoint from Jason Adasiewicz; Ken Vandermark and Fred Lonberg-Holm showing both strength and sensitivity. Paal Nilssen-Love and Mats Gustaffsson brought a muscular swagger. Caspar Brötzmann carved a rugged block of solo guitar noise. And there was bright promise in the contribution of the younger participants: Farida Amadou playing her bass guitar with extraordinary focus and agility; Camille Emaille bringing a captivating poise and precision to her improvisations; twenty-three-year-old saxophonist Zoh Amba blowing tenor with uncompromising commitment and concentration.

It was exciting. It was illuminated by feelings of love and gratitude. In a very real sense, it felt like history. But, above all, it was fiercely alive, refusing to accept that this music can ever die. It left no doubt that, now and always, Brötzmann's energy lives on.

Bibliography

Abish, Walter, *How German Is It (Wie Deutsch ist es)* (New Directions, 1980)

Baraka, Amiri, *The Autobiography of LeRoi Jones* (Freundlich Books, 1984)

Baraka, Amiri; Spellman, A.B.; Neal, Larry (Eds.), *The Cricket: Black Music in Evolution 1968-69* (Blank Forms, 2022)

Barnett, Anthony, *UnNatural Music: John Lennon & Yoko Ono In Cambridge 1969* (Allardyce Book ABP, 2016)

Berendt, Joachim-Ernst, *Ein Fenster aus Jazz: Essays, Portraits, Reflexionen* (Fischer Taschenbuch, 1977)

Boynik, Sezgin; Vitahuhta, Taneli (Eds.), *Free Jazz Communism: Archie Shepp-Bill Dixon Quartet at the 8th World Festival of Youth and Students in Helsinki 1962* (Rab-Rab Press, 2019)

Bradley, Cisco, *Universal Tonality: The Life and Music of William Parker* (Duke University Press, 2021)

Brötzmann, Peter, *The Inexplicable Flyswatter (Works on Paper: 1959–64)* (10th Avenue Freeze Out, 2003)

Brötzmann, Peter, *Arbeiten 1959–2010* (Galerie Epikur, 2011)

Brötzmann, Peter, *We Thought We Could Change the World: Conversations with Gerard Rouy* (Wolke Verlag, 2014)

Brötzmann, Peter, *Graphic Works 1959–2016* (Wolke Verlag, 2016)

Brötzmann, Peter, *Along the Way* (Wolke Verlag, 2021)

Christman, Mark; DiNucci, Celeste; Elms, Anthony (Eds.), *Milford Graves: A Mind-Body Deal* (Inventory Press, 2022)

Collier, Graham, *Inside Jazz* (Quartet Books, 1973)

Corbett, John, *Microgroove: Forays into Other Music* (Duke University Press, 2015)

Heffley, Mike, *Northern Sun, Southern Moon: Europe's Reinvention of Jazz* (Yale University Press, 2005)

Jones, LeRoi, *Black Music* (W. Morrow, 1967)

Jost, Ekkehard, *Europas Jazz: 1960–80* (Fischer Taschenbuch, 1987)

Keshvani, Rozemin; Heil, Axel; Weibel, Peter (Eds.), *Better Books / Better Bookz: Art, Anarchy, Apostasy, Counter-culture & the New Avant-garde* (Koenig Books, 2019)

Kisiedu, Harald, *European Echoes: Jazz Experimentalism in Germany 1950–1975* (Wolke Verlag, 2020)

Kofsky, Frank, *Black Nationalism and the Revolution in Music* (Pathfinder Press, 1970)

Koloda, Richard, *Holy Ghost: The Life & Death of Free Jazz Pioneer Albert Ayler* (Jawbone, 2022)

Kumpf, Lawrence; Karlsson, Naima; Nygren, Magnus (Eds.), *Organic Music Societies* (Blank Forms, 2021)

Lee, Sook-Kyung; Frieling, Rudolph (Eds.), *Nam June Paik* (Prestel, 2020)

Lewis, George E., *A Power Stronger Than Itself: The AACM and American Experimental Music* (The University of Chicago Press, 2008)

Lewis, George E., "*Improvised Music after 1950: Afrological and Eurological Perspectives,*" (Black Music Research Journal, Vol. 16, No. 1, Spring 1996)

Morton, Brian; Cook, Richard, *The Penguin Jazz Guide* (Penguin, 2010)

Müller, Markus (Ed.), *FMP: The Living Music* (Wolke Verlag, 2022)

Neuberger, Susanne (Ed.), *Nam June Paik: Exposition of Music — Electronic Television Revisited* (Buchhandlung Walther Konig GmbH & Co. KG. Abt. Verlag, 2009)

Newton, Francis, *The Jazz Scene* (MacGibbon and Kee, 1959)

Parker, Matt, *Subversion Through Jazz: The Birth of British Progressive Jazz in a Cold War Climate* (Jazz in Britain, 2020)

Saul, Scott, *Freedom Is, Freedom Ain't: Jazz and the Making of the Sixties* (Harvard University Press, 2005)

Shoemaker, Bill, *Jazz in the 1970s: Diverging Streams* (Rowman & Littlefield, 2017)

Sites, William, *Sun Ra's Chicago: Afrofuturism and the City* (The University of Chicago Press, 2020)

Smith, Owen F., *Fluxus: The History of an Attitude* (San Diego State University Press, 1998)

Soejima, Teruto, *Free Jazz in Japan: A Personal History* (Public Bath Press, 2019)

Vague, Tom, *Televisionaries: The Red Army Faction Story 1963–1993* (AK Press, 1994)

Watson, Ben, *Derek Bailey and the Story of Free Improvisation* (Verso, 2004)

Yoshida, Mamoru, *Yokohama Jazz Story: 50 Years of Chigusa* (Kanagawa Shimbun, 1985)

Filmography

Clarke, Shirley (Dir.), *The Connection* (1962)

Croker, C. Martin (Dir.), *Space Ghost Coast to Coast*, Season 3, Episode 5: "Sharrock" (Cartoon Network, 1996)

Jahn, Ebba (Dir.), *Rising Tones Cross* (1985)
Josse, Bernard (Dir.), *Soldier of The Road* (2011)
Meise, Sebastian (Dir.), *Grosse Freiheit* (2021)
Odar, Baran B. (Dir.), *Dark* (Netflix, 2017–2020)
Roth, Alan (Dir.), *Inside Out in The Open* (2001)
Thompson, Ahmir "Questlove" (Dir.), *Summer of Soul (...Or, When the Revolution Could Not Be Televised)* (2021)

Wenders, Wim (Dir.), *Pina* (2001)

Selected Discographies

Brötzmann as leader/co-leader (in order of year recorded)

Peter Brötzmann Trio, *Mayday* (Corbett Vs. Dempsey, 2010, rec. 1966)

Peter Brötzmann Trio, *For Adolphe Sax* (BRÖ, 1967, rec. 1967)

P. Brötzmann Group, *Fuck De Boere (Dedicated to Johnny Diyani)* (Atavistic, 2001 rec. 1968 & 1970)

The Peter Brötzmann Octet, *Machine Gun* (BRÖ, 1968, rec. 1968)

The Peter Brötzmann Sextet / Quartet, *Nipples* (Calig, 1969, rec. 1969)

Brötzmann / Van Hove / Bennink, *Balls* (FMP, 1970, rec. 1970)

Brötzmann / Van Hove / Bennink & Albert Mangelsdorff, *Elements* (FMP, 1971, rec. 1971)

Brötzmann / Van Hove / Bennink & Albert Mangelsdorff, *Couscouss De La Mauresque* (FMP, 1971, rec. 1971)

Brötzmann / Van Hove / Bennink & Albert Mangelsdorff, *The End* (FMP, 1971, rec. 1971)

Brötzmann / Van Hove / Bennink, *Brötzmann / Van Hove / Bennink* (FMP, 1973, rec. 1973)

Brötzmann / Van Hove / Bennink, *Jazz In Der Kammer Nr.71: Deutsches Theater / Berlin / GDR / 04/11/1974* (TROST, 2022, rec. 1974)

Brötzmann / Van Hove / Bennink, *Tschüs* (FMP, 1975, rec. 1975)

Peter Brötzmann, *Brötzmann/Solo* (FMP, 1976, rec. 1976)

Brötzmann / Bennink, *Ein Halber Hund Kann Nicht Pinkeln* (FMP, 1977, rec. 1977)

Brötzmann / Bennink, *Schwarzwaldfahrt* (FMP, 1977, rec. 1977)

Brötzmann / Miller / Moholo, *The Nearer the Bone, the Sweeter the Meat* (FMP, 1979, rec. 1979)

Peter Brötzmann & Han Bennink, *Atsugi Concert* (Gua Bungue, 1980, rec. 1980)

Brötzmann / Miller / Moholo, *Open, But Hardly Touched* (FMP, 1981, rec 1980)

Peter Brötzmann Group, *Alarm* (FMP, 1983, rec. 1981)

Brötzmann, *14 Love Poems* (FMP, 1984, rec. 1984)

Last Exit, *Last Exit* (Enemy, 1986, rec. 1986)

Last Exit, *The Noise of Trouble (Live In Tokyo)* (Enemy, 1986, rec. 1986)

Last Exit, *Köln* (ITM, 1990, rec. 1986)

Last Exit, *Cassette Recordings 87* (Enemy, 1987, rec. 1987)

Brötzmann / Laswell, *Low Life* (Celluloid, 1987, rec 1987)

Peter Brötzmann & Sonny Sharrock, *Whatthefuckdoyouwant* (TROST, 2014, rec. 1987)

No Material, *No Material* (ITM, 1989, rec. 1987)

Last Exit, *Iron Path* (Virgin, 1988, rec. 1988)

Last Exit, *Headfirst into The Flames — Live in Europe* (MuWorks, 1993, rec. 1989)

Caspar Brötzmann / Peter Brötzmann, *Last Home* (Pathological, 1990, rec. 1990)

Peter Brötzmann / Fred Hopkins / Rashied Ali, *Songlines* (FMP, 1994, rec. 1991)

The Peter Brötzmann Tentet, *The März Combo: Live in Wuppertal* (FMP, 1993, rec. 1992)

Peter Brötzmann / Toshinori Kondo / William Parker / Hamid Drake, *Die Like a Dog: Fragments of Music, Life and Death of Albert Ayler* (FMP, 1994, rec. 1993)

Peter Brötzmann & Hamid Drake, *The Dried Rat-Dog* (Okka Disk, 1995, rec. 1994)

Die Like a Dog Quartet, *Close Up* (FMP, 2011, rec. 1994)

Brötzmann / Gania / Drake, *The "WELS" Concert* (Okka Disk, 1997, rec. 1996)

Brötzmann, *The Chicago Octet/Tentet* (Okka Disk, 1998, rec. 1997)

Die Like a Dog Quartet, *Little Birds Have Fast Hearts No. 1* (FMP, 1998, rec. 1997)

Die Like a Dog Quartet, *Little Birds Have Fast Hearts No. 2* (FMP, 1999, rec. 1997)

Die Like a Dog Quartet feat. Roy Campbell, *From Valley to Valley* (Eremite, 1999, rec. 1998)

Die Like a Dog Quartet, *Aoyama Crows* (FMP, 2002, rec. 1999)

Peter Brötzmann Chicago Tentet Plus Two, *Short Visit to Nowhere* (Okka Disk, 2002, rec. 2000)

Peter Brötzmann / William Parker / Hamid Drake, *Never Too Late but Always Too Early* (Eremite, 2003, rec. 2001)

Peter Brötzmann / William Parker / Milford Graves, *Historic Music Past Tense Future* (Black Editions Archive, 2022, rec. 2002)

Peter Brötzmann, *Berg-Und Talfahrt — A Night in Sanàa (Live At 'Deutsches Haus)* (ARM, 2009, rec. 2004)

Full Blast, *Full Blast* (Jazzwerkstatt, 2006, rec. 2006)

Peter Brötzmann / Paal Nilssen-Love / Mats Gustafsson, *The Fat Is Gone* (Smalltown Superjazz, 2007, rec. 2006)

Brötzmann / Kondo / Pupillo / Nilssen-Love, *Hairy Bones* (Okka Disk, 2009, rec. 2008)

Peter Brötzmann / Paal Nilssen-Love, *Woodcuts* (PNL, 2009, rec. 2008)

Full Blast & Friends, *Crumbling Brain* (Okka Disk, 2010, rec. 2008)

Peter Brötzmann Chicago Tentet + 1, *3 Nights in Oslo* (Smalltown Superjazz, 2010, rec. 2009)

Full Blast & Friends, *Sketches and Ballads* (TROST, 2011, rec. 2010)

Brötzmann / Edwards / Noble, *...The Worse the Better* (OTOROKU, 2012, rec. 2010)

Hairy Bones, *Snakelust (To Kenji Nakagami)* (Clean Feed, 2012, rec. 2011)

Brötzmann / Satoh / Moriyama, *Yatagarasu* (Not Two, 2012, rec. 2011)

Brötzmann / Adasiewicz, *Going All Fancy* (BRÖ, 2012, rec. 2011)

Various artists, *Long Story Short* (TROST, 2013, rec. 2011)

Brötzmann / Adasiewicz, *Mollie's in The Mood* (BRÖ, 2014, rec. 2012)

Brötzmann / Noble, *I Am Here Where Are You* (TROST, 2013, rec. 2013)

Brötzmann / Edwards / Noble, *...Soulfood Available* (Clean Feed, 2014, rec. 2013)

Brötzmann / Adasiewicz / Edwards / Noble, *Mental Shake* (OTOROKU, 2014, rec. 2013)

Peter Brötzmann / William Parker / Hamid Drake, *Song Sentimentale* (OTOROKU, 2023, rec. 2015)

Brötzmann / Nilssen-Love, *Chicken Shit Bingo* (TROST, 2024, rec. 2015)

Peter Brötzmann / Heather Leigh, *Ears Are Filled with Wonder* (TROST, 2016, rec. 2015)

Brötzmann / Leigh, *Sex Tape* (TROST, 2017, rec. 2016)

Brötzmann / Leigh, *Sparrow Nights* (TROST, 2018, rec. 2017)

Brötzmann / Schlippenbach / Bennink, *Fifty Years After... (Live at The Lila Eule 26.05.18)* (TROST 2019, rec. 2018)

Peter Brötzmann, *I Surrender Dear* (TROST, 2019, rec. 2018)

Peter Brötzmann / Maâlem Mokhtar Gania / Hamid Drake, *The Catch of A Ghost* (I Dischi Di Angelica, 2020, rec. 2019)

Peter Brötzmann / Farida Amadou / Steve Noble, *B.A.N.* (Dropa Disc, 2022, rec. 2019)

Brötzmann / Leigh / Lonberg-Holm, *Naked Nudes* (TROST, 2023, rec. 2021)

Brötzmann / Bekkas / Drake, *Catching Ghosts* (ACT, 2023, rec. 2022)

Brötzmann as sideman/collaborator (in order of year recorded)

Alexander von Schlippenbach, *Globe Unity* (SABA, 1967, rec. 1966)

Globe Unity Orchestra, *Globe Unity 67/70* (Atavistic, 2001, rec. 1967 & 1970)

Manfred Schoof, *European Echoes* (FMP, 1969, rec. 1969)

Misha Mengelberg / Peter Brötzmann / Evan Parker / Peter Bennink / Paul Rutherford / Derek Bailey / Han Bennink, *Groupcomposing* (FMP, 1978, rec. 1970)

Don Cherry & The New Eternal Rhythm Orchestra / Krzysztof Penderecki, *Actions* (Philips, 1971, rec. 1971)

Globe Unity 73, *Live in Wuppertal* (FMP, 1973, rec 1973)

Globe Unity Orchestra and Guests, *Pearls* (FMP, 1977, rec 1975)

Globe Unity Orchestra, *Jahrmarkt / Local Fair* (Po Torch Records, 1977, rec. 1975 & 1976)

ICP Tentet, *Tetterettet* (ICP, 1977, rec. 1977)

Globe Unity, *Improvisations* (JAPO, 1978, rec 1977)

Cecil Taylor, *Olu Iwa* (Soul Note, 1994, rec. 1986)

OXBOW & Peter Brötzmann, *An Eternal Reminder of Not Today: Live at Moers* (TROST, 2022, rec. 2018)

Others (in alphabetical order; year recorded)

Agitation Free, *Malesch* (Vertigo, 1972, rec. 1972)

AMM, *AMMMusic* (Elektra, 1967, rec. 1966)

Assagai, *Assagai* (Vertigo, 1971, rec. 1971)

Assagai, *Zimbabwe* (Philips, 1971, rec. 1971)

Albert Ayler, *Holy Ghost: Rare & Unissued Recordings (1962–1970)* (Revenant, 2004, rec. 1962–1970)

Albert Ayler, *Something Different!!!!!* (Bird Notes, 1963, rec. 1962)

Albert Ayler, *My Name Is Albert Ayler* (Debut, 1964, rec. 1963)

Albert Ayler, *Spiritual Unity* (ESP-Disk, 1965, rec. 1964)

Albert Ayler, *New York Eye and Ear Control* (ESP-Disk, 1965, rec 1964)

Albert Ayler, *Live at Slug's Saloon* (ESP-Disk, 1982, rec. 1966)

Han Bennink & Willem Breuker, *New Acoustic Swing Duo* (ICP, 1967, rec. 1967)

Carla Bley / Mike Mantler / Steve Lacy, *Jazz Realities* (Fontana, 1966, rec. 1966)

Jaimie Branch, *Fly or Die II: Bird Dogs of Paradise* (International Anthem, 2019, rec. 2018–2019)

Caspar Brötzmann Massaker, *The Tribe* (Zensor, 1987, rec. 1987)

Caspar Brötzmann Massaker, *Black Axis* (Marat, 1989, rec. 1989)

Can, *Delay 1968* (Spoon, 1981, rec. 1968–1969)

Centipede, *September Energy* (RCA, 1971, rec. 1971)

Don Cherry, *Togetherness* (Durium, 1966, rec. 1965)

Don Cherry, *Complete Communion* (Blue Note, 1966 rec. 1965)

Don Cherry, *Symphony for Improvisers* (Blue Note, 1967 rec. 1966)

Don Cherry, *Where Is Brooklyn* (Blue Note, 1969, rec. 1966)

Don Cherry Quintet, *Live at Café Montmartre 1966* (ESP-Disk, 2007, rec. 1966)

Don Cherry / Marion Brown / Evan Parker / John Stevens, *Free Jazz Meeting Baden Baden '67* (Hi Hat, 2018, rec. 1967)

Don Cherry, *Eternal Rhythm* (MPS, 1969, rec. 1968)

Circulasione Totale Orchestra, *Bandwidth* (Rune Grammofon, 2009, rec. 2008–2009)

Ornette Coleman, *Something Else!!!!* (Contemporary, 1958, rec. 1958)

Ornette Coleman, *Change of the Century* (Atlantic, 1960, rec. 1959)

Ornette Coleman, *Dancing in Your Head* (A&M, 1977, rec 1973–1975)

Ornette Coleman, *Body Meta* (Artists House, 1978, rec. 1976)

John Coltrane & Don Cherry, *The Avant-Garde* (Atlantic, 1966, rec. 1960)

John Coltrane, *Coltrane "Live" at the Village Vanguard* (Impulse!, 1962, rec. 1961)

John Coltrane, *Ascension* (Impulse!, 1966, rec. 1965)
John Coltrane, *Interstellar Space* (Impulse!, 1974, rec. 1967)
Miles Davis, *Kind of Blue* (Columbia, 1959, rec. 1959)
Miles Davis, *Jack Johnson* (Columbia, 1971, rec. 1970)
Miles Davis, *Agharta* (CBS/Sony, 1975, rec. 1975)
Decoy, *Spirit* (Bo'Weavil, 2009, rec. 2009)
Decoy, *OTO* (Bo'Weavil, 2011, rec. 2009)
Bill Dixon, *Thoughts* (Soul Note, 1987, rec. 1985)
Bill Dixon, *Vade Mecum* (Soul Note, 1994, rec. 1993)
Eric Dolphy, *Last Date* (Fontana, 1965, rec. 1964)
Eric Dolphy / Misha Mengelberg / Jacques Schols / Han Bennink, *Epistrophy* (ICP, 1974, rec. 1964 & 1972)
Dream / Aktion Unit, *Blood Shadow Rampage* (Volcanic Tongue, 2006, rec. 2005)
Extra Large Unit, *More Fun Please* (PNL, 2018, rec. 2017)
Fire! Orchestra / Krzysztof Penderecki, *Actions* (Rune Grammofon, 2020, rec. 2018)
Charles Gayle / William Parker / Rashied Ali, *Touchin' on Trane* (FMP, 1993, rec. 1991)
Maâlem Mahmoud Ghania with Pharoah Sanders, *The Trance of Seven Colours* (Axiom, 1994, rec. 1994)
Guru Guru, *UFO* (Ohr, 1970, rec. 1970)
Charlie Haden, *Liberation Music Orchestra* (Impulse!, 1970, rec. 1969)
Gunter Hampel Quintet, *Heartplants* (SABA, 1965, rec. 1965)
Herbie Hancock, *Future Shock* (Columbia, 1983, rec. 1983)
Henry Cow, *Concerts* (Compendium, 1976, rec. 1974–1975)
Irreversible Entanglements, *Irreversible Entanglements* (International Anthem, 2017, rec. 2015)
Iskra 1903, *Iskra 1903* (Incus, 1972, rec. 1972)
Ronald Shannon Jackson & The Decoding Society, *Eye on You* (About Time, 1980, rec. 1980)

Ronald Shannon Jackson & The Decoding Society, *Nasty* (Moers Music, 1981, rec. 1981)

Jandek, *Glasgow Sunday 2005* (Corwood Industries, 2008, rec. 2005)

The Jazz Composer's Orchestra, *Communication* (Fontana, 1966, rec. 1965)

King Crimson, *Islands* (Island, 1971, rec. 1971)

Kondo / Kaiser / Oswald, *Moose and Salmon* (Music Gallery Editions, 1978, rec. 1978)

Toshinori Kondo IMA, *Taihen* (Polydor, 1984, rec. 1984)

The Rolf and Joachim Kühn Quartet, *Impressions of New York* (Impulse!, 1967, rec. 1967)

Bill Laswell, *Baselines* (Elektra, 1983, rec. 1982)

Heather Leigh, *I Abused Animal* (Ideologic Organ, 2015, rec. 2014)

Charles Lloyd, *Sangam* (ECM, 2006, rec. 2004)

Mandingo Griot Society, *Mandingo Griot Society* (Flying Fish, 1978, rec. 1978)

Albert Mangelsdorff Quintet, *Tension!* (CBS, 1963, rec. 1963)

Albert Mangelsdorff Quintet, *Now Jazz Ramwong* (CBS, 1964, rec. 1964)

Albert Mangelsdorff / Masahiko Satoh / Peter Warren / Allen Blairman, *Spontaneous* (Enja, 1972, rec. 1971)

Togashi Masahiko Quartet, *We Now Create: Music for Strings, Winds and Percussion* (Victor, 1969, rec. 1969)

Massacre, *Killing Time* (Celluloid, 1981, rec. 1981)

Material, *Memory Serves* (Celluloid, 1981, rec. 1981)

The Chris McGregor Group, *Very Urgent* (Polydor, 1968, rec. 1968)

Joe McPhee, *Nation Time* (CjR, 1971, rec. 1970)

Misha Mengelberg / Han Bennink / John Tchicai, *Instant Composers Pool* (ICP, 1968, rec. 1968)

Harry Miller's Isipingo, *Family Affair* (Ogun, 1977, rec. 1977)

Charles Mingus, *The Black Saint and the Sinner Lady* (Impulse!, 1963, rec. 1963)

Mohel, *Babylon Bypass* (Tyyfus, 2008, rec. 2007)

Louis Moholo Octet, *Spirits Rejoice!* (Ogun, 1978, rec. 1978)

NEW, *NEWtoons* (Bo'Weavil, 2009, rec. 2008)

New York Gong, *About Time* (Charly, 1980, rec. 1979)

Steve Noble / John Edwards / Alan Wilkinson, *Obliquity* (Bo'Weavil, 2007, rec. 2006)

Mike Osborne Trio, *Border Crossing* (Ogun, 1974, rec. 1974)

Painkiller, *Guts of A Virgin* (Earache, 1991, rec. 1991)

Painkiller, *50th Birthday Celebration Volume 12* (Tzadik, 2005, rec. 2003)

Evan ,Parker / Derek Bailey / Han Bennink, *The Topography of the Lungs* (Incus, 1970 rec. 1970)

William Parker Trio, *Painter's Spring* (Thirsty Ear, 2000, rec. 2000)

William Parker & Hamid Drake, *Piercing the Veil* (AUM Fidelity, 2001, rec. 2000)

Ernst-Ludwig Petrowsky Quartet, *Just for Fun* (FMP, 1973, rec. 1973)

Rip, Rig + Panic, *I Am Cold* (Virgin, 1982, rec. 1982)

Rip, Rig + Panic, *Attitude* (Virgin, 1983, rec. 1983)

Sonny Rollins, *Rollins in Holland: The 1967 Studio and Live Recordings* (Resonance, 2020, rec. 1967)

George Russell, *Electronic Sonata for Souls Loved by Nature* (Flying Dutchman, 1971, rec. 1970)

John Russell / Kondo Toshinori / Roger Turner, *Artless Sky* (Caw, 1980, rec. 1979)

Masahiko Satoh & Wolfgang Dauner, *Pianology* (Express, 1971, rec. 1971)

Scorces, *Scorces* (Wholly Other, 2001, rec. 2001)

Alan Skidmore Quintet, *Once Upon a Time* (Deram, 1970, rec. 1970)

Sun Ra, *The Magic City* (Saturn, 1966, rec. 1965)

Sun Ra, *Nuclear War* (Y Records, 1984, rec. 1982)

Manfred Schoof Quintet, *Voices* (CBS, 1966, rec. 1966)

Manfred Schoof Quintet, *The Munich Recordings 1966* (Sireena, 2013, rec. 1966)

Sonny Sharrock, *Black Woman* (Vortex, 1969, rec. 1969)

Sonny Sharrock, *Monkey-Pockie-Boo* (BYG Actuel, 1970, rec. 1970)

Sonny Sharrock & Linda Sharrock, *Paradise* (ATCO, 1975, rec. 1975)

Sonny Sharrock, *Guitar* (Enemy, 1986, rec. 1986)

Sonny Sharrock, *Ask the Ages* (Axiom, 1991, rec. 1991)

Mike Sopko / Bill Laswell / Tyshawn Sorey, *On Common Ground* (M.O.D. Reloaded, 2020, rec. 2020)

Spontaneous Music Ensemble, *Challenge* (Eyemark, 1966, rec. 1966)

Spontaneous Music Ensemble, *Withdrawal* (Emanem, 1997, rec. 1966 & 1967)

Masayuki Takayanagi And New Directions, *Independence: Tread on Sure Ground* (Union, 1970, rec. 1969)

Cecil Taylor, *Jazz Advance* (Transition, 1957, rec. 1956)

Cecil Taylor, *Unit Structures* (Blue Note, 1966, rec. 1966)

Cecil Taylor Unit, *Dark to Themselves* (Inner City/Enja, 1977, rec. 1976)

Cecil Taylor, *Cecil Taylor Unit* (New World, 1978, rec. 1978)

Cecil Taylor, *3 Phasis* (New World, 1978, rec. 1978)

Cecil Taylor, *Live In The Black Forest* (MPS, 1978, rec. 1978)

Cecil Taylor, *One Too Many Salty Swift and Not Goodbye* (Hat Hut, 1980, rec. 1978)

Cecil Taylor, *The Eighth* (Hat Hut, 1986, rec. 1981)

Cecil Taylor, *Winged Serpent (Sliding Quadrants)* (Soul Note, 1985, rec. 1984)

Cecil Taylor, *Cecil Taylor in Berlin '88* (FMP, 1989, rec. 1988)

The Thing, *The Thing* (Crazy Wisdom, 2000, rec. 2000)

The Thing with Joe McPhee, *She Knows...* (Crazy Wisdom, 2001, rec. 2001)

The Thing, *Garage* (Smalltown Superjazz, 2004, rec. 2004)

The Clifford Thornton New Art Ensemble, *Freedom & Unity* (Third World, 1969, rec. 1967)

Keith Tippett's Ark, *Frames (Music for an Imaginary Film)* (Ogun, 1978, rec. 1978)

Charles Tyler Ensemble, *Charles Tyler Ensemble* (ESP-Disk, 1966, rec. 1966)

David S. Ware, *Great Bliss Vols. 1& 2,* (Silkheart, 1991, rec. 1990)

David S. Ware, *Flight of I,* (DIW, 1992, rec. 1991)

Colin Wilkie / Shirley Hart / Albert Mangelsdorff / Joki Freund, *Wild Goose* (MPS, 1969, rec. 1969)

Yosuke Yamashita Trio, *Concert in New Jazz* (Union, 1969, rec. 1969)

Atilla Zoller / Masahiko Satoh, *Duologue* (Express, 1971, rec. 1970)

John Zorn, *Naked City* (Elektra Nonesuch, 1990, rec. 1989)

Zu, *Bromio* (Wide, 1999, rec. 1999)

Zu, *The Zu Side of the Chadbourne* (Felmay, 2000, rec. 1999)

Zu, *Igneo* (Wallace, 2002, rec. 2001)

Zu / Spaceways Inc., *Radiale* (Atavistic, 2004, rec. 2003)

Zu, *How to Raise an Ox* (Atavistic, 2005, rec. 2004)

Notes

Preface

1   Spicer, Daniel, *Jazzwise*, issue 172, March 2013

Long Story Short

1   Interview with author, London, September 2019
2   Wasserbauer, Wolfgang, sleeve notes: Various artists, *Long Story Short* (TROST 2013)
3   Müller, Markus, sleeve notes: Various artists *Long Story Short* (TROST 2013)
4   Phone conversation with author, May 2013
5   Wasserbauer, Wolfgang, sleeve notes: Various artists, *Long Story Short* (TROST 2013)
6   Renfroe, Jessi, & Smirnoff, Marc, *The Oxford American* issue 40, July/August 2001
7   Email correspondence with author, February 2013
8   Heather Leigh's Facebook page, September 2021
9   https://www.youtube.com/watch?v=c_vruhZkAO4   (accessed September 2021)
10 Ibid
11 https://www.rollingstone.com/music/music-news/jimmy-fallon-peter-broetzmann-1223977/ (accessed September 2021)
12 Corbett, John, sleeve notes: Peter Brötzmann, *The Dried Rat-Dog* (Okka Disk 1995)

13 Brötzmann, Peter, *We Thought We Could Change The World: Conversations With Gerard Rouy* (Wolke Verlag 2014)

14 Ibid

15 Corbett, John, *Microgroove: Forays Into Other Music* (Duke University Press 2015)

16 Facebook comment to author, February 2021

17 Email correspondence with author, February 2021

18 Phone conversation with author, July 2020

19 Phone conversation with author, March 2013

20 Phone conversation with author, January 2013

For Adolphe Sax

1 Brötzmann, Peter, *We Thought We Could Change The World: Conversations With Gerard Rouy* (Wolke Verlag 2014)

2 Ibid

3 Ibid

4 Ibid

5 Ibid

6 For illuminating footage of Wuppertal's urban landscape and monorail system, see Wim Wender's film about avant-garde choreographer and fellow Wuppertal resident, Pina Bausch, *Pina*, (2001)

7 Interview with author, Brighton, January 2013

8 Ibid

9 Phone conversation with author, May 2013

10 KIsiedu, Harald, *European Echoes: Jazz Experimentalism in Germany 1950–1975* (Wolke Verlag 2020)

11 Phone conversation with author, May 2013

12 Ibid

13 Ibid

14   Smith, Owen F., *Fluxus: The History of an Attitude* (San Diego State University Press, 1998)

15   Neuberger, Susanne (Ed.), *Nam June Paik: Exposition of Music — Electronic Television Revisited* (Buchhandlung Walther Konig GmbH & Co. KG. Abt. Verlag 2009)

16   Interview with author, Brighton, January 2013

17   Brötzmann, Peter, *The Inexplicable Flyswatter (Works on Paper: 1959–64)* (10th Avenue Freeze Out, 2003)

18   Interview with author, Brighton, January 2013

19   Interview with author, London, September 2019

20   Phone conversation with author, May 2013

21   Keenan, David, *The Wire,* issue 345, November 2012

22   Ibid

23   Ibid

24   Ibid

25   Ibid

26   Phone conversation with author, May 2013

27   Spellman, A. B., sleeve notes: Don Cherry, *Symphony for Improvisers* (Blue Note 1967)

28   Phone conversation with author, May 2013

29   Interview with author, Brighton, January 2013

30   Ibid

31   Ibid

32   https://www.youtube.com/watch?v=zQudZuRT2IA (accessed July 2021)

33   Phone conversation with author, May 2013

34   Müller, Markus (Ed.), *FMP: The Living Music* (Wolke Verlag, 2022)

35   Phone conversation with author, May 2013

36   Müller, Markus (Ed.), *FMP: The Living Music* (Wolke Verlag, 2022)

37   Phone conversation with author, May 2013

38   https://www.thewire.co.uk/in-writing/essays/an-exceptional-human-being-tributes-to-peter-brotzmann (accessed July 2023)

39 *Sounds,* No 1, Winter 1966/67

40 Ibid

41 Ostermann, Robert, *National Observer*, 7 June 1965, from an illuminating article entitled "They Don't Call It Jazz: The Moody Men Who Play the New Music," reproduced in full at http://www. ayler.co.uk/html/article1.html#moody (accessed January 2023)

42 https://www.sounds-archiv.at/styled-180/styled-19/ (accessed January 2023)

43 KIsiedu, Harald, *European Echoes: Jazz Experimentalism in Germany 1950–1975* (Wolke Verlag 2020)

44 https://www.sounds-archiv.at/styled-180/styled-19/styled-137/ (accessed January 2023)

45 Sjerven, Bret, "Interview with Pierre Courbois" (*Amaryllis: A Magazine by We Jazz*, Issue 05, Fall 2022)

46 Von Schlippenbach, Alexander, sleeve notes: Globe Unity Orchestra, *Globe Unity 67/70* (Atavistic, 2001)

47 Ibid

48 Von Schlippenbach, Alexander, sleeve notes: Globe Unity Orchestra, *Globe Unity 67/70* (Atavistic, 2001)

49 Von Schlippenbach, Alexander, sleeve notes: Alexander von Schlippenbach, *Globe Unity* (SABA 1967)

50 Phone conversation with author, May 2013

51 Jost, Ekkehard, *Europas Jazz: 1960–80* (Fischer Taschenbuch, 1987)

52 https://exclaim.ca/music/article/peter_brotzmann (accessed July 2023)

Machine Gun

1 Interview with author, Brighton, January 2013

2 Ibid

3 Gross, Alex, *International Times* number 4, 28 November–11 December 1966

4   Ibid

5   Vague, Tom, *Televisionaries: The Red Army Faction Story 1963–1993* (AK Press, 1994)

6   Jones, LeRoi, *Black Music* (W. Morrow, 1967)

7   Baraka, Amiri, *The Autobiography of LeRoi Jones* (Freundlich Books, 1984)

8   Kofsky, Frank, *Black Nationalism and the Revolution in Music* (Pathfinder Press, 1970)

9   Ibid

10 Christman, Mark; DiNucci, Celeste; Elms, Anthony (Eds.), *Milford Graves: A Mind-Body Deal* (Inventory Press, 2022)

11 Boynik, Sezgin; Vitahuhta, Taneli (Eds.), *Free Jazz Communism: Archie Shepp-Bill Dixon Quartet at the 8th World Festival of Youth and Students in Helsinki 1962* (Rab-Rab Press, 2019)

12 Ibid

13 Newton, Francis, *The Jazz Scene* (MacGibbon and Kee, 1959)

14 Heffley, Mike, *Northern Sun, Southern Moon: Europe's Reinvention of Jazz* (Yale University Press, 2005)

15 Ibid

16 Brötzmann, Peter, *We Thought We Could Change the World: Conversations with Gerard Rouy* (Wolke Verlag, 2014)

17 Kisiedu, Harald, *European Echoes: Jazz Experimentalism in Germany 1950–1975* (Wolke Verlag, 2020)

18 Conversation with author in a car to Kongsberg Jazz Festival, July 2022

19 Josse, Bernard (Dir.), *Soldier of the Road* (2011)

20 Brötzmann, Peter, *We Thought We Could Change the World: Conversations with Gerard Rouy* (Wolke Verlag, 2014)

21 Interview with author, Brighton, January 2013

22 https://www.psychedelicbabymag.com/2019/03/peter-brotzmann-interview.html (accessed May 2022)

23 Phone conversation with author, October 2023

24 Ibid

25 Interview with author, Brighton, January 2013

26 Phone conversation with author, May 2013

27 Josse, Bernard (Dir.), *Soldier of the Road* (2011)

28 Phone conversation with author, August 2009

29 Brötzmann, Peter, *We Thought We Could Change the World: Conversations with Gerard Rouy* (Wolke Verlag, 2014)

30 Ibid

31 Phone conversation with author, May 2013

32 Phone conversation with author, August 2009

33 Watson, Ben, *Derek Bailey and the Story of Free Improvisation* (Verso, 2004)

34 https://www.allmusic.com/artist/spontaneous-music-ensemble-mn0000158979/biography (accessed June 2022)

35 Heffley, Mike, *Northern Sun, Southern Moon: Europe's Reinvention of Jazz* (Yale University Press, 2005)

36 Watson, Ben, *Derek Bailey and the Story of Free Improvisation* (Verso, 2004)

37 Brötzmann, Peter, *We Thought We Could Change the World: Conversations with Gerard Rouy* (Wolke Verlag, 2014)

38 Email correspondence with author, July 2020

39 Ibid

40 Ibid

41 Ibid

42 Brötzmann, Peter, *We Thought We Could Change the World: Conversations with Gerard Rouy* (Wolke Verlag, 2014)

43 Interview with author, London, September 2019

44 Brötzmann, Peter, *We Thought We Could Change the World: Conversations with Gerard Rouy* (Wolke Verlag, 2014)

45 Phone conversation with author, March 2013

46 Phone conversation with author, May 2013

47 Heffley, Mike, *Northern Sun, Southern Moon: Europe's Reinvention of Jazz* (Yale University Press, 2005)

48 Interview with author, Brighton, January 2013

49 Phone conversation with author, March 2013

50 *https://www.youtube.com/watch?v=TS-6flJdz2I* (accessed June 2022)

51 Email correspondence with author, July 2020

52 *https://downbeat.com/news/detail/when-sonny-rollins-went-dutch* (accessed June 2022)

53 Email correspondence with author, July 2020

54 Phone conversation with author, March 2013

55 Interview with author, London, September 2019

56 Phone conversation with author, August 2009

57 Kisiedu, Harald, *European Echoes: Jazz Experimentalism in Germany 1950–1975* (Wolke Verlag, 2020)

58 Phone conversation with author, August 2009

59 Phone conversation with author, September 2008

60 Heffley, Mike, *Northern Sun, Southern Moon: Europe's Reinvention of Jazz* (Yale University Press, 2005)

61 Email correspondence with author, July 2020

62 Phone conversation with author, March 2013

63 Phone conversation with author, September 2008

64 Phone conversation with author, August 2009

65 Ibid

66 Josse, Bernard (Dir.), *Soldier of the Road* (2011)

67 Cover: The Peter Brötzmann Octet, *Machine Gun* (BRÖ, 1968)

68 *https://downbeat.com/news/detail/machine-gun-turns-50* (accessed June 2022)

69 Phone conversation with author, September 2008

70 Email correspondence with author, July 2020

71 Phone conversation with author, September 2008

72 Miles, Barry, *International Times*, No 39, 6–19 September 1968

73 Caux, Daniel, sleeve notes: Albert Ayler, *Holy Ghost: Rare & Unissued Recordings (1962–1970)* (Revenant, 2004)

74 Lewis, George E., *A Power Stronger Than Itself: The AACM and American Experimental Music* (The University of Chicago Press, 2008)

75 Phone conversation with author, September 2008

76 *https://de-academic.com/dic.nsf/dewiki/660470* (accessed June 2022)

77 Brötzmann, Peter, *We Thought We Could Change the World: Conversations with Gerard Rouy* (Wolke Verlag, 2014)

78 Phone conversation with author, July 2020

79 Email correspondence with author, January 2013

80 Phone conversation with author, July 2020

Schwarzwaldfahrt

1 Müller, Markus (Ed.), *FMP: The Living Music* (Wolke Verlag, 2022)

2 Heffley, Mike, *Northern Sun, Southern Moon: Europe's Reinvention of Jazz* (Yale University Press, 2005)

3 Saul, Scott, *Freedom Is, Freedom Ain't: Jazz and the Making of the Sixties* (Harvard University Press, 2005)

4 Email correspondence with author, June 2022

5 *The Quasimodo Club Broadcast 1968* on Spotify (accessed September 2022)

6 Müller, Markus (Ed.), *FMP: The Living Music* (Wolke Verlag, 2022)

7 Email correspondence with author, June 2022

8 Müller, Markus (Ed.), *FMP: The Living Music* (Wolke Verlag, 2022)

9 Phone conversation with author, August 2009

10 Interview with author, Brighton, January 2013

11 https://herri.org.za/7/aryan-kaganof-i/ (accessed November 2022)

12 Phone conversation with author, August 2009

13 Brötzmann, Peter, *We Thought We Could Change the World: Conversations with Gerard Rouy* (Wolke Verlag, 2014)

14 Müller, Markus (Ed.), *FMP: The Living Music* (Wolke Verlag, 2022)

15 Ibid

16 Ibid

17 Email correspondence with author, July 2020

18 Brötzmann, Peter, *We Thought We Could Change the World: Conversations with Gerard Rouy* (Wolke Verlag, 2014)

19 Ibid

20 http://www.incusrecords.force9.co.uk/features/history.html (accessed February 2023)

21 Heffley, Mike, *Northern Sun, Southern Moon: Europe's Reinvention of Jazz* (Yale University Press, 2005)

22 Insert: Evan Parker / Derek Bailey / Han Bennink, *The Topography Of The Lungs* (Incus, 1970)

23 Free Music Production Partnership Agreement: Müller, Markus (Ed.), *FMP: The Living Music* (Wolke Verlag, 2022)

24 Ibid

25 Lewis, George E., *A Power Stronger Than Itself: The AACM and American Experimental Music* (The University of Chicago Press, 2008)

26 Phone conversation with author, March 2013

27 Sleeve notes: Brötzmann / Van Hove / Bennink, *Brötzmann / Van Hove / Bennink* (FMP, 1973)

28 https://www.youtube.com/watch?v=58qSR3Cg8Mg   (accessed February 2023)

29 Josse, Bernard (Dir.), *Soldier of the Road* (2011)

30 Ibid

31 https://www.youtube.com/watch?v=dFa0oyF63d0   (accessed February 2023)

32   Nogllk, Bert, sleeve notes: Brötzmann / Van Hove / Bennink, *Jazz In Der Kammer Nr.71: Deutsches Theater / Berlin / GDR / 04/11/1974* (TROST, 2022)

33   Ibid

34   Sleeve notes: Brötzmann / Van Hove / Bennink, *Tschüs* (FMP, 1975)

35   Brötzmann, Peter, *We Thought We Could Change the World: Conversations with Gerard Rouy* (Wolke Verlag, 2014)

36   Email correspondence with author, July 2020

37   Interview with author, London, September 2019

38   Brötzmann, Peter, *We Thought We Could Change the World: Conversations with Gerard Rouy* (Wolke Verlag, 2014)

39   https://www.allaboutjazz.com/fmp-records-a-snapshot-of-german-jazz-history-by-clifford-allen (accessed April 2023)

40   Müller, Markus (Ed.), *FMP: The Living Music* (Wolke Verlag, 2022)

41   https://destination-out.bandcamp.com/album/sgsch-nk (accessed April 2023)

42   Brötzmann, Peter, *We Thought We Could Change the World: Conversations with Gerard Rouy* (Wolke Verlag, 2014)

43   Interview with author, London, September 2019

44   Email correspondence with author, July 2020

45   Keenan, David, *The Wire*, issue 345, November 2012

46   Phone conversation with author, March 2013

47   Sleeve notes: Brötzmann / Bennink, *Schwarzwaldfahrt* (FMP, 1977)

48   Abish, Walter, *How German Is It (Wie Deutsch ist es)* (New Directions, 1980)

49   Phone conversation with author, March 2013

50   Interview with author, London, September 2019

51   Phone conversation with author, September 2009

52   Interview with author, London, September 2019

53   Email correspondence with author, July 2020

54   Interview with author, Brighton, January 2013

55   Ibid

56   Ibid

57   Brötzmann, Peter, *We Thought We Could Change the World: Conversations with Gerard Rouy* (Wolke Verlag, 2014)

58   Spicer, Daniel, *Plan B*, issue 18, February 2007

59   Interview with author, Brighton, January 2013

60   Ibid

61   Brötzmann, Peter, *We Thought We Could Change the World: Conversations with Gerard Rouy* (Wolke Verlag, 2014)

The Nearer the Bone, the Sweeter the Meat

1   Phone conversation with author, May 2013

2   Interview with author, London, May 2022

3   Sleeve notes: Mike Osborne Trio, *Border Crossing* (Ogun, 1974)

4   Barnett, Anthony, *UnNatural Music: John Lennon & Yoko Ono In Cambridge 1969* (Allardyce Book ABP, 2016)

5   Barnes, Mike, *The Wire*, issue 400, June 2017

6   Ibid

7   Interview with author, Brighton, January 2013

8   Ibid

9   Soejima, Teruto, *Free Jazz in Japan: A Personal History* (Public Bath Press, 2019)

10   Ibid

11   Yoshida, Mamoru, *Yokohama Jazz Story: 50 Years Of Chigusa* (Kanagawa Shimbun, 1985)

12   Soejima, Teruto, *Free Jazz in Japan: A Personal History* (Public Bath Press, 2019)

13   Cummings, Alan, sleeve notes: Masayuki Takayanagi and New Directions, *Independence: Tread on Sure Ground* (Tiliqua, 2007)

14   Soejima, Teruto, *Free Jazz in Japan: A Personal History* (Public Bath Press, 2019)

15   Ibid

16   Phone conversation with author, May 2013

17   Ibid

18   Ibid

19   Soejima, Teruto, *Free Jazz in Japan: A Personal History* (Public Bath Press, 2019)

20   Phone conversation with author, May 2013

21   Ibid

22   Soejima, Teruto, *Free Jazz in Japan: A Personal History* (Public Bath Press, 2019)

23   https://www.redbullmusicacademy.com/lectures/peter-brotzmann (accessed June 2023)

24   Phone conversation with author, May 2013

25   Ibid

26   Email to author, May 2021

27   Phone conversation with author, May 2013

28   Interview with author, Brighton, January 2013

29   Sleeve notes: Don Cherry, *Eternal Rhythm* (MPS, 1969)

30   https://web.archive.org/web/20041010181237/http://www.martinos.org/~reese/joetest/articles/articles_v01_j.html (accessed July 2023)

31   Sleeve notes: Don Cherry, *Eternal Rhythm* (MPS, 1969)

32   https://www.youtube.com/watch?v=RFYJP1DbWjs (accessed July 2023)

33   Sleeve notes: Don Cherry, *Eternal Rhythm* (MPS, 1969)

34   Sleeve notes: Don Cherry & The New Eternal Rhythm Orchestra / Krzysztof Penderecki, *Actions* (Philips, 1971)

35   Ibid

36   Ibid

37   Nygren, Magnus, "Don Cherry" (*Shadow Shapes: A Magazine By We Jazz*, issue 08, Summer 2023)

38   Sleeve notes: Don Cherry & The New Eternal Rhythm Orchestra / Krzysztof Penderecki, *Actions* (Philips, 1971)

39 Ibid

40 https://www.youtube.com/watch?v=Or8zLGaqBIs   (accessed
    September 2023)

41 Interview with author, Brighton, January 2013

42 Keenan, David, *The Wire*, issue 345, November 2012

43 Sleeve notes: Peter Brötzmann Group, *Alarm* (FMP, 1983)

44 Morton, Brian; Cook, Richard, *The Penguin Jazz Guide* (Penguin,
    2010)

45 Ibid

46 Sleeve notes: Peter Brötzmann Group, *Alarm* (FMP, 1983)

47 Ibid

48 Phone conversation with author, May 2013

49 Conversation with author in a car to Kongsberg Jazz Festival, July
    2022

The Noise of Trouble

1 Witherden, Barry, *The Wire*, issue 73, March 1990

2 Brötzmann, Peter, *We Thought We Could Change the World:
   Conversations with Gerard Rouy* (Wolke Verlag 2014)

3 https://www.thewire.co.uk/in-writing/essays/p=10864   (accessed
   November 2023)

4 Brötzmann, Peter, *We Thought We Could Change the World:
   Conversations with Gerard Rouy* (Wolke Verlag 2014)

5 https://web.archive.org/web/20070505171709/http://www.
   joemcphee.com/jny/sharrock/ratliff89.html (accessed November
   2023)

6 https://www.innerviews.org/inner/bill-laswell4   (accessed
   November 2023)

7 https://www.thewire.co.uk/in-writing/essays/an-exceptional-
   human-being-tributes-to-peter-brotzmann (accessed November
   2023)

8   Ibid

9   Phone conversation with author, February 2019

10   Interview with author, Brighton, January 2013

11   https://www.thewire.co.uk/in-writing/essays/an-exceptional-human-being-tributes-to-peter-brotzmann (accessed November 2023)

12   Interview with author, Brighton, January 2013

13   Ibid

14   Brötzmann, Peter, *We Thought We Could Change the World: Conversations with Gerard Rouy* (Wolke Verlag 2014)

15   Interview with author, Brighton, January 2013

16   https://web.archive.org/web/20101206105844/http://www.reocities.com/jeff_l_schwartz/chpt3.html (accessed November 2023)

17   Interview with author, Brighton, January 2013

18   Brötzmann, Peter, *We Thought We Could Change the World: Conversations with Gerard Rouy* (Wolke Verlag 2014)

19   Interview with author, Brighton, January 2013

20   Phone conversation with author, February 2019

21   Brötzmann, Peter, *We Thought We Could Change the World: Conversations with Gerard Rouy* (Wolke Verlag 2014)

22   Lake, Steve, *The Wire*, issue 29, July 1986

23   Interview with author, Brighton, January 2013

24   https://www.youtube.com/watch?v=FKYq4H3-iKM (accessed December 2023)

25   Email correspondence with author, January 2013

26   Witherden, Barry, *The Wire*, issue 73, March 1990

27   Phone conversation with author, February 2019

28   Lake, Steve, *The Wire*, issue 29, July 1986

29   Interview with author, London, September 2019

30   Lake, Steve, *The Wire*, issue 29, July 1986

31   Interview with author, London, September 2019

32 Phone conversation with author, February 2019

33 Lake, Steve, *The Wire*, issue 29, July 1986

34 Ibid

35 Sleeve notes: Last Exit, *The Noise of Trouble (Live in Tokyo)* (Enemy, 1986)

36 Phone conversation with author, February 2019

37 Email correspondence with author, February 2021

38 Lake, Steve, *The Wire*, issue 29, July 1986

39 Interview with author, Brighton, January 2013

40 Phone conversation with author, May 2013

41 Interview with author, Brighton, January 2013

42 Witherden, Barry, *The Wire*, issue 73, March 1990

43 Witherden, Barry, *The Wire*, issue 41, July 1987

44 Phone conversation with author, February 2019

45 Interview with author, Brighton, January 2013

46 Brötzmann, Peter, *We Thought We Could Change the World: Conversations with Gerard Rouy* (Wolke Verlag 2014)

47 Interview with author, Brighton, January 2013

48 Phone conversation with author, February 2019

49 Sleeve notes: Last Exit, *Iron Path* (Virgin, 1988)

50 https://www.youtube.com/watch?v=9CsvcJ3f3yw   (accessed December 2023)

51 Barnes, Mike, *The Wire*, issue 395, January 2017

52 Ibid

Never Too Late but Always Too Early

1 Phone conversation with author, February 2019

2 Interview with author, London, September 2019

3 Ibid

4 Corbett, John, *Microgroove: Forays Into Other Music* (Duke University Press, 2015)

5   Interview with author, Brighton, January 2013

6   Shoemaker, Bill, *Jazz in the 1970s: Diverging Streams* (Rowman & Littlefield, 2017)

7   All quotes translated from https://www.youtube.com/watch?v=8iR6wbdIylA (accessed March 2024)

8   Interview with author, Brighton, January 2013

9   Berendt, Joachim-Ernst, *Ein Fenster aus Jazz: Essays, Portraits, Reflexionen* (Fischer Taschenbuch, 1977)

10 Heffley, Mike, *Northern Sun, Southern Moon: Europe's Reinvention of Jazz* (Yale University Press, 2005)

11 Brötzmann, Peter, *We Thought We Could Change the World: Conversations with Gerard Rouy* (Wolke Verlag, 2014)

12 Ibid

13 Lewis, George E., "Improvised Music after 1950: Afrological and Eurological Perspectives" (*Black Music Research Journal*, Vol 16, No 1, Spring 1996)

14 Ibid

15 Ibid

16 Ibid

17 Kisiedu, Harald, *European Echoes: Jazz Experimentalism in Germany 1950–1975* (Wolke Verlag, 2020)

18 "Three-Night Jazz Festival Set," *The New York Times*, 1 June, 1984

19 Jahn, Ebba (Dir.), *Rising Tones Cross* (1985)

20 Ibid

21 http://www.pointofdeparture.org/archives/PoD-23/PoD23FarCry.html (accessed April 2024)

22 Press release: Peter Brötzmann / William Parker / Milford Graves, *Historic Music Past Tense Future* (Black Editions Archive, 2022)

23 Sleeve notes: Die like a Dog Quartet, *Aoyama Crows* (FMP, 2002)

24 Sleeve notes: Peter Brötzmann / Toshinori Kondo / William Parker / Hamid Drake, *Die like a Dog: Fragments of Music, Life and Death of Albert Ayler* (FMP, 1994)

25 Interview with author, Brighton, January 2013

26 Corbett, John, *Microgroove: Forays into Other Music* (Duke University Press, 2015)

27 Sleeve notes: Peter Brötzmann / Toshinori Kondo / William Parker / Hamid Drake, *Die like a Dog: Fragments of Music, Life and Death of Albert Ayler* (FMP, 1994)

28 Interview with author, Brighton, January 2013

29 Ibid

30 Ibid

31 Sleeve notes: Die like a Dog Quartet, *Aoyama Crows* (FMP, 2002)

32 Ibid

33 Phone conversation with author, May 2013

34 Ibid

35 Conversation with author in a car to Kongsberg Jazz Festival, July 2022

36 Sleeve notes: Peter Brötzmann / Toshinori Kondo / William Parker / Hamid Drake, *Die like a Dog: Fragments of Music, Life and Death of Albert Ayler* (FMP, 1994)

37 Phone conversation with author, December 2013

38 Phone conversation with author, May 2013

39 Sleeve notes: Peter Brötzmann / Toshinori Kondo / William Parker / Hamid Drake, *Die like a Dog: Fragments of Music, Life and Death of Albert Ayler* (FMP, 1994)

40 Phone conversation with author, December 2013

41 Sleeve notes: Die like a Dog Quartet, *Aoyama Crows* (FMP)

42 Sleeve notes: Peter Brötzmann / Toshinori Kondo / William Parker / Hamid Drake, *Die like a Dog: Fragments of Music, Life and Death of Albert Ayler* (FMP, 1994)

43 Sleeve notes: Die like a Dog Quartet, *Aoyama Crows* (FMP, 2002)

44 Ibid

45 Meyer, Bill, *The Wire*, issue 466, December 2022

46 Spicer, Daniel, *Jazzwise*, issue 195, April 2015

47 https://www.thewire.co.uk/in-writing/essays/an-exceptional-human-being-tributes-to-peter-brotzmann (accessed April 2024)

48 Phone conversation with author, December 2013

49 https://chicagoreader.com/music/peter-brotzmann-corbett-constellation/ (accessed April 2024)

50 Ibid

Short Visit To Nowhere

1 https://chicagoreader.com/music/peter-brotzmann-corbett-constellation/ (accessed April 2024)

2 Phone conversation with author, December 2013

3 https://www.thewire.co.uk/in-writing/essays/an-exceptional-human-being-tributes-to-peter-brotzmann (accessed April 2024)

4 Skype conversation with author, December 2018

5 Ibid

6 Ibid

7 Ibid

8 Skype conversation with author, January 2013

9 Email correspondence with author, January 2013

10 Ibid

11 Skype conversation with author, January 2013

12 Phone conversation with author, January 2013

13 Skype conversation with author, January 2013

14 Ibid

15 Phone conversation with author, January 2013

16 Ibid

17 Interview with author, Brighton, January 2013

18 Ibid

19 Ibid

20 ibid

21 Phone conversation with author, February 2020

22 Phone conversation with author, January 2013

23 Brötzmann, Peter, *We Thought We Could Change the World: Conversations with Gerard Rouy* (Wolke Verlag, 2014)

24 Sleeve notes: Peter Brötzmann / William Parker / Hamid Drake, *Never Too Late but Always Too Early* (Eremite, 2003)

25 Phone conversation with author, August 2009

26 Phone conversation with author, February 2020

27 https://www.trost.at/artist-steamboat-switzerland.html (accessed April 2024)

28 Phone conversation with author, February 2020

29 Ibid

30 https://www.thewire.co.uk/in-writing/essays/an-exceptional-human-being-tributes-to-peter-brotzmann (accessed April 2024)

31 Phone conversation with author, February 2020

32 https://www.thewire.co.uk/in-writing/essays/an-exceptional-human-being-tributes-to-peter-brotzmann (accessed April 2024)

33 Phone conversation with author, February 2020

34 Phone conversation with author, August 2009

35 https://www.thewire.co.uk/in-writing/essays/an-exceptional-human-being-tributes-to-peter-brotzmann (accessed April 2024)

36 Barnes, Mike, *The Wire*, issue 400, June 2017

37 Phone conversation with author, August 2009

38 Phone conversation with author, January 2013

39 Phone conversation with author, August 2009

40 Phone conversation with author, May 2013

41 Phone conversation with author, January 2013

42 Collier, Graham, *Inside Jazz* (Quartet Books, 1973)

43 Phone conversation with author, August 2009

44 Brötzmann, Peter, *We Thought We Could Change the World: Conversations with Gerard Rouy* (Wolke Verlag, 2014)

45 Ibid

46 Watson, Ben, *Derek Bailey and the Story of Free Improvisation* (Verso, 2004)

47 Phone conversation with author, July 2020

48 Brötzmann, Peter, *We Thought We Could Change the World: Conversations with Gerard Rouy* (Wolke Verlag, 2014)

49 Phone conversation with author, May 2013

50 Ibid

51 Email correspondence with author, January 2013

52 Phone conversation with author, August 2009

53 Ibid

54 Ibid

55 Phone conversation with author, January 2013

56 Ibid

57 Phone conversation with author, May 2013

58 Ibid

59 Phone conversation with author, January 2013

60 Ibid

I Surrender Dear

1 Sleeve notes: Brötzmann / Satoh / Moriyama, *Yatagarasu* (Not Two, 2012)

2 Phone conversation with author, January 2013

3 Phone conversation with author, May 2013

4 Interview with author, London, September 2019

5 Zoom conversation with author, April 2024

6 Ibid

7 Ibid

8 Ibid

9 Ibid

10 Phone conversation with author, July 2020

11 Ibid

12 Ibid

13 https://www.15questions.net/interview/fifteen-questions-interview-heather-leigh/page-1/ (accessed April 2024)

14 Ibid

15 Interview with author, London, September 2019

16 Ibid

17 Ibid

18 Ibid

19 Zoom conversation with author, April 2024

20 Ibid

21 Ibid

22 Ibid

23 Phone conversation with author, July 2020

24 Interview with author, London, September 2019

25 Phone conversation with author, July 2020

26 Interview with author, London, September 2019

27 Ibid

28 Ibid

29 Phone conversation with author, May 2013

30 Boynik, Sezgin; Vitahuhta, Taneli (Eds.), *Free Jazz Communism: Archie Shepp-Bill Dixon Quartet at the 8th World Festival of Youth and Students in Helsinki 1962* (Rab-Rab Press, 2019)

31 Interview with author, Brighton, January 2013

32 Interview with author, London, September 2019

33 Ibid

34 Ibid

35 Phone conversation with author, August 2009

36 Brötzmann, Peter, *We Thought We Could Change the World: Conversations with Gerard Rouy* (Wolke Verlag, 2014)

37 Interview with author, London, September 2019

38 Phone conversation with author, August 2009

39 Interview with author, London, September 2019

40 Ibid
41 Phone conversation with author, December 2013
42 Brötzmann, Peter, *The Inexplicable Flyswatter (Works on Paper: 1959–64)* (10th Avenue Freeze Out, 2003)
43 Brötzmann, Peter, *Along The Way* (Wolke Verlag, 2021)
44 Phone conversation with author, May 2013
45 Interview with author, Brighton, January 2013
46 Brötzmann, Peter, *We Thought We Could Change the World: Conversations with Gerard Rouy* (Wolke Verlag, 2014)
47 Phone conversation with author, February 2021
48 Email correspondence with author, February 2021
49 Interview with author, Brighton, January 2013
50 Phone conversation with author, July 2020
51 Phone conversation with author, February 2020
52 Liner notes: Peter Brötzmann, *I Surrender Dear* (TROST, 2019)
53 https://www.thewire.co.uk/in-writing/essays/an-exceptional-human-being-tributes-to-peter-brotzmann (accessed April 2024)
54 Peter Brötzmann's Facebook page, November 2021
55 Conversation with author in a car to Kongsberg Jazz Festival, July 2022
56 Email correspondence with author, July 2022
57 Zoom conversation with author, April 2024
58 Ibid
59 Ibid
60 Spicer, Daniel, *Jazzwise*, issue 283, April 2023
61 Zoom conversation with author, April 2024
62 Peter Brötzmann's Facebook page, March 2023
63 Interview with author, Brighton, January 2013
64 Email correspondence with author, June 2023
65 https://www.zeit.de/kultur/musik/2023-06/peter-broetzmann-freejazz-saxofon-tod (accessed April 2024)

INDEX

REPEATER BOOKS

is dedicated to the creation of a new reality. The landscape of twenty-first-century arts and letters is faded and inert, riven by fashionable cynicism, egotistical self-reference and a nostalgia for the recent past. Repeater intends to add its voice to those movements that wish to enter history and assert control over its currents, gathering together scattered and isolated voices with those who have already called for an escape from Capitalist Realism. Our desire is to publish in every sphere and genre, combining vigorous dissent and a pragmatic willingness to succeed where messianic abstraction and quiescent co-option have stalled: abstention is not an option: we are alive and we don't agree.